MW00825020

ETHICAL test preparation *in the* classroom

Robert J. Marzano   Julia A. Simms
Christopher W. Dodson   Jacob P. Wipf

MARZANO
Resources

555 North Morton Street
Bloomington, IN 47404
888.849.0851
FAX: 866.801.1447

email: info@MarzanoResources.com
MarzanoResources.com

Printed in the United States of America

Library of Congress Cataloging-in-Publication Data

Names: Marzano, Robert J., author. | Dodson, Christopher W., author. |
  Simms, Julia A., author. | Wipf, Jacob P., author.
Title: Ethical test preparation in the classroom / Robert J. Marzano,
  Christopher W. Dodson, Julia A. Simms, Jacob P. Wipf.
Description: Bloomington, IN : Solution Tree Press, [2022] | Includes
  bibliographical references and index.
Identifiers: LCCN 2021032335 (print) | LCCN 2021032336 (ebook) | ISBN
  9781943360512 (paperback) | ISBN 9781943360529 (ebook)
Subjects: LCSH: Educational tests and measurements--United States. |
  Educational tests and measurements--Moral and ethical aspects--United
  States. | Language arts--United States--Examinations. | English
  language--Study and teaching--United States--Evaluation.
Classification: LCC LB3051 .M4574 2022 (print) | LCC LB3051 (ebook) | DDC
  371.26--dc23
LC record available at https://lccn.loc.gov/2021032335
LC ebook record available at https://lccn.loc.gov/2021032336

Production Team

President and Publisher: Douglas M. Rife
Associate Publisher: Sarah Payne-Mills
Managing Production Editor: Kendra Slayton
Editorial Director: Todd Brakke
Art Director: Rian Anderson
Copy Chief: Jessi Finn
Senior Production Editor: Laurel Hecker
Content Development Specialist: Amy Rubenstein
Copy Editors: Evie Madsen and Mark Hain
Proofreader: Jessi Finn
Editorial Assistants: Sarah Ludwig and Elijah Oates

Table of Contents

About the Authors

 **Robert J. Marzano, PhD,** is cofounder and chief academic officer of Marzano Resources in Denver, Colorado. During his fifty years in the field of education, he has worked with educators as a speaker and trainer and has authored more than fifty books and two hundred articles on topics such as instruction, assessment, writing and implementing standards, cognition, effective leadership, and school intervention. His books include *The New Art and Science of Teaching, Leaders of Learning, Making Classroom Assessments Reliable and Valid,* the *Classroom Strategies* series, *Managing the Inner World of Teaching, A Handbook for High Reliability Schools, A Handbook for Personalized Competency-Based Education,* and *The Highly Engaged Classroom.* His practical translations of the most current research and theory into classroom strategies are known internationally and are widely practiced by both teachers and administrators.

He received a bachelor's degree from Iona College in New York, a master's degree from Seattle University, and a doctorate from the University of Washington.

To learn more about Dr. Marzano, visit www.marzanoresources.com.

 **Christopher W. Dodson** is a proficiency scale analyst at Marzano Resources. His primary focus is assessment and grading, with work in areas such as standards-based grading and classroom assessment. He helped develop both the Marzano Compendium of Instructional Strategies and the Critical Concepts proficiency scales, and is the author of the report *The Critical Concepts in Social Studies.* He received a BS in English from the University of Southern Indiana.

 **Julia A. Simms** is vice president of Marzano Resources in Denver, Colorado. A former classroom teacher, Julia and her team develop research-based resources and provide support to educators as they implement them. Her areas of expertise include effective instruction, learning progressions and proficiency scales, assessment and grading,

argumentation and reasoning skills, and literacy development. She has coauthored and contributed to ten books, including *Coaching Classroom Instruction*, *Vocabulary for the Common Core*, *Questioning Sequences in the Classroom*, *A Handbook for High Reliability Schools*, *The New Art and Science of Teaching Reading*, and *Improving Teacher Development and Evaluation*.

Julia received a bachelor's degree from Wheaton College and master's degrees in educational administration and K–12 literacy from Colorado State University and the University of Northern Colorado.

 **Jacob P. Wipf** is a proficiency scale analyst at Marzano Resources in Denver, Colorado. He helps develop resources for assessment and grading, with a particular focus on standards-based grading and classroom assessment. He was involved in the creation of the Critical Concepts proficiency scales and authored a report on the alignment of the Critical Concepts and Northwest Evaluation Association's MAP assessments. He received bachelor's degrees in history and journalism from Arizona State University and a master's degree in history from the University of Colorado.

Introduction

The central premise of this book is quite simple—large-scale assessments (that is, tests) are important determiners of how educators judge students on their knowledge of content. These judgments are significant in students' lives and can either open doors to the future or close those same doors. While large-scale assessments are intended as objective measures of students' knowledge and skill, educators unwittingly design them in ways that sometimes detract from this goal. Specifically, large-scale assessments contain items which, in and of themselves, add an artificial component to the test-taking process. Stated differently, taking a test requires ways of thinking that can have little to do with what an educator designed a particular test to measure.

If students are unaware of these different ways of thinking, they will most probably answer some items incorrectly even if they are skilled at what those items purportedly measure. To illustrate, consider a fourth-grade English language arts (ELA) item in which the teacher presents students with an excerpt of eight paragraphs from *The Wonderful Wizard of Oz* (Baum, 1900). Each paragraph is numbered. After students read the passage, they answer the two questions, part A and part B, as figure I.1 (page 2) shows.

On the surface it might seem like these items are designed to measure a student's ability to read and comprehend the paragraphs taken from *The Wonderful Wizard of Oz.* Traditionally, assessing reading comprehension has been thought of as assessing a student's ability to ascertain the main idea of a passage, which usually involves some type of summary of the information. If that were the case, this item would require a fourth grader to select a statement from the alternatives that best summarizes the action in the eight paragraphs. However, this fourth-grade item clearly does not focus on what is traditionally thought of as *main idea*. Rather, the item highlights a specific incident involving Dorothy and Scarecrow (that is, Scarecrow asking Dorothy to help him get down from the pole he is displayed on) and asks the student to discern why the incident took place.

Also note the content of the part B item related to the part A item. Part B asks students to identify the specific paragraph that provides support for the answer they provided in part A. Of course, if a student incorrectly answers part A, he or she cannot correctly answer part B.

Associated Text: *The Wonderful Wizard of Oz*

Part A

Why does the Scarecrow ask Dorothy to help him down from the pole?

　○ A. He wants to go to Oz to get brains in his head instead of straw.

　○ B. He wants to go to Oz to get real arms and legs so he can feel things.

　○ C. He is afraid of being left alone in the field and hurt by crows.

　○ D. He is bored being perched in a field scaring away crows.

Part B

Which paragraph in the passage **best** supports the answer to Part A?

　○ A. paragraph 3

　○ B. paragraph 5

　○ C. paragraph 6

　○ D. paragraph 8

Figure I.1: Grade 4 ELA item.

If students understood the basic nature of this item from the outset, they would read it differently than they would if they were trying to discern the main idea of the passage. Rather than reading with an eye toward summarizing what happened, they would be looking for specific events and for evidence as to why these events occurred. Without such awareness on the part of students, their inability to answer the item might be a simple lack of awareness of what the item requires of them as opposed to an inability to execute what the item requires.

This phenomenon also occurs in mathematics tests. To illustrate, consider the seventh-grade mathematics item in figure I.2. In one sense, this item is relatively simple. Students must determine how much money is left from $15.00 to buy markers. If the notebooks and folders cost $10.80, then $4.20 remains to buy markers. If markers cost $0.70 each, then students can purchase from one to six markers. But to communicate this calculation the students must understand the meaning of the solution set indicators, select the one that would indicate that the numbers 1 through 6 all represent correct answers, and then know how to drag and drop that indicator to the correct portion on the number line.

Finally, items on science tests include the same issues. To illustrate, consider a fifth-grade science example (see figure I.3). On the surface, this item looks quite straightforward. It involves iron filings in sand and tools. The item initially stimulates the image of someone using a tool with sand that has some iron in it. A fifth-grade student would probably not think of a magnet (which is the correct answer) as a tool, whereas the other alternatives (a scale, a thermometer, and a magnifying glass) all fit well within the category of tool.

In effect, test items are not straightforward queries into students' knowledge and skill regarding a specific topic. Rather, along with specific knowledge and skills, test items frequently require students to discern the nuances and idiosyncrasies of the item format itself

Jonathon has $15.00 to spend on notebooks, folders, and markers. The total cost of the notebooks and folders is $10.80. The cost of each marker is $0.70. Graph the solution set of the inequality that could be used to determine m, the number of markers Jonathon could choose to purchase.

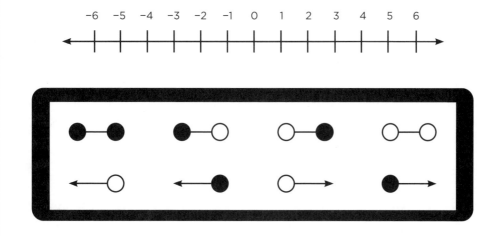

Select a solution set indicator. Drag the points on the indicator to the appropriate locations on the number line.

Figure I.2: Grade 7 mathematics item.

Which tool would work best to separate iron filings from sand?
- ○ A. a scale
- ○ B. a refrigerator magnet
- ○ C. a thermometer
- ○ D. a magnifying glass

Figure I.3: Grade 5 science item.

and the actual intent of those who designed the items. We believe it is not only useful but also necessary to provide K–12 students with an understanding of some of these nuances and idiosyncrasies so they have a fair chance at interpreting what the test requires of them when confronted with such items. Along with effective content instruction, such familiarization with the features of test items constitutes what testing experts regard as *ethical test preparation*. By removing artificial impediments to demonstrating their knowledge and skills, such preparation makes the test fairer for students while also increasing the test's effectiveness as a measurement tool. To provide educators with a systematic means of teaching students to navigate features of test items while simultaneously deepening their content knowledge, we undertook a study of state and national tests in ELA, mathematics, and science that involved over eight thousand items.

Our Study

We began our study by identifying a representative group of 8,804 items from state, national, and international large-scale assessments. These included the American College Testing (ACT), the Scholastic Aptitude Test (SAT), the National Assessment of Educational Progress (NAEP), state and international science tests, and assessments from the Partnership for Assessment of Readiness for College and Careers (PARCC) and the Smarter Balanced Assessment Consortium (SBAC), the two state-led consortia that developed assessments aligned to the Common Core State Standards (CCSS). We selected assessments that not only meet high standards of validity and reliability but also reflect what most students in the United States will encounter over the course of their K–12 education. The tests we studied serve a variety of purposes and occur at different times and frequencies throughout a student's education, but collectively they cover grades 3–12, the typical span during which students take large-scale standardized assessments. Within this sample, we analyzed the characteristics of each item, in terms of not just what content it required students to know, but how it asked them to demonstrate that knowledge. The analysis was somewhat different for each of the three content areas (ELA, mathematics, and science), as the assessments approached each area in different ways (see table I.1).

Table I.1: Assessment Items Analyzed

Subject Area	Number of Items	Assessments Analyzed
ELA	1,684	PARCC, SBAC, NAEP, ACT, SAT
Mathematics	2,629	PARCC, SBAC, NAEP, ACT, SAT
Science	4,491	State science tests, NAEP, ACT, Trends in International Mathematics and Science Study (TIMSS), Program for International Student Assessment (PISA)
Total	8,804	

The primary limitations of our study are related to an uneven sampling of items among assessments and the diversity of the assessments themselves. While PARCC and SBAC released items were abundantly available, the SAT and ACT each make only one practice test available at any one time, so the study included very few items from those assessments. For the science component of the study, while sampling from across every state with publicly available items created a large and diverse sample, not all states provided items, and the number of items available varied widely state to state. The international assessments used in the study also provided comparatively few items. Additionally, the purposes and forms of the assessments we analyzed vary. For example, the SAT and ACT are designed to measure individual students' preparedness for college, while NAEP ("The Nation's Report Card") is meant to assess the overall growth and condition of U.S. students as a group. While the various assessments share some characteristics, such as a high frequency of selected-response items, the content sampled and the complexity of items are not equivalent across assessments, even at the same grade level. Thus, while this study enables us to draw conclusions about features typical to large-scale assessment as a whole, these conclusions are unlikely to fit any single assessment perfectly.

The following sections detail our methodology for each of the content areas we analyzed.

English Language Arts

In ELA, we analyzed 1,684 items from the ACT, SAT, NAEP, PARCC, and SBAC. We organized these items into three broad categories: reading, language, and writing, with reading items constituting the vast majority. We further categorized these items by response format: selected-response, short constructed-response, and extended constructed-response, with selected-response items being by far the most prevalent format. Altogether, about 80 percent of the ELA items in our study address reading using a selected-response item format. The remaining 20 percent of items fall into three additional composite types: short constructed-response items on reading, selected-response items on language, and extended constructed-response items on writing.

Within each item type, we observed basic structures or *frames* used to assess specific aspects of a student's comprehension of a text. For example, the *big idea frame* in reading selected-response items asks students to identify main ideas and themes of a text, in line with traditional conceptions of reading comprehension. This frame encompasses around a quarter of these types of items. The remaining reading selected-response items comprise five more frames addressing topics such as how the author conveys a message or the identification of specific details in text. This granular unpacking of texts reflects the growing emphasis on *close reading* to aid student comprehension of more complex texts.

Most reading selected-response items have two parts, which we categorized separately. The second parts of items predominantly ask students to provide evidence for their response in the first part of the item, meaning that answering the second part of an item correctly often depends on a correct response to the first part.

Short constructed-response reading items make up only about 3 percent of all ELA items in our study. The five frames for this item type are similar to those used with selected-response reading items, encompassing both main ideas and more detailed aspects of the text and its structure. However, students must provide their own answers without the aid of multiple-response options cues.

Selected-response language items are the second-most common item type, though they still make up only 9 percent of the items studied. These items deal with conventions related to the use of the English language, such as word choice, clarity, sentence structure, and spelling. Such items comprise four frames: expression, content, grammar, and mechanics, with a relatively even distribution among the frames.

Extended constructed-response writing items account for the final 8 percent of ELA items in the study. These items are designed to assess students' writing abilities by having them compose their own texts. The frames comprise the different types of writing tests ask students to produce: narrative, analytic, informative, argumentative, and comparative. Scorers typically evaluate student responses to these items on the basis of both content and quality of writing rather than the ability to simply produce a correct answer. While the time required to complete and score these items precludes test makers from including many of them on large-scale assessments, the low frequency of this item type is somewhat deceptive relative to its importance. In real terms, writing ability is a core component of a student's overall proficiency in ELA, and even in terms of assessment results themselves, a single item of this type is likely to be weighted far more heavily than a single selected-response or short constructed-response item.

Mathematics

The mathematics analysis drew on items from PARCC, SBAC, NAEP, SAT, and ACT. Because of the variety in secondary course progressions across schools and districts, items at the high school level were placed together in one large group. Items from the SAT and ACT were analyzed separately due to differences in the designs and uses of those tests.

Like ELA, a large portion of the mathematics items consisted of two or more parts. Unlike ELA, we found that these multiple parts typically asked questions that were significantly distinct from one another. Whereas the second part of an ELA item might ask a student to explain or support his or her answer to the first part, the successive parts of a mathematics item often asked students to perform new calculations within the same mathematical scenario, sometimes requiring the use of entirely different skills. Because of the heterogeneity in multipart items, we decided to analyze these distinct parts separately, resulting in a total of 2,629 mathematics items.

Also in contrast to the ELA analysis, we found the mathematics items displayed extreme diversity in terms of item format, leading us to categorize items primarily by content rather than form. Many items asked students to draw on multiple areas of mathematical content in solving a problem, and in such cases, we categorized the item by what raters considered its most prominent content. We identified nine broad content categories, further divided into a total of sixty subcategories. Almost 70 percent of the items belonged to the categories of expressions, equations, inequalities, and functions (EEIF); operations; or geometry. As expected, different grade levels displayed an emphasis on different categories, with operations peaking in grades 3–5 and EEIF rising to prominence in the secondary grades.

Science

Because the consortia-built assessments (PARCC and SBAC) that comprised the bulk of our mathematics and ELA analyses did not include science, we built the majority of our science analysis on publicly released items from available science tests from thirty-eight individual states and Washington, DC. We supplemented this analysis of 4,140 state test items with items from the NAEP and ACT, as well as two international tests—the Trends in

International Mathematics and Science Study (TIMSS) and the Program for International Student Assessment (PISA)—resulting in a sample of 4,491 items overall.

Our analysis produced a conceptual framework with two broad categories: items that required declarative knowledge about science and items that did not require declarative knowledge about science. That is, while a substantial majority (about 86 percent) of the items assessed students' understanding of scientific concepts, generalizations, and principles, the remaining items only required students read and understand provided scientific information, analyze and interpret data, or utilize mathematics skills and procedures within the context of science without calling on any external scientific knowledge.

Items that required knowledge of scientific concepts, generalizations, and principles fell into five distinct content categories: (1) physical science, (2) life science, (3) earth and space science, (4) engineering and technology, and (5) scientific investigation. While reading comprehension, data analysis, and mathematics were also sometimes called for in these items, we grouped all items that required declarative science knowledge together, regardless of the other skills involved. Among the content categories, earth and space science, physical science, and life science each encompassed a substantial portion of the items, while engineering and technology and scientific investigation items were relatively infrequent. To a greater extent than mathematics or ELA items, science items required students to know and recall specific content rather than determine what knowledge or procedures to apply to a given problem or reason through provided information.

We divided the items that did not require declarative science knowledge into three categories: data analysis, calculation using formulas, and reading comprehension. While these items typically appeared within a scientific context, they did not require students have any specific scientific knowledge outside of information provided in the item itself. Among these items, data analysis (involving the interpretation or creation of data sets and displays) was the most frequently needed skill. Reading comprehension items, which asked students to understand and interpret text, illustrations, and models (not including data displays), were the second-most frequent, with items involving mathematics calculations or concepts being the least frequent. Given the relative homogeneity of science item formats and the fact that most require specific scientific knowledge, success on large-scale science assessments depends primarily on ensuring students know the most critical content at each grade level.

What You Will Find in This Book

In the book's six chapters, you will find discussions of the nature and impact of large-scale assessments and actions you can take to mitigate the potential negative effects of those assessments on students. In particular, we focus on how teachers can make students aware of the idiosyncrasies of standardized test items by exposing them to similar items on classroom assessments. Thus, you can use test items to deepen students' understanding of the content as well as prepare them to demonstrate that knowledge on large-scale tests. You will also find a detailed analysis of our findings for ELA, mathematics, and science.

Specifically, chapter 1 addresses the history of large-scale assessment in the United States and the impact such assessment can have on students' educational careers. Chapter 2 addresses our findings and recommendations for ELA. Using the frames for each item type that our study revealed, educators can construct ELA items that reflect the typical form and content of those in large-scale assessments.

Chapter 3 addresses our findings and recommendations for mathematics. The diversity of item formats in mathematics did not allow for the more general item-creation guidelines the ELA analysis produced. To facilitate the creation of classroom assessment items in mathematics, we developed a set of templates that represent the most common item formats present within each subcategory (see appendix A, page 187). These templates allow educators to quickly create multiple distinct items that share the same general form and content as the test items in our analysis.

Chapter 4 addresses our findings and recommendations for science. For items that draw on students' knowledge of science, we explain how educators can use proficiency scales to identify and address the most important content. Given the presence of items that do not require prior declarative science knowledge on science tests, we suggest that educators should instruct students to identify this type of item, and we provide strategies for creating items of this type.

In chapter 5, we consider the issue of test preparation and how this book forms the basis for an approach that follows the recommendations of those who create large-scale assessments. In chapter 6, we describe a step-by-step process to create a school- or districtwide approach to help K–12 students understand various item formats and gain experience with the critical content educators will assess them on. Additionally, there are two appendices that provide resources and information educators can use to implement the recommendations made in this book.

As you engage with the next six chapters, we hope that you will leverage our analysis and recommendations as appropriate to your role as an educator. For K–12 classroom teachers, the recommendations found in the following chapters can be used in at least three transformational ways. First, using the item frames described in chapters 2, 3, and 4 allows teachers to create high-quality assessment items quickly and efficiently. Second, teaching students to use the item frames to create their own test items is a strategy that can deepen students' understanding of the content, while simultaneously familiarizing them with the structures of the items they'll encounter on large-scale assessments. Finally, even in grades K–2, the recommendations in the following chapters can inform teachers about which content may take a higher priority over more supplemental content in the standards. For K–12 educational leaders, we encourage you to consider the impact of this book's recommendations when implemented across an entire school or district. While these practices have the potential to transform classroom instruction, implementing them systemwide across content areas and grade levels can revolutionize educators' approach to teaching and test preparation.

CHAPTER 1

A Brief Overview of Large-Scale Assessments in the United States

Large-scale assessments have been a part of the educational landscape in the United States since the mid-1800s. Reformers who believed schools should serve the masses of American society advocated common written assessments both as a more equitable and efficient means of evaluating and managing increasingly large school systems, and as a spur to what they perceived as other needed improvements in education. Secretary of the Massachusetts Board of Education Horace Mann became the first to implement this type of examination on a broad scale when he directed a common written assessment be given to several hundred students in the Boston area in 1845 (Mann, 1845). Mann was a leading proponent of free public schooling and other progressive ideas in education, embodied in the common school movement. To Mann (1845), common schools represented the fulfillment of the American democratic ideal, as students would be "educated in a truly republican manner, educated together, under the same roof, on the same seats, with the same encouragements, rewards, punishments, and to the exclusion of adventitious and artificial distinctions" (p. 80).

Faced with a large and rapidly growing student population and local schoolmasters reluctant to change long-held practices, Mann (1845) and his reform-minded colleagues, including physician Samuel Gridley Howe, scholar Theophilus Parsons, and minister Rollin H. Neale, hoped to use common written assessments to address both issues. They enumerated the advantages of a common set of printed questions demanding written answers over the public oral exhibitions and recitations prevalent in the evaluation of schools to that time (Mann, 1845). First, they asserted that such written assessments were perfectly objective and impartial. In contrast to the impressionistic reports generated from previous inspections and oral examinations, timed written examinations would offer "positive information, in black and white" about student learning (Mann, 1845, p. 291).

This standardization and generation of hard data in turn allowed for an equitable comparison among students and schools, which was a central purpose of the assessments (Mann, 1845). These comparative data were intended not only for the use of school and state officials but also for public consumption. Adherents of the new science of statistics, the reformers carefully tabulated the results of the exams "so that the common eye can compare them, and determine at a glance the relative standing of each school" (Mann, 1845, p. 289). Generally speaking, students fared poorly on the exams, with average scores ranging from 26 percent in history to 39 percent in grammar (Reese, 2013). Mann and his allies saw publicizing test results as a way to garner community support for their mission to change entrenched and (as they perceived them) unsound practices in schools.

In this respect, the early uses of large-scale assessment seem to follow the sequence of postulating a problem, then administering tests to obtain evidence of that problem. This inaugurated a pattern in educational reform in which "tests are often administered not just to discover how well schools or kids are doing, but rather to obtain external confirmation-validation—of the hypothesis that they are not doing well at all" (U.S. Congress, Office of Technology Assessment, 1992, p. 108). This sort of confirmation bias may also have led the reformers to overlook or minimize the host of complicating factors surrounding the administration of the written exams. For example, Mann and his colleagues gave scant consideration to the effect the novelty of their method would have had on student responses. The examiners showed up to schools without prior notice (Mann, 1845), and administered timed written exams to students whose writing experience was largely "confined to copybooks and slates" (Kaestle, 2012, p. 5).

Confident in the virtues of their new assessments, Mann and his colleagues used the results to inform what today would be termed *high-stakes decisions* about public school education and educators. Though not explicitly using the language of *accountability*, the reformers held schools and teachers responsible for students' poor performance on the examination.

The motives that drove the Boston reformers seemed to intensify through the rest of the 19th century and into the 20th century. Immigration, mandatory attendance laws, and the demands of a rapidly industrializing economy drove up enrollment, and large, urban school systems in particular turned increasingly to standardized written tests to help educators make decisions about student placement and promotion (Gallagher, 2003; Kaestle, 2012). By 1878, a Chicago-area administrator remarked that America had entered "an age of examinations" (Reese, 2013, p. 1). With the proliferation of tests came a flurry of now-familiar critiques: testing cut into valuable instructional time, focused on recall rather than comprehension and analysis, and harmed students' health by forcing them into stressful cramming and "over-study" (Reese, 2013). While testing as a whole was largely unaffected, such criticisms did have the effect of temporarily shifting emphasis away from high-stakes, year-end promotion exams to a system of more frequent smaller examinations throughout the year (Reese, 2013).

Intelligence Testing in the Early 20th Century

In the early 20th century, testing shifted focus to the measurement of intelligence and spawned some of the most extraordinary abuses in the history of assessment. Following an intellectual tradition that posited intelligence was "hereditary, unitary, and largely immutable," American psychologists such as Henry Goddard and Lewis Terman sought to devise and use intelligence tests to sort people into the roles in which they would be the most socially useful (Gallagher, 2003, p. 87). Ironically, the famous Stanford-Binet intelligence test Terman created in 1916 to determine IQ was an adaptation of the test and scales created in 1905 by French psychologist Alfred Binet, who believed intelligence was neither fixed nor a single, unified entity (Kaestle, 2012).

The use of intelligence testing for classifying people into roles gained popularity and prestige particularly after the U.S. Army administered its Alpha test to sort recruits into various jobs during World War I (Kaestle, 2012). Those who achieved the highest scores were recommended for officer training, promotion, or specialized tasks, while those with low scores were either discharged or assigned to menial work or regular service (Yoakum & Yerkes, 1920). The Army Alpha test also constituted the first significant use of the multiple-choice question format, which made scoring more objective and efficient, encouraging the use of standardized tests on ever greater scales (U.S. Congress, Office of Technology Assessment, 1992).

One of the most unfortunate consequences of the increased propensity to systematically classify large groups of people through testing was the use of test data to support racist, xenophobic, and eugenicist policies and attitudes. For several of the most prominent social scientists of the era, patterns of test scores among immigrants justified a belief in the innate superiority of people of Northern European descent over people from Slavic, Mediterranean, African, and other backgrounds. These attitudes manifested themselves in support for restrictive and discriminatory immigration policies. For some, the ultimate implication of a desire for social improvement combined with the belief that education and environment could not meaningfully improve intelligence was support for eugenics, including such policies as the forced sterilization of the "feeble-minded" (Kaestle, 2012, p. 9).

In an educational context, intelligence tests enabled schools to place students on different curricular tracks according to their tested capabilities (Clarke, Madaus, Horn, & Ramos, 2000). But some observers also saw value in ranking and classifying students. In 1913, psychologist Edward Thorndike, who helped bring greater standardization to educational measurement, commented:

> Educational agencies are a great system of means not only of making men good and intelligent and efficient but also of picking out and labeling those who for any reason are good and intelligent and efficient. . . .

They help society by providing it not with better men but with the knowledge of which men are good. (as cited in Gallagher, 2003, p. 86)

In addition to these tests of general intelligence, achievement tests also gained in popularity during the 1920s and 1930s, benefitting from the pervasive obsession with efficiency
and scientifically supported decision making. School systems sought to assess both student
progress and instructional effectiveness in a more systematic and correlated fashion. Under
the direction of education professor E. F. Lindquist, the University of Iowa created the Iowa
Test of Basic Skills and the Iowa Test of Educational Development in 1929 and used them
in the first-ever statewide administration of student-achievement tests. They remained the
most popular commercial achievement test in the United States for more than fifty years
(Gallagher, 2003).

A final innovation of the early 20th century was the SAT, designed to assess students'
readiness for college-level work. The test, first administered in 1926, was the work of the
College Board, a group of higher education officials seeking to standardize and streamline
admissions procedures at colleges across the United States. A hybrid between a curriculum-
based achievement test and a general-intelligence test, the comprehensive SAT was meant
to establish that students had a baseline of content knowledge, while also filtering out
those of meager intellectual ability who merely crammed for tests (U.S. Congress, Office
of Technology Assessment, 1992). The SAT carried over to the realm of college admissions
the need to systematically discriminate among and classify students, which drove the explo-
sion of standardized testing in the early 20th century. A new set of imperatives would help
shape testing policy and practice in the years after World War II.

Post–World War II Educational Assessment Policies and Trends

The urgency of international competition and concerns about equity in American society
drove significant changes in educational assessment in the decades following World War II.
The launch of the Sputnik satellite by the Soviet Union in 1957 aroused anxiety among the
American public and government that the nation's education system was falling behind
that of the Soviet Union, particularly in the domains of mathematics, science, and technology. In response, Congress passed the National Defense Education Act of 1958, which
poured hundreds of millions of dollars into education and provided for testing programs
to identify gifted students (Clarke et al., 2000). At around the same time, the invention of
a high-speed optical scanner enabled the proliferation of multiple-choice exams by making
scoring cheaper and faster (U.S. Congress, Office of Technology Assessment, 1992).

The Elementary and Secondary Education Act (ESEA) of 1965, which president Lyndon
B. Johnson signed as part of his War on Poverty, gave further impetus to large-scale testing.
Title I of the act directed federal funds toward schools with high numbers of students from
low-income families in an effort to close achievement gaps among students of different
backgrounds. In an attempt to ensure the money was being spent effectively, however,

ESEA mandated testing to evaluate the impact of its funded programs (Wigdor & Garner, 1982), part of a larger trend toward the use of cost-benefit analysis in policy making (Kaestle, 2012).

As part of the broader push for data collection and evaluation, the federal government instituted NAEP in 1969. States followed suit in instituting their own testing programs, but declining SAT scores, economic anxiety, and concerns over the perceived diminishing value of a high school diploma prompted a shift from using these tests as system diagnostic tools to employing them to ensure minimum competencies among students over the course of the 1970s (Shepard, 2008).

The pendulum swung away from minimum competency with the publication of the 1983 report "A Nation at Risk," but the use of large-scale assessments only intensified. The report warned a "rising tide of mediocrity" would swamp American students in an increasingly competitive and globalized economic environment (National Commission on Excellence in Education, 1983, p. 5). In addition to raising graduation requirements, many states expanded testing programs in the name of increasing oversight and accountability (Kaestle, 2012). The increased frequency and higher stakes of large-scale assessments in turn led to concerns about a narrowing of the curriculum and the cost of testing in terms of both time and resources (Shepard, 2008).

In the 1990s, educational reformers devoted increased attention to the nature of curricula and assessments with an emphasis on more uniform, rigorous standards that emphasized reasoning and inquiry alongside content knowledge. Various groups of specialists developed bodies of standards for their respective subject areas, and states were encouraged to develop their own content standards and aligned assessments through the passage of the Goals 2000: Educate America Act in 1994 (Clarke et al., 2000; Kaestle, 2012). The more complex cognitive skills the new standards demanded were accompanied by a push toward new modes of assessment, such as portfolios and extended constructed-response tasks that would better reflect real-world situations (Kaestle, 2012). While these performance assessments enjoyed initial enthusiasm among assessment experts, they quickly fell out of widespread favor due to issues of cost, reliability, validity, and generalizability of the results (Pearson & Hamm, 2005).

The standards movement continued into the 2000s, while the stakes of accountability testing became ever higher for districts, schools, teachers, and students. No Child Left Behind (NCLB), the 2001 reauthorization of ESEA, mandated yearly statewide testing for students in grades 3–8 (and once in high school), and included severe sanctions for schools that did not demonstrate "adequate yearly progress" toward reading and mathematics proficiency goals (Gallagher, 2003, p. 94). President Barack Obama's administration granted states more flexibility in structuring their accountability systems, but left the yearly testing requirements in place. Federal Race to the Top grants incentivized additional education reforms, including the adoption of high-quality state standards and aligned assessments. While some states devised their own standards, most adopted the Common Core State Standards that the National Governors Association and the Council of Chief State School

Officers developed. The standards were released in 2010, and the Smarter Balanced and PARCC consortia of states created assessments aligned to the Common Core in subsequent years (Kaestle, 2012). In 2021, while many states still use the Common Core standards or modified versions of them, only around a third of states still use the consortia-built assessments (Gewertz, 2019). Though the form and scope of large-scale educational assessment have changed significantly over its 150-year history, its use as not only a measure of performance but also a spur to reform has remained remarkably consistent.

Consequences of Standardized Testing for Individual Students

Large-scale standardized tests can have profound consequences for individual students. Throughout a student's K–12 career, test results can influence educators' decisions about placement and grouping, grade promotion or retention, and graduation from high school. For postsecondary education, test scores factor into admissions decisions, scholarship opportunities, and determinations of career readiness. The precise ways educators use testing to inform these decisions vary widely among states and institutions, but with U.S. federal legislation mandating testing every year from third to eighth grade and once in high school, large-scale standardized assessment constitutes a major part of every student's educational experience.

Ability Grouping and Tracking

Decisions about placement and grouping are among the first consequences of testing for schoolchildren. While testing for the purpose of educational grouping has gone through various iterations since its first widespread use in schools in the 1920s, contemporary practice encompasses two primary forms: ability grouping and tracking. *Ability grouping* refers to the practice of dividing students within a class into smaller, more homogenous instructional groups based on ability level. This is typically done in elementary school, often for reading in early grades and reading or mathematics in later grades (Loveless, 2013). Ability grouping is intended to be more flexible and less formal than tracking, with instructional-unit changes and frequent reassessment leading to reorganization of groups throughout the school year. In its modern formulation, *tracking* refers to the practice of dividing students into separate classes, subject by subject, according to ability or prior achievement. It generally no longer entails dividing students among entirely distinct curricular pathways, such as college preparatory, general, and vocational tracks (Loveless, 2013). Tracking is most common in high schools, as in the placement of students into honors, advanced placement (AP), or International Baccalaureate (IB) courses, and it also remains prevalent for mathematics courses in middle school (Loveless, 2016).

Much of the research on tracking and ability grouping suggests the practices benefit students in higher tracks and groups (Card & Giuliano, 2016; Loveless, 2016), but often with the caveat that these gains for high achievers accompany losses for students in lower tracks and groups (Fu & Mehta, 2018; Jean, 2016; Lleras & Rangel, 2009). Research on the effects of within-class ability grouping in particular yields mixed results, in part because educators can implement it in many different ways. One point of general consensus is, if teachers use ability grouping, flexibility and fluidity of group assignments based on changes in instructional content and constant reassessment are important to ensure students receive instruction targeted to their specific needs. Students can and should move up to a more complex level of content as soon as they are prepared to do so (Gamoran, 1992; Jean, 2016; Olszewski-Kubilius, 2013; Ward, 1987).

For these approaches, test results inform educational judgments of students' achievement and preparedness levels, and thus their placement in a given group, course, or track. While the consequences of grouping may no longer be as enduring as assignment to immutable curricular sequences, the continued prevalence of grouping and tracking and the possibility of their differential effects on students make it important to ensure the measurements informing these decisions are valid and reliable.

Promotion and Retention

Testing also influences students' progress from grade to grade. As of the 2019–2020 school year, fifteen states used test scores to determine a student's eligibility for promotion to the next grade at least once between kindergarten and twelfth grade. The most common version of such a policy (adopted in fourteen states) requires students to pass a reading test at the end of third grade to advance to fourth grade. Five states used test scores for promotion at more than one grade level, as table 1.1 (page 16) shows. The exact specifications of the retention policies vary from state to state, with *good-cause exemptions* allowed for many of the reading requirements. These exemptions can include limited proficiency in English, special education status, educational interventions, educator or parent recommendations, previous retention, proficiency demonstrated through a portfolio, or the passage of an alternative reading assessment (Weyer, 2019).

These mandatory retention policies aim to limit the practice of *social promotion*, which refers to the promotion of students to the next grade with their age group rather than according to their academic proficiency. However, research conflicts on the relative merits of social promotion and grade retention. While some researchers and policy advocates cite increased scores on achievement tests among some retained students relative to their nonretained peers (Greene & Winters, 2007; Ladner & Burke, 2010), many studies have indicated students do not benefit academically from retention, especially over the long term, and retained students are substantially more likely to drop out of school than their promoted peers (Jimerson, 2001; Penfield, 2010; Xia & Kirby, 2009).

Other researchers point out that the debate over social promotion versus retention represents a false dichotomy, with neither strategy being effective in isolation (Jimerson, 2001; National Research Council, 1999; University of Northern Colorado, 2011). For example, beyond test-based retention, Florida's state policy mandates retained students receive instruction from a high-performing teacher, carry out an individualized

Table 1.1: States With Test-Based Mandatory Grade-Retention Policies

State	Promotion Test Grades	Promotion Test Subjects
Arizona	3	Reading
California	3	Reading
	4	Reading, ELA, Mathematics
	End of elementary school	Reading, ELA, Mathematics
	End of middle school	Reading, ELA, Mathematics
Connecticut	K	Reading
	1	Reading
	2	Reading
	3	Reading
Delaware	3	Reading
	5	Reading
	8	Reading, Mathematics
Florida	3	Reading
Georgia	3	Reading
	5	Reading, Mathematics
	8	Reading, Mathematics
Indiana	3	Reading
Iowa	3	Reading
Michigan	3	Reading
Mississippi	3	Reading
Missouri	3	Reading
North Carolina	3	Reading
Ohio	3	Reading
South Carolina	3	Reading
Texas	5	Reading, Mathematics
	8	Reading, Mathematics

Source: Adapted from Weyer, 2019.

academic-improvement plan, and receive other specialized interventions as needed (University of Northern Colorado, 2011).

Regardless of their relative efficacy, neither social promotion nor retention appears to be a desirable outcome, given that each reflects a response to an observed deficiency in learning over a given time period. Some educational policy researchers (National Research

Council, 1999; University of Northern Colorado, 2011) suggest that rather than obsessing over the merits or defects of mandatory retention or social promotion, researchers and educators should focus on strategies to reduce the need for such either-or choices, such as early identification and support for struggling students. Yet assessment results still at least partially inform such identifications and decisions about the provision of support services and interventions. Therefore, valid test interpretations remain critical to ensuring students' progress through school at an appropriate rate, even in the absence of a test-based mandatory retention policy.

Graduation

For many students, standardized test results also determine whether or not they will graduate from high school. The use of large-scale tests to determine graduation eligibility has declined sharply since the early 2010s, when around half of U.S. states required students to pass an exit exam (Hyslop, 2014; Mathews, 2017; McIntosh, 2012). However, ten states maintain the practice, including three of the five most populous: Florida, New York, and Texas. See table 1.2 (page 18) for a complete list of states that include standardized testing as a graduation requirement.

As with many other uses of standardized tests, exit exams remain contested and policies on them fluctuate year to year. Some states have incorporated alternative nontest pathways to graduation, such as gaining college admission, passing certain college-level or dual-credit classes, or completing career and technical education course sequences (Nadvornick, 2019).

The drop in states' use of graduation tests has accompanied a debate over their value. Exit-exam policies are intended to improve students' achievement, especially among the lowest performers, by increasing students' motivation and prompting schools to provide them with greater resources and more effective instruction (Greene & Winters, 2004; Holme, Richards, Jimerson, & Cohen, 2010). They are also meant to reinforce the value of a diploma in the eyes of employers and colleges by certifying that students have mastered a baseline of knowledge and skill, thereby improving postsecondary outcomes such as college admissions and completion, and employment and earnings among high school graduates (Greene & Winters, 2004; Holme et al., 2010; Hyslop, 2014).

In a 2010 review of the literature on exit exams, writers Jennifer Jellison Holme, Meredith P. Richards, Jo Beth Jimerson, and Rebecca W. Cohen concluded such policies largely failed to achieve these intended outcomes and were associated with negative consequences for disadvantaged students. Increases in high school achievement, college attendance or completion, or employment or earnings did not accompany exit-exam policies. However, higher drop-out rates, especially among low-achieving students, racial minorities, and students in high-poverty urban schools, did accompany more rigorous exit exams (Holme et al., 2010). A National Research Council (2011) report using studies that enabled causal conclusions rather than mere correlations made similar determinations regarding a lack of effect on achievement and negative impacts on graduation rates. As states adopted the

Table 1.2: States With Tests as a Graduation Requirement

State	Exit Exam	Notes
Florida	Florida Standards Assessments (FSA)	Students must pass exit exams or achieve specified scores on ACT or SAT.
Louisiana	Louisiana Educational Assessment Program (LEAP 2025)	Students must pass one subject in each of three subject pairs.
Maryland	Maryland Comprehensive Assessment Program (MCAP)	Can substitute AP or IB test scores. A *Bridge Plan* project-based alternative is available after failing an MCAP exam test twice.
Massachusetts	Massachusetts Comprehensive Assessment System (MCAS)	Students who do not pass the requisite MCAS exams can fulfill the requirement through completion of a portfolio and an Educational Proficiency Plan. There is also an MCAS performance-appeals process.
New Jersey	New Jersey Student Learning Assessments (NJSLA)	Students must pass NJSLA or pass alternative assessments, including the ACT or SAT. There is a portfolio-based appeal process for those who fail the requisite exams.
New Mexico	New Mexico Measures of Student Success and Achievement (NM-MSSA)	Students must pass NM-MSSA or alternative assessments or complete competency-based alternatives.
New York	Regents Examinations	Students must pass five exams.
Ohio	Ohio's State Tests	Students must pass end-of-course exams or achieve specified scores on other tests, such as ACT or SAT. Ohio also has a graduation pathway requiring an industry credential and minimum score on the WorkKeys career-readiness assessment.
Texas	State of Texas Assessments of Academic Readiness (STAAR)	Students must pass five end-of-course exams.
Virginia	Standards of Learning (SOL)	Students must pass SOL exams or achieve specified scores on other tests, including ACT, SAT, AP, or IB.

Source: Adapted from Gewertz, 2019.

Common Core or other more rigorous standards, existing exit exams no longer aligned to the curriculum (Harrington & Freedberg, 2017), and schools switching to Common Core–aligned assessments faced the prospect of lower graduation rates if they used those tests' higher proficiency standard as the bar for graduation eligibility (Barnum, 2016; Hyslop, 2014; Strauss, 2014). Exit exams' lack of proven positive impact, combined with their potentially adverse effects for some students, provided little incentive for most states to replace or reconstitute their graduation tests (Barnett, 2013; Barnum, 2016).

Changes in high school graduation policies since the early 2000s have heeded calls for multiple measures of student achievement rather than reliance on a single test score (Darling-Hammond, Rustique-Forrester, & Pecheone, 2005). Yet the states still using exit exams as of 2019 enroll more than a third of public school students in the United States (National Center for Education Statistics, 2018a), and many of the alternate pathways in other states still involve standardized tests in some form. Even with the decline in exit exams, large-scale testing remains an important component of determining students' eligibility for graduation.

College Admission

The use of large-scale standardized tests in college admissions is one of the oldest and most prominent ways testing can affect the educational lives of individual students. Major universities' goal of unifying their admissions standards produced the College Board's first common entrance exam in 1901 (Clarke et al., 2000). The SAT and ACT are the dominant large-scale assessments educators use to determine a student's preparedness for college. However, such determinations now affect a far greater proportion of the American public than they did in the early 20th century. In 2017, more than 40 percent of eighteen- to twenty-four-year-olds in the United States were enrolled in college (National Center for Education Statistics, 2018b), compared to 2 percent in 1900 (National Center for Education Statistics, 1993).

Educators most often judge (and promote) the SAT and ACT for their capacity to predict college performance, particularly first-year grades. The idea that the SAT could "gauge students' general analytic ability, as distinct from their mastery of specific subject matter" was the key component of the College Board's assertion that it could predict future performance (Atkinson & Geiser, 2009, p. 666). Research generally supports the ACT and SAT as predictive of college success, but most studies find high school GPA is the single best predictor, for both first-year grades and longer-term outcomes such as college graduation and cumulative college grades (Atkinson & Geiser, 2009; Galla et al., 2019; Geiser & Santelices, 2007).

The value of the large-scale admissions tests primarily derives from supplementing information from high school transcripts, as test scores used in conjunction with grades have often been found to have higher predictive validity than grades alone (Atkinson & Geiser, 2009; Zwick, 2013). Combining test scores with grades also helps mitigate concerns about grade inflation, variability in quality and rigor from school to school (Gershenson, 2018; Jaschik, 2017), and high school grades' possible overprediction of college performance among certain groups (Zwick, 2013).

Nevertheless, concerns that large-scale admissions testing replicates existing inequalities in educational and social opportunities prompted more colleges and universities to adopt test-optional admissions policies, particularly since the mid-2010s. More than one thousand schools have now made SAT and ACT scores an optional component of their application or otherwise de-emphasized test scores in admissions criteria (FairTest, 2021). This group includes numerous small liberal arts colleges, several large public universities, and a few high-profile institutions, such as the University of Chicago and George Washington University. Admissions officials at many of these colleges and universities frame these policies to increase diversity on their campuses by encouraging more applications from groups historically underrepresented in U.S. higher education (Syverson, Franks, & Hiss, 2018). When large-scale admissions assessments were first widely adopted in the mid-20th century, proponents such as Educational Testing Service founder Henry Chauncey conceived of them as possible equalizing agents that could allow students from disadvantaged circumstances to access college through demonstrated academic aptitude rather than elevated social status (Lemann, 1999). But some subsequent research indicates admissions test scores are even more closely correlated to socioeconomic characteristics than high school grades and are, therefore, more likely to hinder minority students, who disproportionately come from disadvantaged backgrounds (Atkinson & Geiser, 2009; Geiser & Santelices, 2007; Rothstein, 2004). In a 2018 study, a majority of participating institutions with test-optional policies reported a greater increase in applications and freshman-class representation among underrepresented minority students and students from lower socioeconomic backgrounds than matched schools that required test scores (Syverson et al., 2018). Beyond the direct effects of admitting students who choose not to submit scores, some observers suggest that test-optional policies create a welcoming environment by indicating to low-income and minority students that the school is sensitive to issues affecting them (Jaschik, 2018).

Advocates of large-scale standardized testing and the testing companies themselves question the effectiveness of such policies. Some research suggests test-optional schools have not, on average, outpaced their test-requiring peers in increasing diversity within the student body (Belasco, Rosinger, & Hearn, 2015). In test-optional cases in which diversity has increased at a higher rate, testing supporters point out that other institutional changes besides a test-optional policy might have contributed (Jaschik, 2018). Though most students still submit scores even when doing so is optional (Syverson et al., 2018), critics also contend that elite schools may benefit in terms of higher perceived selectivity by making test-score reporting optional. Lower-scoring students would tend not to submit their scores, thereby increasing the average admissions test scores for the institution (Belasco et al., 2015). Still, the major admissions testing companies have acknowledged that socioeconomic factors are related to performance on their exams (College Board, 2018b; Wilkinson, 2014).

More broadly, the trend in college-admissions testing has been toward curriculum-oriented assessment of achievement rather than pure ability testing. The ACT was introduced in 1959 as an achievement-based alternative to the SAT, a hybrid assessment of ability and achievement (Atkinson & Geiser, 2009). The SAT itself more explicitly emphasized a link to classroom instruction in its latest redesign in 2016 (College Board, 2015).

Achievement-oriented AP and IB exams also factor into college admissions, especially at more selective institutions. The inherent appeal of achievement-based admissions tests lies in creating closer alignment with curriculum, instruction, and assessment, though the lack of unified national standards means admissions tests administered nationwide could not perfectly align with teaching at any particular school. Though the form and intended function of large-scale admissions assessments continues to evolve, their prevalence remains. More than 2.1 million students in the graduating class of 2018 took the SAT (College Board, 2018b), and around 1.9 million took the ACT (2018), an increase from the prior year for both tests.

COVID-19's Impact on Large-Scale Assessment

The COVID-19 pandemic disrupted the entire American education system, including large-scale assessments. With schools across the United States forced to close or move to remote learning near the end of the 2019–2020 school year, the U.S. Department of Education waived the requirement for state-accountability testing (Sparks, 2020). School officials cancelled or postponed spring and summer SAT and ACT testing opportunities, and many colleges dropped admissions-testing requirements, at least temporarily, as a result (Selingo, 2020).

As the pandemic continued through the fall and winter of 2020 and into 2021, some states sought accountability-testing waivers for the 2020–2021 school year as well. Proponents of these waivers raised concerns about the safety of in-person testing, as well as the validity and usefulness of any form of large-scale assessment during such an unsettled period in education. Others argued that a two-year gap in testing would deprive educators, parents, and governments of the valuable data they need to monitor and improve schools (Ujifusa, 2020). Meanwhile, the National Center for Education Statistics delayed the planned 2021–2022 administration of NAEP (Woodworth, 2020). In admissions, while some colleges planned to only pause their testing requirements, others, including the massive University of California system, committed to eliminating those requirements permanently (Selingo, 2020). The long-term effects of the coronavirus on large-scale standardized assessments remain to be seen, but the pandemic again brought the utility and fairness of such assessments to the forefront of public discussion.

Summary

In this chapter we provided a panoramic view of the history of large-scale assessments in the United States and an overview of the implications such assessments have for students. Large-scale assessments have been part of American public education since its earliest years. While the methods and purposes of assessment have shifted along with changes in society and new understanding about the nature of learning and intelligence, many of the concerns around high-stakes testing remain the same. Meanwhile, the prevalence of large-scale assessments and the impact they can have on students' lives have increased over time, with test results potentially affecting placement and grouping, promotion from one grade to the next, graduation, and admission to college. Given the importance large-scale assessments retain in the American education system and the lives of students, it is essential that students learn to navigate the idiosyncratic nature of large-scale assessment items.

CHAPTER 2

Analysis of English Language Arts Assessment Items

As described in the introduction (page 1), analysts at Marzano Resources undertook a study of large-scale assessment items with the goal of helping educators equip students to succeed on such tests. In our study, we analyzed 1,684 ELA items. We organized those items into three broad categories: reading, language, and writing. Table 2.1 (page 24) depicts the general findings from our ELA study.

An obvious inference from table 2.1 is that reading items make up the majority of items (83 percent) across the three domains of reading, language, and writing. More nuanced inferences are observable when you consider the types of items within these three domains. Table 2.2 (page 24) depicts two main categories of item types: selected-response items and constructed-response items, and the three ELA domains: reading, language, and writing. Perhaps the most salient finding is that over 80 percent of the items in the study dealt with reading using a selected-response item format. Therefore, we consider these items first.

Selected-Response Reading Items

If a school or district were to use the findings from our study to develop a strategy for ensuring students do well on externally developed assessments in ELA, educators would be well advised to focus on reading items that employ a selected-response format, since over 80 percent of the items in our study fit this profile.

As their name implies, *selected-response items* present students with possible right answers and they select the answer they believe is the best. These include traditional multiple-choice items with a single correct answer, but also encompass variants such as multiple-select, text highlighting, matching, and true/false. There are six basic structures or *frames* in selected-response reading items. In all situations, students read a passage and then respond

Table 2.1: General Findings From ELA Study

	Reading	Language	Writing	Total	Percentage of Items
Grade 3	94	5	10	109	6
Grade 4	156	6	19	181	11
Grade 5	119	5	13	137	8
Grade 6	166	6	14	186	11
Grade 7	121	5	11	137	8
Grade 8	145	5	15	165	10
Grade 9	148	0	13	161	10
Grade 10	129	0	9	138	8
Grade 11	204	4	18	226	13
Grade 12 (NAEP)	25	0	6	31	2
SAT	52	44	1	97	6
ACT	40	75	1	116	7
Total	1,399	155	130	1,684	100
Percentage of Items	83	9	8	100	

Table 2.2: General Findings by Item Types

Item Type	Domain	Number of Items	Percentage of Items
Selected response	Reading	1,344	80
	Language	155	9
Short constructed response	Reading	55	3
Extended constructed response	Writing	130	8
Total		1,684	100

to the selected-response items. Table 2.3 depicts the six frames. Note that table 2.3 focuses on part A of the 1,344 analyzed selected-response reading items. This is because the majority of selected-response reading items we analyzed have two parts: part A and part B. Student responses to part B of an item are dependent on how they answer part A. We discuss this in depth later (page 26).

Table 2.3: Reading Frames in Selected-Response Items (Part A)

Frame	Number of Items	Percentage of Items	Most Common Stems
Big Idea	314	23.36	What is a central idea of the [Text]? What is the main idea of the [Text]? What is a theme of the [Text]?
Detail	290	21.58	According to the text, [Who, What, When, Where, Why, or How]? Based on the text, [Who, What, When, Where, Why, or How]?
Meaning	285	21.21	What is the meaning of [Word or Phrase] as it is used in the text?
Function	258	19.20	How does [Textual Element] do [Literary Element]? How does [Textual Element] affect [Literary Element]? How does [Textual Element] influence [Literary Element]? What is the relationship between [Textual Element] and [Literary Element] in terms of understanding the overall passage?
Purpose	108	8.04	What is the purpose of [Textual Element]? What is the author's purpose in this section of the text?
Evidence	89	6.62	What evidence supports [Claim]? What evidence supports [Conclusion]? What evidence supports [Opinion]? What evidence supports [Statement]?
Total	1,344	100	

Of the six reading frames, the big idea frame represents what you might consider the traditional conception of the main idea. Indeed, understanding the main idea of a passage is probably what most people associate with reading comprehension. It makes intuitive sense that if students understand the main idea of a passage, then they comprehend the passage. In table 2.3, this type of item accounted for only about 23 percent of the items we analyzed. The other five types of frames accounted for the remaining 77 percent. A reasonable question is, therefore, Where did an emphasis on the other five types of reading frames originate? The answer is that they have their roots in the close-reading movement.

Although close reading can be traced to the New Criticism movement (which focused on finding the "correct" reading of a passage in the 20th century), it became prominent at the beginning of the 21st century. In 2006, ACT released "Reading Between the Lines," a report warning that only 51 percent of U.S. high school graduates were ready for college-level reading, the lowest point in more than a decade. The ability to read and understand complex texts explained the disparity between students who met the ACT reading benchmark and those who did not, not the comprehension level or textual elements tested. The report defined a *complex text* as having subtle, involved, or deeply embedded relationships among ideas or characters; richness in the amount and sophistication of information conveyed; elaborate or unconventional structure; intricate style; demanding and highly context-dependent vocabulary; and an implicit or ambiguous purpose. The ability to discern the meaning of these texts was found to be "the clearest differentiator in reading between students who are likely to be ready for college and those who are not"—a relationship that held true across genders, racial and ethnic groups, and family income levels (ACT, 2006, pp. 16–17). The effects extended beyond reading. Of those students who did not meet the ACT reading benchmark, only 16 percent met the benchmark for college readiness in mathematics and only 5 percent in science. The ability to understand complex texts and the subsequent link to reading skill impacted success across the entire curriculum (Student Achievement Partners, 2015).

Research into the importance of complex texts heavily influenced the development of the Common Core State Standards and close reading emerged as a practice strongly associated with the instructional shifts in the standards (Student Achievement Partners, 2015). The CCSS Anchor Standard for Reading 1 asks students to "Read closely to determine what the text says explicitly" (National Governors Association Center for Best Practices & Council of Chief State School Officers [NGA & CCSSO], 2010, p. 10) and the authors note, "Students who meet the Standards readily undertake the close, attentive reading that is at the heart of understanding and enjoying complex works of literature" (p. 3). Because it was not widely practiced prior to the adoption of the standards, close reading has not been studied directly (Student Achievement Partners, 2015). However, close reading is based on well-researched components found to promote comprehension, including vocabulary (National Center for Education Statistics, 2012), syntax (Goff, Pratt, & Ong, 2005), fluency (National Reading Panel, 2000; Paige, 2011), deliberate practice (Ericsson, Krampe, & Tesch-Römer, 1993), and a high standard for coherence (Pearson & Liben, 2013).

Close reading, then, has changed the landscape of what educators expect of students as they read. Rather than simply discerning the gist of rather large sections of text, the focus of reading comprehension is analyzing sections of text. This actually makes good sense from a practical perspective, particularly with expository content. One rarely, if ever, reads a chapter of a textbook with the simple intent of summarizing its main idea. Rather, readers of such texts identify sections they perceive include the most important information and then parse those sections into granular detail. This is why expository texts have section headings; they break up the content into meaningful chunks.

As mentioned previously, many selected-response reading items have multiple parts. In these situations, students first respond to an item regarding the passage they just read. They then respond to a second item based on their response to the first item. In a few cases, a third item expands on the first two. Table 2.4 depicts the distribution of such items.

Table 2.4: Distribution of Selected-Response Reading Items With One, Two, or Three Parts

Number of Parts	Number of Items	Percentage of Total Items
One-Part Items (part A only)	333	24.78
Two-Part Items (parts A and B only)	1,005	74.78
Three-Part Items (parts A, B, and C)	6	0.45
Total	1,344	100

According to table 2.4, almost 75 percent of selected-response reading items have two parts, with only about 25 percent involving one part and less than 1 percent involving three parts. Examining part B items discloses a strong pattern in terms of the distribution of the six reading frames, as shown in table 2.5 (page 28).

As table 2.5 depicts, 70.25 percent of the items in the part B section of selected-response reading items involve students providing evidence for their answers in the part A section. This provides a very different perspective on the importance of the evidence frame. As table 2.3 (page 25) shows, the evidence frame is least frequently used when one considers part A items only. Specifically, in part A items, the evidence frame accounted for only 6.62 percent of the 1,344 items we analyzed, while the big idea frame accounted for 23.36 percent. From this perspective, evidence frames do not seem as important as the other frames. However, in part B items, the evidence frame accounted for nearly three-quarters of the 1,005 part B items we analyzed.

The general trends regarding the distribution of selected-response reading item frames become more useful to classroom teachers when they examine them at specific grade levels, as table 2.6 (page 28) shows. Even a cursory analysis of this distribution demonstrates that the importance of specific item frames changes from grade level to grade level.

Next, we consider each of the six frames from a grade-level perspective. Each of the following sections indicates the distribution of each frame across grade levels and provides step-by-step directions on how teachers can use each frame to create practice items.

The Big Idea Frame in Selected-Response Items

The most recognizable reading frame is the big idea frame. Table 2.7 (page 29) shows this frame distributed across the grade levels. As table 2.7 shows, the frequency of the big idea frame ranges from 19.13 percent to 30.41 percent across tests given in grades 3–11. The big idea frame is also commonly found in items from the NAEP given in grade 12, SAT, and ACT. Figure 2.1 (page 29) shows an example of a big idea frame from a grade 8 sample item.

Table 2.5: Reading Frames in Selected-Response Items (Part B)

Frame	Number of Items	Percentage of Items	Most Common Stems
Evidence	706	70.25	What evidence or information (best) supports the answer to part A (the previous question)?
Function	145	14.43	Which [Textual Element] does [Literary Element]?
Meaning	115	11.44	Which information helps the reader understand the meaning of a word or phrase?
Detail	19	1.89	According to or based on the text, [Who, What, When, Where, Why, or How]?
Big Idea	18	1.79	Which sentences, details, or paragraphs belong in, relate to, or provide a summary of the text?
Purpose	2	0.20	What is the purpose of [Textual Element]?
Total	1,005	100	

Table 2.6: Selected-Response Reading Items by Grade (Part A Frames)

	3	4	5	6	7	8	9	10	11	12 (NAEP)	SAT	ACT	Total
Big Idea	19	35	22	42	27	26	45	30	55	2	7	4	314
Detail	23	42	26	23	20	25	34	33	18	6	16	24	290
Meaning	20	43	26	34	20	21	29	29	44	8	7	4	285
Function	15	13	26	33	31	29	31	22	55	0	2	1	258
Purpose	4	2	4	18	9	20	7	13	14	1	9	7	108
Evidence	8	10	11	10	8	14	2	2	13	0	11	0	89
Total	89	145	115	160	115	135	148	129	199	17	52	40	1,344
Percentage of Items*	7	11	9	12	9	10	11	10	15	1	4	3	

*Totals do not sum to 100 percent due to rounding.

As we described previously, the big idea frame items determine if students can identify what is traditionally referred to as the *main idea* of a passage. In these items, students read a passage and identify a statement that best represents the main idea of the passage they just read. To provide students with an understanding of this frame and practice for using it,

Table 2.7: Big Idea Frame in Selected-Response Reading Items

Most Common Stems	Grade or Test	Percentage of Items*
What is a central idea of the [Text]? What is the main idea of the [Text]? What is a theme of the [Text]?	3	21.34
	4	24.14
	5	19.13
	6	26.25
	7	23.48
	8	19.26
	9	30.41
	10	23.26
	11	27.64
	12 (NAEP)	11.76
	SAT	13.46
	ACT	10.00

*Percentages indicate how many selected-response reading items for a grade or test use the big idea frame in part A.

Part A

Which statement **best** summarizes the central idea of the text?

○ A. Medieval rulers always treated their subjects humanely.

○ B. Peasants' lives were difficult in medieval Europe.

○ C. Medieval European villages were dirty and dangerous.

○ D. Plague was one of the hazards faced by medieval Europeans.

Figure 2.1: Grade 8 example of a big idea frame.

teachers use the reading material students encounter in their day-to-day classes. For example, assume a seventh-grade teacher assigns students to read a passage about New Year's resolutions. In an introduction and three subsequent sections with headings, the passage describes experiments social scientists conducted about various ways to make good habits stick. The teacher might conclude this text is a good candidate for the big idea frame. This should be a well-thought-out decision, because not all texts are good candidates as practice texts. For the big idea frame, a text should have a relatively clear structure to the information in the text, and formatting and linguistic clues regarding the structure of the text. Once the teacher appropriately identifies the text, he or she can use the protocol in figure 2.2 (page 30) to create a selected-response practice item.

1. Select a text with a relatively clear structure, along with formatting and linguistic clues that signal its structure.

2. Write part A using one of the following stems.

   • What is a central idea of [Text]?

   • What is the main idea of [Text]?

   • What is a theme of [Text]?

3. Create a correct choice.

4. Create alternative choices that are incorrect.

5. Write part B using one of the following stems.

   • What evidence best supports the answer to part A?

   • What information best supports the answer to part A?

6. Create a correct choice.

7. Create alternative choices that are incorrect.

Figure 2.2: Big idea frame protocol for creating selected-response reading practice items.

Steps 2–4 of the protocol deal with generating part A of an item. The question stem in part A cues students that they are to identify the main idea; this cue can take many forms, including, What is a central idea of the text? What is the main idea of the text? What is a theme of the text? For the example passage, assume the teacher selects the question, What is the main idea of the text? Next, the teacher creates a clear answer to the question. In this case, that answer might be the following.

A. Research shows specific strategies are most likely to cause people to change their habits.

The teacher then creates alternative choices that are incorrect. Typically, there are three such choices, like the following.

B. Setting goals with friends helps people follow through on good intentions.

C. Focusing on success rather than failure is a good strategy for lasting change.

D. Most people only stick with their New Year's resolutions for a short time; lasting change requires a long-term commitment.

Steps 5–7 of the protocol address part B of the item, which involves evidence. The question stem for this part should involve statements such as, What evidence best supports the answer to part A? What information best supports the answer to part A? Again, the teacher generates a correct answer. In this case, that answer might be the following.

A. "Social science has some insights into how to break a bad habit or start a good one." (paragraph 2)

Finally, the teacher creates three alternative answers that are incorrect. In this case, those alternatives might be the following.

B. "Failure is discouraging and can lead us to give up on our goals." (paragraph 5)

C.   "On New Year's, we look back on past failures and feel an uncommon burst of optimism." (paragraph 1)

D.   "Even if you cannot promise yourself to stick with something for long, there is a huge benefit in putting in a burst of energy for a few weeks." (paragraph 7)

Once the teacher composes this item, he or she administers it to students. Obviously, the order of answers should be random; that is, choice A should not always be the correct response. To complete the exercise, the teacher leads a discussion of how students responded and the process they used to arrive at correct or incorrect answers.

The Detail Frame in Selected-Response Items

As its name implies, the detail frame requires students to identify details in a passage. These details are usually important facts integral to the content of a text. Table 2.8 (page 32) shows the distribution of detail frames across the grade levels. As table 2.8 shows, the frequency of the detail frame ranges from 9.05 percent to 28.97 percent across grades 3–11. The detail frame is also very frequently found in items from the NAEP, SAT, and ACT. Notably, 60 percent of the SAT items we analyzed utilized the detail frame. Figure 2.3 (page 32) shows an example of a detail frame from a grade 3 item.

Items that use the detail frame determine if students can recall significant bits of information from a passage including who was featured; what was said or done; when, where, and why events occurred; and how action unfolded. As with the big idea frame, teachers can use the reading material students encounter daily in school to provide practice with the detail frame. Candidate passages should include a great deal of detail, including examples and illustrations. Narratives are good for this, as are texts about events. To illustrate the process, assume a fourth-grade teacher has selected a passage describing the winning entry in a local pumpkin contest. The passage describes how the grower of the 2,300-pound winning pumpkin raised it during the COVID-19 pandemic and drove it across the country to enter it in the competition, where it won a $16,450 prize.

Once the teacher identifies an appropriate text, he or she can use the protocol in figure 2.4 (page 33) to create a selected-response practice item.

Again, steps 2–4 of the protocol involve part A of the item. The question stem in part A cues students that they are to identify details. For this passage, the question might be: According to the text, what did the grower do to make his pumpkin grow so large? The teacher then creates a clear answer to the question. In this case, that answer might be the following.

A.   He watered it up to ten times a day and fertilized it at least twice a day.

The teacher then creates alternative choices that are incorrect. Typically, there are three such choices, like the following.

B.   He spent a lot of his free time in the pumpkin patch in his backyard.

C.   He is a landscape and horticulture teacher at a local college.

D.   He drove the pumpkin across the country to enter it in the pumpkin contest.

Table 2.8: Detail Frame in Selected-Response Reading Items

Most Common Stems	Grade or Test	Percentage of Items*
According to the text, [Who, What, When, Where, Why, or How]? Based on the text, [Who, What, When, Where, Why, or How]?	3	25.84
	4	28.97
	5	22.61
	6	14.38
	7	17.39
	8	18.52
	9	22.97
	10	25.58
	11	9.05
	12 (NAEP)	35.29
	SAT	60.00
	ACT	30.77

*Percentages indicate how many selected-response reading items for a grade or test use the detail frame in part A.

Part A

What event happens that leads to the wolf being killed by the shepherd?

    A.   The shepherd keeps a close eye on the sheep.

    B.   A lamb begins to follow the wolf around.

    C.   A lamb outruns the wolf.

    D.   The wolf dresses itself in sheepskin.

Part B

Which sentence in the story supports the answer to Part A?

    A.   sentence 1

    B.   sentence 3

    C.   sentence 4

    D.   sentence 7

Figure 2.3: Grade 3 example of a detail frame.

Steps 5–7 of the protocol address part B of the item, which involves evidence. The question stem for this part should involve statements such as, What evidence best supports the answer to part A? What information best supports the answer to part A? In many cases, it is useful to number either the sentences or paragraphs of a passage. If the teacher does this, part B can refer to specific paragraphs or sentences, rather than direct quotes. Again, the teacher generates a correct answer. In this case, that answer might be the following.

    A.   Paragraph 2

1. Select a text that includes a great deal of detail, including examples and illustrations.

2. Write part A using one of the following stems.

   • According to the text, [Who, What, When, Where, Why, or How]?

   • Based on the text, [Who, What, When, Where, Why, or How]?

3. Create a correct choice.

4. Create alternative choices that are incorrect.

5. Write part B using one of the following stems.

   • What evidence best supports the answer to part A?

   • What information best supports the answer to part A?

6. Create a correct choice.

7. Create alternative choices that are incorrect.

Figure 2.4: Detail frame protocol for creating selected-response reading practice items.

Finally, the teacher creates three alternative answers that are incorrect. In this case, those alternatives might be the following.

B.   Paragraph 3

C.   Paragraph 4

D.   Paragraph 5

After randomizing the order of the answers for both parts of the practice item, the teacher administers the item to students, and the class discusses various responses and the rationales for each.

The Meaning Frame in Selected-Response Items

The meaning frame requires students to determine the meaning of specific words or phrases in a text by using context clues. Table 2.9 (page 34) shows how this frame is distributed across the grade levels. As table 2.9 shows, the frequency of the meaning frame ranges from 15.56 percent to 29.66 percent across grades 3–11. While the meaning frame is slightly less frequent in items from the SAT and ACT, it was quite prominent in the items we analyzed from the NAEP, appearing in almost half of those items. Figure 2.5 (page 34) shows an example of a meaning frame from a grade 12 item.

To construct meaning frame items, the teacher starts by identifying an appropriate passage. Candidate passages should include at least one word or phrase students probably don't know or that has an unusual meaning as used in the text. To illustrate the process, assume that a high school teacher has selected a passage about the use of meditation to treat major depression. The passage includes the phrase "In spite of an arsenal of available treatments—including medication, counseling, and other types of therapy—these interventions don't work for every patient." The teacher decides to focus on this use of the word *arsenal*.

Table 2.9: Meaning Frame in Selected-Response Reading Items

Most Common Stems	Grade or Test	Percentage of Items*
What is the meaning of [Word or Phrase] as it is used in the text?	3	22.47
	4	29.66
	5	22.61
	6	21.25
	7	17.39
	8	15.56
	9	19.59
	10	22.48
	11	22.11
	12 (NAEP)	47.06
	SAT	13.46
	ACT	10.00

*Percentages indicate how many selected-response reading items for a grade or test use the meaning frame in part A.

22. On page 1, the passage describes English vocabulary as **malleable**. This means that English

    A. is constantly changing

    B. is a rich and colorful language

    C. sounds familiar to speakers of other languages

    D. is difficult for most students to learn

Source: U.S. Department of Education, Institute of Education Sciences, National Center for Education Statistics, National Assessment of Educational Progress (NAEP), 2013 Reading Assessment. Item 2013-12R16 #2 R0V0802.

Figure 2.5: Grade 12 example of a meaning frame.

Once the teacher identifies an appropriate text and word, he or she can use the protocol in figure 2.6 to create a selected-response practice item.

Steps 2–4 of the protocol deal with generating part A of an item. The question stem in part A cues students that they are to determine the meaning of a word or phrase; this cue can take many forms, including, What is the meaning of the following word as it is used in the text? What is the meaning of the following phrase as it is used in the text? For this passage, the question would be: What is the meaning of the word *arsenal* as it is used in line 6 of the text? Note that numbering lines, sentences, or paragraphs will help students to find the target word or phrase in the text more quickly, and doing this also facilitates

1. Select a text that includes at least one word or phrase students don't know or that has an unusual meaning as used in the text.

2. Write part A using the following stem.
   - What is the meaning of [Word or Phrase] as it is used in the text?

3. Create a correct choice.

4. Create alternative choices that are incorrect.

5. Write part B using one of the following stems.
   - What evidence best supports the answer to part A?
   - What information best supports the answer to part A?

6. Create a correct choice.

7. Create alternative choices that are incorrect.

Figure 2.6: Meaning frame protocol for creating selected-response reading practice items.

the generation of part B of the practice item. The teacher then creates a clear answer to the question. In this case, that answer might be the following.

    A.   A repertoire or supply of available options

The teacher then creates alternative choices that are incorrect. Typically, there are three such choices, like the following.

    B.   A place where weapons are manufactured and stored

    C.   A vandalistic act involving setting fire to buildings or property

    D.   The use of poison to treat a condition or disease

Steps 5–7 of the protocol address part B of the item, which involves evidence. The question stem for this part should involve statements such as, What evidence best supports the answer to part A? What information best supports the answer to part A? Again, the teacher generates a correct answer. In this case, that answer might be the following.

    A.   Paragraph 3

Finally, the teacher creates three alternative answers that are incorrect. In this case, those alternatives might be the following.

    B.   Paragraph 5

    C.   Paragraph 7

    D.   Paragraph 10

Particularly with the meaning frame, asking students to explain their answers before revealing the correct answer can be very informative and lead to fruitful discussions about the proper use of context clues when trying to discern the meaning of a specific word as it is used in the passage.

The Function Frame in Selected-Response Items

The function frame requires students to determine the role specific aspects of a text play in the overall message. Table 2.10 shows how this frame is distributed across the grade levels. While function frames are rare on the SAT and ACT, and did not appear at all in our analysis of NAEP items, they comprise about a tenth to a quarter of selected-response reading items across grades 3–11.

Table 2.10: Function Frame in Selected-Response Reading Items

Most Common Stems	Grade or Test	Percentage of Items*
How does [Textual Element] do [Literary Element]?	3	16.86
	4	8.97
	5	22.61
How does [Textual Element] affect [Literary Element]?	6	20.63
	7	26.97
How does [Textual Element] influence [Literary Element]?	8	21.48
	9	20.95
What is the relationship between [Textual Element] and [Literary Element] in terms of understanding the overall passage?	10	17.05
	11	27.64
	12 (NAEP)	0
	SAT	3.85
	ACT	2.50

*Percentages indicate how many selected-response reading items for a grade or test use the function frame in part A.

Questions with function frames can be more difficult to identify than those with big idea frames, detail frames, or meaning frames because they involve aspects of a text that are not as obvious. To determine the focus of a function frame, students must view the text as a piece of literature with rhetorical features that have an influence on the interpretation of the text. At the most abstract level, a function frame can be described as *How does* X *do* Y? where *X* stands for a textual element and *Y* is its literary effect. Figures 2.7 and 2.8 show examples of function frames from grades 6 and 7.

The item in figure 2.7 highlights a paragraph and requires students to determine whether its function relates to rising action, falling action, a turning point in the action, or a resolution to some conflict. The item in figure 2.8 highlights a specific phrase and requires students to determine what information it provides about a specific character.

Recall that the template form of a function frame is, How does [Textual Element] do [Literary Element]? Function items always involve highlighting a specific element or elements of the text (represented by [Textual Element] in the frame's item stem). The

Part A

How does paragraph 6 contribute to the plot of "King Midas and the Golden Touch"?

    A. It is part of the rising action and explains how the conflict develops.

    B. It is the turning point of the story and explains how the conflict is addressed.

    C. It is part of the falling action and explains the consequences of the characters' actions.

    D. It is the resolution of the story and explains the lessons that have been learned.

Part B

Which paragraph in "Daedalus and Icarus" contributes to the plot in the same way as the answer to Part A?

    A. paragraph 14

    B. paragraph 15

    C. paragraph 20

    D. paragraph 21

Figure 2.7: Grade 6 example of a function frame.

Read the sentence from the text.

Kate shifted apprehensively as she waited to begin, but as she sprinted toward the platform and launched herself into the air, her <u>worries fell away</u>, and, flipping and twisting and soaring, she remembered the pure, unbridled joy that had made her fall in love with gymnastics in the first place.

How does the author's use of the phrase, <u>worries fell away</u>, help the reader understand Kate's experience as a gymnast?

    A. The phrase tells the reader that Kate has been doing gymnastics for a long time.

    B. The phrase shows the reader that Kate feels a lot of pressure to perform.

    C. The phrase emphasizes that Kate is a very skilled gymnast.

    D. The phrase indicates that Kate no longer enjoys gymnastics.

Figure 2.8: Grade 7 example of a function frame.

preceding examples highlight a specific paragraph and a specific phrase. Other textual elements a teacher might highlight include the following.

- The overall structure of a section of text

- The actions or attitudes of a character

- A specific sentence

- A specific event

- The artistic choices of an author

- The apparent point of view a text expresses

- The description of a specific characteristic of a person, place, thing, event, or concept
- Photographs or images in a text
- Dialogues or conversations
- Interactions the text describes

The literary component of a text or the effect of the textual element can come in many forms. That notwithstanding, the most common forms of [Literary Element] include the following.

- An important idea in the text, to which [Textual Element] contributes information
- A general understanding of the text, where [Textual Element] contributes to that understanding
- An argument developed in the text, where [Textual Element] is a part of that argument
- The plot, where [Textual Element] is a part of that plot
- An explicit structure or organizational scheme in the text, where [Textual Element] is a part of that structure or organizational scheme

Finally, it is important to be aware of possible confusions between function frames and detail frames. Detail frames focus on explicit information about the content of the text, whereas function frames address how elements of a text function as literary devices. For example, an item might start with the phrase "How do" or "How does," which is a typical marker of the function frame. But if the rest of the item is simply asking about a detail in the passage (for example, How does a barometer help meteorologists predict the weather?), it is not a function frame, but a detail frame.

To construct function frame items, the teacher starts by identifying an appropriate passage. Candidate passages should include elements with an identifiable function. To illustrate the process, assume a third-grade teacher selected a passage about how the military is using trained rats to find hidden land mines. The passage focuses specifically on one rat that was recently awarded a medal for its work clearing land mines and other unexploded items from fields in Cambodia; the passage contains a quote from the director general of the British charity that awarded the medal. The teacher decides to focus on the function of this quote in the passage.

Once the teacher identifies an appropriate text and specific element, he or she can use the protocol in figure 2.9 to create a selected-response practice item.

Steps 2–4 of the protocol deal with generating part A of an item. The question stem in part A cues students that they are to determine the function of a specific element. For this passage, the question might be: How does the quote in paragraph 5 support the idea that land mine–sniffing rats are highly trained, working animals? The teacher then creates a clear answer to the question. In this case, that answer might be the following.

1. Select a text that includes at least one element, [Textual Element], with an identifiable function, [Literary Element].

2. Write part A using one of the following stems.
   - How does [Textual Element] do [Literary Element]?
   - How does [Textual Element] affect [Literary Element]?
   - How does [Textual Element] influence [Literary Element]?
   - What is the relationship between [Textual Element] and [Literary Element] in terms of understanding the overall passage?

3. Create a correct choice.

4. Create alternative choices that are incorrect.

5. Write part B using one of the following stems.
   - What evidence best supports the answer to part A?
   - What information best supports the answer to part A?

6. Create a correct choice.

7. Create alternative choices that are incorrect.

Figure 2.9: Function frame protocol for creating selected-response reading practice items.

    A.   The director general mentions the rat's work harness.

The teacher then creates alternative choices that are incorrect. Typically, there are three such choices, like the following.

    B.   The director general mentions the rat's name.

    C.   The director general mentions the medal.

    D.   The director general mentions how the medal was designed.

The second part of the protocol addresses part B of the item that involves evidence. The question stem for this part should involve statements such as, What evidence best supports the answer to part A? What information best supports the answer to part A? It is acceptable to modify these stems as appropriate. For this practice item, the teacher uses the following verbiage for part B: What other evidence in the passage supports the idea that land mine–sniffing rats are highly trained, working animals? Again, the teacher generates a correct answer. In this case, that answer might be the following.

    A.   Paragraphs 6–7

Finally, the teacher creates three alternative answers that are incorrect. In this case, those alternatives might be the following.

    B.   Paragraphs 2–3

    C.   Paragraphs 4–5

    D.   Paragraphs 8–9

After randomizing each set of alternative answers, the teacher administers the practice item and leads a discussion regarding correct and incorrect responses.

The Purpose Frame in Selected-Response Items

The purpose frame requires students determine the purpose of an entire text or sections of a text. Table 2.11 shows how this frame is distributed across the grade levels. It is useful to contrast the purpose frame with the function frame. The *function frame* always focuses on a specific element that functions in a specific way within the text. While the *purpose frame* sometimes focuses on the purpose of specific elements of a text (represented by [Textual Element] in the stems in table 2.11), it also commonly asks about the author's purpose across the entire text.

Table 2.11: Purpose Frame in Selected-Response Reading Items

Most Common Stems	Grade or Test	Percentage of Items*
What is the purpose of [Textual Element]? What is the author's purpose in this section of the text?	3	4.49
	4	1.38
	5	3.48
	6	11.25
	7	7.83
	8	14.81
	9	4.73
	10	10.08
	11	7.04
	12 (NAEP)	5.88
	SAT	17.31
	ACT	17.50

*Percentages indicate how many selected-response reading items for a grade or test use the purpose frame in part A.

To illustrate, consider the item in figure 2.10. Notice in this purpose frame item that the focus is on the purpose of the dialogue in the text. Purpose frame items are easy to identify because they almost always use the term *purpose* in the text of the item.

To construct purpose frame items, the teacher starts by identifying an appropriate passage. Because this type of item explicitly addresses choices made by the author, candidate passages should have an overt author and, in many cases, specific elements that serve a clear purpose in the passage. Speeches are ideal for the purpose frame because of their clear authorship and use for a variety of purposes. To illustrate the process, assume that a sixth-grade teacher has selected as a text a grade-level appropriate adaptation of Kamala Harris's vice president–elect acceptance speech. Delivered on November 7, 2020, by the first woman to be elected vice president, the speech serves several purposes, including to signal a change in presidential administrations, to thank her family for their support, to recognize the contributions and victories by women of color throughout history, to

---

Part A

What is the purpose of the dialogue between the woman and the man at the end of the story?

- ○ A. to highlight the contrast between the woman's version of events and the man's

- ○ B. to resolve the disagreement the woman and man had earlier in the story

- ○ C. to explain the woman's background and experiences before she met the man

- ○ D. to provide a review of the major events in the relationship between the woman and the man

Part B

Which sentence from the story best supports the answer in Part A?

- ○ A. "'When we met, I was working as a waitress. That's the only part that's true,' she said." (paragraph 5)

- ○ B. "'You've changed your mind, haven't you?' he asked. 'You should change it back.'" (paragraph 6)

- ○ C. "She knew that whether she had met him or not, she would have been successful." (paragraph 8)

- ○ D. "Over seven years, they had experienced so many of life's ups and downs together." (paragraph 10)

Figure 2.10: Example of purpose frame.

articulate goals of the new presidential administration, and to introduce president-elect Joe Biden. The teacher decides to focus on the purpose of the section of the speech that recognizes historical contributions and victories by women of color.

Once the teacher identifies an appropriate text, he or she can use the protocol in figure 2.11 (page 42) to create a selected-response practice item.

Steps 2–4 of the protocol deal with generating part A of an item. The question in part A cues students that they are to determine the purpose of a specific element or section of the text; this cue can take many forms including, What is the purpose of [Textual Element]? What is the author's purpose in this section of the text? For this passage, the question might be: What is the author's purpose in lines 27–36 of Kamala Harris's vice president–elect acceptance speech? The teacher then creates a clear answer to the question. In this case, that answer might be the following.

A.   To recognize the contributions of women of color throughout history

The teacher then creates alternative choices that are incorrect. Typically, there are three such choices, like the following.

B.   To let young girls know that she is aware that they are watching her

C.   To identify those groups that form the backbone of American democracy

D.   To express her wish that the next president be a woman

1. Select a text with a clear author and either an element, [Textual Element], in the text with a specific purpose or a section of the text that serves a specific purpose.
2. Write part A using one of the following stems.
   - What is the purpose of [Textual Element]?
   - What is the author's purpose in this section of the text?
3. Create a correct choice.
4. Create alternative choices that are incorrect.
5. Write part B using one of the following stems.
   - What evidence best supports the answer to part A?
   - What information best supports the answer to part A?
6. Create a correct choice.
7. Create alternative choices that are incorrect.

Figure 2.11: Purpose frame protocol for creating selected-response reading practice items.

The second part of the protocol addresses part B of the item that involves evidence. The question stem for this part should involve statements such as, What evidence best supports the answer to part A? What information best supports the answer to part A? Again, the teacher generates a correct answer. In this case that answer might be the following.

   A.　Line 30

Finally, the teacher creates three alternative answers that are incorrect. In this case, those alternatives might be the following.

   B.　Line 29

   C.　Line 32

   D.　Line 33

As with the meaning frame, waiting to share correct answers until students have shared their responses and the evidence for each response provides unique opportunities to discuss the relationships between evidence and conclusions.

The Evidence Frame in Selected-Response Items

The evidence frame requires students to identify and examine the evidence for an implicit or explicit claim in a text. Table 2.12 shows how this frame is distributed across the grade levels. It is important to remember that the distribution reported is based on part A of items that we analyzed. If you consider these data in isolation, it would be reasonable to conclude that evidence frames are not that frequent in selected-response reading items. However, recall the evidence frame comprises the majority of part B items. In effect, when you consider part A and part B items jointly, the evidence frame rises to the top of the list in terms of frames teachers should ensure students understand. Figure 2.12 shows an example of an evidence frame from a grade 5 item.

Table 2.12: Evidence Frame in Selected-Response Reading Items

Most Common Stems	Grade or Test	Percentage of Items*
What evidence supports [Claim]? What evidence supports [Conclusion]? What evidence supports [Opinion]? What evidence supports [Statement]?	3	8.99
	4	6.90
	5	9.57
	6	6.25
	7	6.97
	8	10.37
	9	1.35
	10	1.55
	11	6.53
	12 (NAEP)	0
	SAT	21.15
	ACT	0

*Percentages indicate how many selected-response reading items for a grade or test use the evidence frame in part A.

> Which detail from the article **best** supports the idea that ice skates are an old invention?
>
>   A. The first ice skates were made out of animal bones.
>
>   B. Ice skates were used to help save energy during hunts.
>
>   C. The first ice skates were invented by the Finns.
>
>   D. Ice skating remains popular in many countries today.

Figure 2.12: Grade 5 example of an evidence frame.

To construct evidence frame items, the teacher starts by identifying an appropriate passage. Candidate passages are those with distinct pieces of evidence for a conclusion (or conclusions) either explicit or implicit in the text. To illustrate the process, assume a high school teacher has selected a passage about whether or not it is racist to mimic foreign accents for comedic purposes. The passage presents evidence on both sides of the issue and refrains from drawing an explicit conclusion at the end.

Once the teacher identifies an appropriate text, he or she can use the protocol in figure 2.13 (page 44) to create a selected-response practice item.

1. Select a text with distinct pieces of evidence related to an explicit or implicit conclusion.

2. Write part A using one of the following stems.

   • What evidence supports [Claim]?

   • What evidence supports [Conclusion]?

   • What evidence supports [Opinion]?

   • What evidence supports [Statement]?

3. Create a correct choice.

4. Create alternative choices that are incorrect.

5. Write part B using one of the following stems.

   • What evidence best supports the answer to part A?

   • What information best supports the answer to part A?

6. Create a correct choice.

7. Create alternative choices that are incorrect.

Figure 2.13: Evidence frame protocol for creating selected-response reading practice items.

Steps 2–4 of the protocol deal with generating part A of an item. The question stem in part A cues students that they are to determine what evidence best supports a specific statement. For this passage, the question might be: Which evidence from the text best supports the conclusion that using a foreign accent for comedic purposes is racist behavior? The teacher then creates a clear answer to the question. In this case, that answer might be the following.

A.　Recent survey results showing that 50 percent of those surveyed reported that imitating an accent was either always or usually racist

The teacher then creates alternative choices that are incorrect. Typically, there are three such choices, like the following.

B.　Diana Nguyen's expert opinion that the intention of the speaker determines whether or not the behavior is racist

C.　Factual information regarding the use of blackface to mock and degrade Black people

D.　Poll results from a Greek newspaper showing that many Greek people gave a high approval rating to a TV show where a White person imitated a Greek accent

For items in our analysis where the evidence frame appeared in the first or only part of the item, many did not include a part B. Therefore, educators may choose to present evidence frame practice items without a part B as well.

Short Constructed-Response Reading Items

As their name implies, *short constructed-response reading items* require students to write out their responses to questions after they read a passage. As opposed to selected-response items, which provide students with already constructed answers, with short constructed-response items, students must design their answers without the alternative answers providing any cueing in the item. By definition, this requires more of students in that they must produce their own text to answer these questions correctly.

There are five types of frames typically used for short constructed-response items: (1) detail, (2) evidence, (3) big idea, (4) function, and (5) meaning. Table 2.13 depicts the distribution of these types of short constructed-response items across the grade levels, in order of prevalence. As with selected-response items, short constructed-response items have unique characteristics in terms of what is required to answer them, which we detail in the following sections.

Table 2.13: Short Constructed-Response Reading Items by Grade

	3	4	5	6	7	8	9	10	11	12 (NAEP)	SAT	ACT	Total
Detail	4	7	2	1	1	4	0	0	1	1	0	0	21
Evidence	1	1	1	2	1	2	0	0	2	2	0	0	12
Big Idea	0	1	0	3	2	2	0	0	2	1	0	0	11
Function	0	1	1	0	2	2	0	0	0	3	0	0	9
Meaning	0	1	0	0	0	0	0	0	0	1	0	0	2
Total	5	11	4	6	6	10	0	0	5	8	0	0	55
Percentage of Items	9	20	7	11	11	18	0	0	9	15	0	0	

The Detail Frame in Short Constructed-Response Items

Table 2.14 (page 46) depicts the distribution of the detail frame in short constructed-response items across the grade levels. Figure 2.14 (page 46) provides an example of a short constructed-response reading item that uses the detail frame.

Like selected-response items, short constructed-response items refer to specific passages of text. As mentioned previously, for the detail frame, teachers should select passages that include a great deal of detail, including examples and illustrations. Narratives are good for this, as are texts about events. Once the teacher identifies an appropriate text, he or she can use the protocol in figure 2.15 (page 46) to create a short constructed-response practice item.

Table 2.14: Detail Frame in Short Constructed-Response Reading Items

Most Common Stems	Grade or Test	Percentage of Items*
What inference can be made about [Detail From Text]? According to the text, [Who, What, When, Where, Why, or How]?	3	80.00
	4	63.34
	5	50.00
	6	16.67
	7	16.67
	8	40.00
	9	0
	10	0
	11	20.00
	12 (NAEP)	12.50
	SAT	0
	ACT	0

*Percentages indicate how many short constructed-response reading items for a grade or test use the detail frame.

> What inference can be made about Norah's opinion of Gideon's actions? Support your answer with details from the text.

Figure 2.14: Grade 7 short constructed-response item using the detail frame.

1. Select a text that includes a great deal of detail, including examples and illustrations.
2. Write an item using one of the following stems.
   - What inference can be made about [Detail From Text]?
   - According to the text, [Who, What, When, Where, Why, or How]?
3. Add a prompt for evidence, such as:
   - Support your answer with details from the text.
   - Use details from the text to support your answer.
   - Use two details from the source to support your explanation.

Figure 2.15: Detail frame protocol for creating short constructed-response practice items.

To illustrate the process, assume a fifth-grade teacher selected a passage about the discovery of ancient rock art in the Amazon rainforest. The passage describes the discovery and the paintings in detail and includes several photographs. The teacher then creates a question such as, According to the text, about how long ago do archaeologists think the rock art was created? Finally, the teacher adds a prompt for evidence, such as, Support your answer with details from the text.

The Big Idea Frame in Short Constructed-Response Items

Table 2.15 depicts the distribution of big idea frame short constructed-response items across the grade levels. Figure 2.16 provides an example of a short constructed-response reading item that uses the big idea frame.

Table 2.15: Big Idea Frame in Short Constructed-Response Reading Items

Most Common Stems	Grade or Test	Percentage of Items*
What is the author's message?	3	0
	4	9.09
	5	0
	6	50.00
	7	33.33
	8	20.00
	9	0
	10	0
	11	40.00
	12 (NAEP)	12.5
	SAT	0
	ACT	0

*Percentages indicate how many short constructed-response reading items for a grade or test use the big idea frame.

What is the author's message about apparent contradictions in one's opinions? Use details from the text to support your answer.

Figure 2.16: Grade 11 short constructed-response item using the big idea frame.

Like selected-response items, short constructed-response items refer to specific passages of text. As mentioned previously, for the big idea frame, teachers should select passages with the following characteristics: a relatively clear structure to the information in the text and formatting and linguistic clues regarding the structure of the text. Once the teacher identifies an appropriate text, he or she can use the protocol in figure 2.17 to create a short constructed-response practice item.

---

1. Select a text with a relatively clear structure, along with formatting and linguistic clues that signal its structure.

2. Write an item using the following stem.

   • What is the author's message?

3. Add a prompt for evidence, such as:

   • Support your answer with details from the text.

   • Use details from the text to support your answer.

   • Use two details from the source to support your explanation.

Figure 2.17: Big idea frame protocol for creating short constructed-response practice items.

To illustrate the process, assume a seventh-grade teacher has selected a passage about the benefits of forest fires. The passage includes four subheadings with sections describing various ways forest fires can be ecologically beneficial under the right conditions. The teacher then creates a question such as, What is the author's message about forest fires? Finally, the teacher adds a prompt that asks students to support their answers with specific details and examples of the message from the passage such as, Use two details from the text to support your answer.

The Evidence Frame in Short Constructed-Response Items

Table 2.16 depicts the distribution of evidence frame short constructed-response items across the grade levels. Figure 2.18 provides an example of a short constructed-response reading item that uses the evidence frame.

As table 2.16 and figure 2.18 show, most evidence frame short constructed-response items actually reference multiple passages of text, asking the student to determine which one provides the best or most helpful or most relevant information about a topic. Therefore, for the short constructed-response evidence frame, teachers should select two or more passages on the same topic, with one of the passages clearly offering better evidence or information about one facet of the topic. Once the teacher identifies appropriate texts, he or she can use the protocol in figure 2.19 to create a short constructed-response practice item.

Table 2.16: Evidence Frame in Short Constructed-Response Reading Items

Most Common Stems	Grade or Test	Percentage of Items*
Which source is most helpful or relevant?	3	20.00
	4	9.09
	5	25.00
	6	33.33
	7	16.67
	8	20.00
	9	0
	10	0
	11	40.00
	12 (NAEP)	25.00
	SAT	0
	ACT	0

*Percentages indicate how many short constructed-response reading items for a grade or test use the evidence frame.

Which source would **most likely** be the most helpful in understanding how erosion changes the features of a landscape over time? Explain why this source is **most likely** the most helpful. Use **two** details from the source to support your explanation.

Figure 2.18: Grade 4 short constructed-response item using the evidence frame.

1. Select two or more texts on the same topic, with one text clearly focusing on a specific facet of the topic.
2. Write an item using the following stem.
   - Which source is most helpful or relevant?
3. Add a prompt for evidence, such as:
   - Support your answer with details from the text.
   - Use details from the text to support your answer.
   - Use two details from the source to support your explanation.

Figure 2.19: Evidence frame protocol for creating short constructed-response practice items.

To illustrate the process, assume a high school teacher has selected two passages on vaccines. One passage describes how medicated patches could be used to administer vaccines without needles. The other describes what vaccines are and how they are developed, tested, and approved. The teacher then creates a question such as, Which source would be most helpful in understanding why a fear of needles can lead to lower rates of vaccination? Finally, the teacher adds a prompt that asks students to support their answers with specific details such as, Use details from the source to support your answer.

The Function Frame in Short Constructed-Response Items

Table 2.17 depicts the distribution of function frame short constructed-response items across the grade levels. Figure 2.20 provides an example of a short constructed-response reading item that uses the function frame.

Table 2.17: Function Frame in Short Constructed-Response Reading Items

Most Common Stems	Grade or Test	Percentage of Items*
Explain how [Textual Element] does [Literary Element].	3	0
	4	9.09
	5	25.00
	6	0
	7	33.33
	8	20.00
	9	0
	10	0
	11	0
	12 (NAEP)	37.50
	SAT	0
	ACT	0

*Percentages indicate how many short constructed-response reading items for a grade or test use the function frame.

---

7. You have read passages from Chapters 1 and 2 of *The Hobbit*. Explain how the narrator's point of view affects how the events in the chapters are described. Be sure to use details from **both** Chapters 1 and 2 of *The Hobbit* to support your answer.

Figure 2.20: Grade 5 short constructed-response item using the function frame.

As mentioned previously, for the function frame, teachers should select text passages with elements that serve a clear function in terms of contributing to the meaning of the text. Once the teacher identifies an appropriate text, he or she can use the protocol in figure 2.21 to create a short constructed-response practice item.

1. Select a text with at least one element, [Textual Element], with an identifiable function, [Literary Element].
2. Write an item using the following stem.
   • Explain how [Textual Element] does [Literary Element].
3. Add a prompt for evidence, such as:
   • Support your answer with details from the text.
   • Use details from the text to support your answer.
   • Use two details from the source to support your explanation.

Figure 2.21: Function frame protocol for creating short constructed-response practice items.

To illustrate the process, assume a fourth-grade teacher has selected a passage about prejudice based on skin color in India. In the passage, the author describes her and her family's experiences of prejudice, and explains why she started a social media campaign against it. The passage includes specific instances of prejudice the author's daughter encountered at school. The teacher then creates a question such as, How do the experiences the author's daughter encountered at school influence the author's decision to start a campaign against prejudice based on skin color? Finally, the teacher adds an evidence prompt asking students to support their answers with specific details, such as, Support your answer with details from the text.

The Meaning Frame in Short Constructed-Response Items

Table 2.18 (page 52) depicts the distribution of meaning frame short constructed-response items across the grade levels. Figure 2.22 (page 52) provides an example of a short constructed-response reading item that uses the meaning frame.

As mentioned previously, for the meaning frame, teachers should select text passages with at least one word or phrase students probably don't know or that has an unusual meaning as used in the text. Once the teacher identifies an appropriate text, he or she can use the protocol in figure 2.23 (page 52) to create a short constructed-response practice item.

To illustrate the process, assume a sixth-grade teacher selected a passage that describes how a twelve-year-old boy discovered a comet. The passage includes the following phrase in the fourth paragraph: "Amateur astronomers . . . trawl through images from spacecraft or missions to help make scientific discoveries." The teacher then creates a question such as, What is the meaning of the word *trawl* as it is used in the fourth paragraph of the text? Finally, the teacher adds an evidence prompt such as, Use details from the text to support your answer.

Table 2.18: Meaning Frame in Short Constructed-Response Reading Items

Most Common Stems	Grade or Test	Percentage of Items*
Explain what [Phrase From Text] means.	3	0
	4	9.09
	5	0
	6	0
	7	0
	8	0
	9	0
	10	0
	11	0
	12 (NAEP)	12.50
	SAT	0
	ACT	0

*Percentages indicate how many short constructed-response reading items for a grade or test use the meaning frame.

Explain what the author means when she says, "Fun is a rare jewel."

Source: U.S. Department of Education, Institute of Education Sciences, National Center for Education Statistics, National Assessment of Educational Progress (NAEP), 2013 Reading Assessment. Item 2103-12R4 #1 R060301.

Figure 2.22: Grade 12 short constructed-response item using the meaning frame.

---

1. Select a text with at least one word or phrase students don't know or that has an unusual meaning as used in the text.

2. Write an item using the following stem.

   • Explain what [Phrase From Text] means.

3. Add a prompt for evidence, such as:

   • Support your answer with details from the text.

   • Use details from the text to support your answer.

   • Use two details from the source to support your explanation.

Figure 2.23: Meaning frame protocol for creating short constructed-response practice items.

Selected-Response Language Items

The ELA domain of language addresses conventions relative to the use of the English language. Such items account for 9 percent of the items we analyzed in our study. While this is a relatively small segment of the items addressed in the ELA domain, it still represents an important aspect of English language proficiency. The items we analyzed fit into four general categories: (1) expression, (2) content, (3) grammar, and (4) mechanics. Table 2.19 depicts the distribution of these categories. While the distribution is fairly evenly spread across the four categories, expression items are the most frequent. We consider each category separately.

Table 2.19: Language Categories in Selected-Response Items

Category	Number of Items	Percentage of Items	Subcategories
Expression	50	32.26	Relationship signal words Vocabulary terms Word choice
Content	42	27.10	Addition Deletion Appropriate placement
Grammar	39	25.16	Sentence structure Verb tense Pronoun usage Modifier placement and formation Agreement
Mechanics	24	15.48	Punctuation Capitalization Spelling
Total	155	100	

Expression Category

Expression items accounted for 32 percent of the language items and about 3 percent (50 of 1,684) of the total ELA items. Table 2.20 (page 54) depicts the distribution of expression category items across the grade levels. Expression items fall into three subcategories: relationship signal words, vocabulary terms, and word choice.

Table 2.20: Expression Category in Short Constructed-Response Language Items

Subcategories	Grade or Test	Percentage of Items*
Relationships Vocabulary Word choice	3	40.00
	4	33.33
	5	20.00
	6	16.67
	7	20.00
	8	20.00
	9	0
	10	0
	11	25.00
	12 (NAEP)	0
	SAT	38.64
	ACT	32.00

*Percentages indicate how many selected-response language items for a grade or test use the expression category.

Relationship items require students to select the best word or phrase that most accurately represents the relationship between two ideas. For example, in figure 2.24, the phrases *Even so* and *Despite this* each indicate an unexpected causal relationship. These phrases make sense in the context of the surrounding passage, creating a logical relationship between a "disappointing" outcome and an "interesting" one. In these items, students must first determine the nature of the relationship between two ideas in a passage, and then select the word or phrase that best describes the identified relationship.

Items classified as addressing vocabulary require students to determine if a highlighted word or short phrase in a passage should be changed or is better than the provided alternatives. One characteristic of vocabulary items is they sometimes ask students to identify the "best" alternative. This adds cognitive complexity; it implies that more than one answer might correctly fit in the passage, but one option is the best. Another characteristic of some of these items is they offer the option to leave the highlighted part of the passage unchanged. Thus, the pre-existing word or phrase becomes one of the options to consider. Figure 2.25 presents an example.

A student is writing a report about her experience learning to ride a horse. Read the draft of the report and complete the task that follows.

When I met Chestnut, she was very timid. My instructor helped me climb into the saddle, and Chestnut whinnied and tossed her head. I was worried Chestnut didn't like me very much. Eventually, she calmed down, and we started to walk slowly around the corral. After I got used to riding slowly, my instructor tried to get Chestnut to trot faster, but Chestnut just kept walking. My instructor said Chestnut would have to learn to trust me. It was disappointing that I did not get to ride Chestnut very fast. _____, learning to ride a horse has been very interesting so far.

Choose the **best two** phrases to connect "It was disappointing that I did not get to ride Chestnut very fast" and "learning to ride a horse has been very interesting so far."

- ☐ Even so
- ☐ Later on
- ☐ Let alone
- ☐ Despite this
- ☐ For example
- ☐ In other words

Figure 2.24: Example of language expression relationship item.

A student is writing an essay for social studies class about a famous historical figure. Read the draft of the essay and complete the task that follows.

Marie Curie made many significant contributions to science. In 1903, she became the first woman to win a Nobel prize when she, her husband Pierre, and the physicist Henri Becquerel were recognized with the award for their pioneering work on radioactivity. She won a second Nobel prize in 1911 after discovering the elements polonium and radium. During World War I, she worked as a radiologist, providing X-ray services to field hospitals. Though she disliked public honors and attention, Curie became one of the most <u>legendary</u> scientists in history.

Choose the **best** way to revise the underlined word so that the essay maintains a consistent tone.

- ○ A. brilliant
- ○ B. productive
- ○ C. renowned
- ○ D. fabled

Figure 2.25: Example of language expression vocabulary item.

Word choice items are similar to vocabulary items, but deal with larger language structures. For example, the item in figure 2.26 (page 56) asks students to select more descriptive sentences to revise a narrative.

Figure 2.27 (page 56) shows the general protocol for constructing a selected-response expression item.

Maria is writing a story for her class about a day hiking in the woods. She wants to revise her story to use more descriptive words. Read the draft and complete the task that follows.

It was Maria's last day of summer vacation. She zoomed into the backyard and yelled, "Dad, we have to go hiking today! It's our last chance this summer to pick flowers and chase butterflies together!"

Dad smiled happily and, together, Maria and Dad drove an hour to the trailhead. Once there, they put on their backpacks and hiking boots. Dad looked for birds and Maria walked.

Maria continued collecting flowers for about half an hour. Then, she noticed that her dad had spent that entire time looking for birds. She felt annoyed. She tugged at Dad's binoculars. She looked at him.

Dad grinned and put his binoculars down. Together, the two chased delicate, brightly colored butterflies. They laughed with excitement.

Select **two** of the choices that have the **best** descriptive sentences to replace Dad looked for birds and Maria walked and She looked at him.

☐ Dad enjoyed spotting new birds while Maria wandered through the woods gathering wildflowers. / She gave him a look that said, "I want you to spend time with me."

☐ Dad helped Maria pick wildflowers. / She gave him a look that said, "I'm glad you like your birds."

☐ Dad pointed out birds to Maria and then they chased butterflies. / She looked at the birds.

☐ Dad looked for birds for a while and then picked wildflowers. / She looked at the delicate, brightly colored butterflies.

☐ Dad had a wonderful time birdwatching while Maria gathered a bunch of wildflowers. / She gave him a look that said, "It's time to have some fun, now!"

☐ Dad decided that he did not like looking for birds. / She gave him a look that said, "You are the best dad."

Figure 2.26: Example of language expression word choice item.

1. Select a subtype.
   - Relationships
   - Vocabulary
   - Word choice
2. Pick a passage with the subtype present.
3. Adjust the passage to be wrong, if desired.
4. Write a correct option (if the passage was made incorrect).
5. Write two or three incorrect options and a NO CHANGE option.

Figure 2.27: Expression category protocol for creating selected-response language practice items.

To illustrate how teachers might use this protocol, consider a high school teacher who wishes to construct an expression item for the subcategory vocabulary. First, the teacher selects a passage and changes a word within it to a phrase that does not express the intended meaning as well as the original, as in the following passage:

> Oxford University researchers conducted a study on how playing video games affects mental health, which is the emotional well-being of a person. Their study used data from video game makers. This was a rare <u>working together</u> between scientists and the game industry. (Associated Press, 2020a)

The teacher then creates the following question: Which of the following best describes the interaction between the scientists and the video game makers? In this case, the original word from the passage serves as the correct answer.

A. collaboration

The teacher then creates alternative choices that are incorrect. Typically, there are three such choices, like the following.

B. NO CHANGE

C. teamwork

D. agreement

As with other selected-response items, the teacher randomizes the order of the answers for the practice item, then administers the item to students, and the class discusses various responses and the rationales for each.

Content Category

Content category items accounted for about 27 percent of the language items and about 2.5 percent (42 of 1,684) of the total ELA items. Table 2.21 (page 58) depicts the distribution of content category items across the grade levels. Content category items fall into three subcategories: addition, deletion, and appropriate placement.

As their name implies, addition items involve adding content to a passage to make the passage "better" in some respect. To illustrate, consider the items in figures 2.28 (page 58) and 2.29 (page 59). In these addition items, teachers ask students to identify content to add that improves a passage. This may be by providing additional evidence or detail, adding relevant information, or deciding whether or not a given addition will improve the passage.

Table 2.21: Content Category in Short Constructed-Response Language Items

Subcategories	Grade or Test	Percentage of Items*
Addition **Deletion** **Appropriate placement**	3	20.00
	4	33.33
	5	40.00
	6	50.00
	7	40.00
	8	40.00
	9	0
	10	0
	11	25.00
	12 (NAEP)	0
	SAT	25.00
	ACT	24.00

*Percentages indicate how many selected-response language items for a grade or test use the content category.

Riley is writing a story for her class about a man who sits on a park bench and helps people feel better by listening to their problems and worries. Riley wants to revise her story to add better detail about the main character. Read the draft paragraphs of her story and complete the task that follows.

About two years ago, a man began spending an hour every day sitting on a park bench reflecting on his life. The man was named Andrew, and he had recently retired from his job as a janitor.

Each morning, Andrew would walk down to the park and sit on the bench. He enjoyed the quiet and solitude, and he used the time to consider what was truly important to him. He knew he wanted to find a way to help others find the peace of mind that he had achieved, but he wasn't sure how he would be able to. He wasn't very outgoing by nature, and he preferred listening to talking. As it turned out, the solution to his problem would show up when he least expected.

As Andrew sat deep in thought one day, an older woman sat down on the bench next to him and began to talk about the recent loss of her husband. She explained that since her husband had passed, she had no one left to talk to. As Andrew listened, the woman became happier, and when she had finished, she said how wonderful it felt to have someone to talk to again. Before long, more people began to approach Andrew to talk, and everyone came away feeling much better than when they sat down.

Choose the **best** sentence to add detail to show or explain who the main character is.

A. The other people who came to chat with Andrew talked to him about all sorts of subjects.

B. Andrew was a kind, patient, and compassionate man.

C. The older woman had never had any children, and the rest of her family lived far away.

D. Riley met Andrew one day when she went for a walk in the park.

Figure 2.28: Example one of language content addition item.

These days, many students majoring in English have no intention of becoming writers or teachers; instead they plan to apply those skills to other careers. Law and public relations careers specifically benefit from the understanding of communication developed in the study of English, but an English degree can be useful in any part of the business world requiring analytical thinking skills. **32** Many of these skills are transferable across professions.

32

At this point, the writer is considering adding the following line.

Many CEOs, for instance, began their careers with a degree in English.

Should the writer make this addition here?

A) Yes, because it reinforces the passage's main point about the career prospects of English majors.

B) Yes, because it recognizes a frequent counterargument to the central claim of the passage.

C) No, because it introduces a new idea without explaining how it relates to the paragraph's focus.

D) No, because it undermines the passage's claim about the employability of English majors.

Figure 2.29: Example two of language content addition item.

Not surprisingly, deletion items require students identify content that should be deleted to make the passage better. To illustrate, consider the items in figures 2.30 and 2.31 (page 60). As these figures show, some deletion items ask students to identify irrelevant information or distracting content that should be deleted. Others ask students to decide whether a given deletion will improve the passage.

The article explained that storage units are locations that, for a rental fee, individuals can use to store their belongings. The units are typically accompanied by a small retail counter that sells cardboard boxes, packing tape, and other moving supplies. The facilities often include small units as well as larger storage areas. **18** The cost of renting an average storage unit in the United States is estimated to be approximately $150 per month.

The writer is considering deleting the underlined sentence. Should the sentence be kept or deleted?

A) Kept, because it provides a detail that supports the main topic of the paragraph.

B) Kept, because it sets up the main topic of the paragraph that follows.

C) Deleted, because it blurs the paragraph's main focus with a loosely related detail.

D) Deleted, because it repeats information that has been provided in an earlier paragraph.

Figure 2.30: Example one of language content deletion item.

A student is revising a paragraph from a history report she is writing. Read the draft of the paragraph and complete the task that follows.

The Lowell mill girls played an important role in the history of industry and labor in the United States. During the 19th century, they made up a large part of the workforce in textile factories in Massachusetts. Instead of living at home, these women lived together in boardinghouses near the factories. This reminds me of my friend who went to boarding school in Massachusetts. The women came from farms and villages around New England to earn money for themselves and their families. While they had new social opportunities and some economic independence, their lives were tightly controlled by the factory owners. They also worked long hours in dangerous environments. Sometimes, the women organized protests to push for shorter hours, better pay, or safer working conditions.

Choose the sentence that is distracting or does not maintain the focus of the paragraph.

    A. Instead of living at home, these women lived together in boardinghouses near the factories.

    B. This reminds me of my friend who went to boarding school in Massachusetts.

    C. The women came from farms and villages around New England to earn money for themselves and their families.

    D. Sometimes, the women organized protests to push for shorter hours, better pay, or safer working conditions.

Figure 2.31: Example two of language content deletion item.

Appropriate placement items ask students to identify where they should place specific text for maximum impact or literary effect. To illustrate, consider the items in figures 2.32 and 2.33. As shown in the figures, these items sometimes ask students to identify which topical heading is the best fit for given information, and other times ask them to place information at a specific place in a passage.

A student is writing a report about meerkats. Read the passage from a source and the directions that follow.

Meerkats are a type of mongoose found in the southern part of Africa. They are about 20 inches long, including their tails, and weigh around two pounds, making them about the size of squirrels. Meerkats are covered in bushy, light brown, striped fur, with dark patches around their eyes. They use their sharp claws to dig burrows, where they live in groups of up to 40. Their legs also allow them to stand upright to keep watch for predators. Meerkats use their pointy snouts and keen sense of smell to sniff for food, including various bugs and plants.

The parts of the student's report are shown below. In which part of the report would the facts from the source **best** fit?

    A. Part A: Meerkat Physical Characteristics

    B. Part B: Meerkat Diet

    C. Part C: Meerkat Social Patterns

    D. Part D: Meerkat Habitat

Figure 2.32: Example one of language content appropriate placement item.

[1] Thus, even though I had some extra space at home, I decided to rent a storage unit in my city. [2] Because I was interested in storing some temperature-sensitive items, I chose a facility that offered climate-controlled units where I could adjust the temperature and even the humidity. [3] That morning, I visited the facility and signed the rental agreement. [4] The other renters filtered in and out during the day, but it was largely quiet in the warehouse-like building. **21**

21

The writer wants to add the following sentence to the paragraph.

After filling out the paperwork and taking a quick tour of the facility, I pulled my truck around to the loading dock and began moving my things into the storage unit.

The best placement for the sentence is immediately

    A) before sentence 1.

    B) after sentence 1.

    C) after sentence 2.

    D) after sentence 3.

Figure 2.33: Example two of language content appropriate placement item.

Figure 2.34 shows the general protocol for constructing a selected-response content item.

1. Select a subtype.
    - Addition
    - Deletion
    - Appropriate placement
2. Pick a passage.
3. Select or generate content to add, delete, or move.
4. Write a correct option.
5. Write three incorrect options.

Figure 2.34: Content category protocol for creating selected-response language practice items.

To illustrate how teachers might use this protocol, consider a fifth-grade teacher who wishes to construct a content item for the subcategory of deletion. The teacher selects a passage and adds a sentence that distracts from the central focus of the text, as in the following passage:

> The U.S. Olympic and Paralympic Committee (USOPC) announced December 10 that it won't punish athletes for raising their fists or kneeling as they accept medals at next year's Tokyo, Japan Games and beyond. The Tokyo Olympic Games were delayed from 2020 to 2021 due to the coronavirus pandemic. The decision is a response to a set of recommendations from a USOPC athlete group. It seeks changes to the much-criticized Rule 50 of the IOC Olympic Charter. It bans protests inside venues at the Games. (Associated Press, 2020b)

The teacher then writes a question like: Select the sentence that is not relevant to the main topic of the paragraph. The correct answer would be the following.

A. The Tokyo Olympic Games were delayed from 2020 to 2021 due to the coronavirus pandemic.

The teacher then creates three incorrect alternative choices using other sentences in the passage, like the following.

B. The U.S. Olympic and Paralympic Committee (USOPC) announced December 10 that it won't punish athletes for raising their fists or kneeling as they accept medals at next year's Tokyo, Japan Games and beyond.

C. The decision is a response to a set of recommendations from a USOPC athlete group.

D. It seeks changes to the much-criticized Rule 50 of the IOC Olympic Charter.

The teacher randomizes the order of the answers, then administers the item to students, and discusses various responses and their rationales with the class.

Grammar Category

Grammar items accounted for about 25 percent of the language items and about 2.3 percent (39 of 1,684) of the total ELA items. Table 2.22 depicts the distribution of grammar items across the grade levels. As indicated in table 2.22, grammar involves five subcategories: sentence structure, verb tense, pronoun usage, modifier placement and formation, and agreement. We consider each briefly.

Table 2.22: Grammar Category in Short Constructed-Response Language Items

Subcategories	Grade or Test	Percentage of Items*
Sentence structure Verb tense Pronoun usage Modifier placement and formation Agreement	3	20.00
	4	0
	5	20.00
	6	33.33
	7	0
	8	0
	9	0
	10	0
	11	25.00
	12 (NAEP)	0
	SAT	27.27
	ACT	29.33

*Percentages indicate how many selected-response language items for a grade or test use the grammar category.

Sentence structure items require students to recognize proper and improper sentence construction. In some cases, students determine if any construction errors are present—and if so, fix them—and in others, students are alerted to the presence of errors and must identify them. Figures 2.35 and 2.36 depict some sample items.

Guinness, realizing how lucrative **68** the opportunity might be, agreed to star in the film despite his skepticism about the quality of the writing.	**68. A.** NO CHANGE **B.** Guinness would realize **C.** Guinness, a realization of **D.** Guinness realized

Figure 2.35: Example one of language grammar sentence structure item.

Which sentence uses **incorrect** parallel structure?

    A. Students who participate in theater learn public speaking, confidence, and they learn to express themselves creatively.

    B. Preparing my breakfast typically includes frying three eggs, cooking four sausage links, and making two slices of toast.

    C. Before going on a long backpacking trip, a person needs to be in good physical condition, pack carefully, and check the weather.

    D. Regretting having eaten such a big lunch, Sharon tried to ward off the worst effects by taking some antacid tablets, drinking water, and going for a walk.

Figure 2.36: Example two of language grammar sentence structure item.

Verb tense items require students to identify correct versus incorrect uses of tense. These items commonly provide students with alternatives for a highlighted section of text, along with a *no change* option. To illustrate, consider the items in figures 2.37 and 2.38 (page 64).

Because a liberal arts degree typically **36** teaching students not what to think but how to think, the classic disciplines offer contemporary and useful tools for academic and professional achievement.	**36** A) NO CHANGE B) teaches C) to teach D) and teaching

Figure 2.37: Example one of language grammar verb tense item.

Edit the sentences by clicking on the sentence that does **not** use verb tense correctly.

Michaela asked her dad, "Can I borrow the car after school? I want to go see a movie with my friends."

"Michaela, you may not have the car, but the theater is close enough that you can ride your bike there," her dad replied.

Michaela frowned and said, "If I wanted to ride my bike, I would not have asked to have took the car!"

Figure 2.38: Example two of language grammar verb tense item.

Pronoun usage items require students recognize correct and incorrect uses of pronouns in terms of characteristics like person and number. Again, students must determine whether to make specific changes to highlighted content or to make no change in these items. The item in figure 2.39 exemplifies this.

Read the following pairs of sentences that include one mistake in pronoun usage. Then read the question that follows.

For **each** pair of similar sentences, choose the sentence with the correct pronoun.

Gabe and I came home for dinner on Sunday, and after we finished eating, Mom split the leftovers between him and me. / Gabe and I came home for dinner on Sunday, and after we finished, Mom split the leftovers between he and I.

John, Mitch, and myself quit the hockey team after the season. / John, Mitch, and I quit the hockey team after the season.

Rachel and me went fishing and caught trout and salmon. / Rachel and I went fishing and caught trout and salmon.

Figure 2.39: Example of language grammar pronoun usage item.

Modifier placement and formation items deal with the structure and placement of modifying phrases, clauses, and sentences. Items in this category range from focusing on a single word to relatively lengthy clauses. The items in figures 2.40 and 2.41 show typical examples.

Art Pranks

Some street artists have put their own adaptations of famous works of art on display in museums. Surprised, these new pieces are placed secretly and sometimes left hanging for days until staff notice they do not belong.

1

Such works include a copy of the Mona Lisa with a smiley face painted in place of her face and a pastoral scene with police tape in the foreground.

1. **A.** NO CHANGE

   B. These new pieces are placed secretly and sometimes remain hanging for days until surprised staff notice they do not belong.

   C. Placed secretly and sometimes left hanging for days until staff notice they do not belong, these new pieces are surprised.

   D. Secretly surprised, these new pieces are sometimes left hanging for days until staff notice they do not belong.

Figure 2.40: Example one of language grammar modifier placement and formation item.

Long viewed by many as a useless major, English is now seen by many students and employers as a practical and advantageous major, offering a collection of useful skills with applicability to the modern workplace. In general terms, an English degree involves the study of the content and structure of communication. But **45** more simply, the discipline encourages students to analyze complex material and build solid arguments.	**45** A) NO CHANGE B) speaking in a more simple way, C) speaking in a way more simply, D) in a more simple-speaking way

Figure 2.41: Example two of language grammar modifier placement and formation item.

Agreement items require students to recognize correct and incorrect agreement between phrases, clauses, and sentences in terms of their agreement in characteristics like proper reference and number. The item in figure 2.42 is a typical example. Notice that the choices limit the options students have to correct such an error; in this case, they must change the number of both the noun and the verb.

As he walks around the pond, he notices a frog sitting on <u>a lily pad as fly buzzes</u> nearby. Children fish from a
        1
small dock as their parents look on from the shore. He looks up at the sky and sees nothing but a few wispy clouds and a pair of geese in flight. The scene seems completely tranquil.
	1. **A.** NO CHANGE
	   B. lily pads as fly's buzzes
	   C. a lily pad as flies buzz
	   D. lily pad's as fly buzzes

Figure 2.42: Example of language grammar agreement item.

Figure 2.43 (page 66) shows the general protocol for constructing a selected-response grammar item.

To illustrate how teachers might use this protocol, consider a sixth-grade teacher who wishes to construct a grammar item for the subcategory of verb tense. The teacher selects a passage and changes a verb to the incorrect tense, as in the following:

> When the people of one country take control over an Indigenous population of another, they are said to have colonizing that population. When they take the Indigenous people's ideas and practices and make them their own, they are said to have appropriated them. Food was often appropriated because the ingredients weren't native to the colonizers' home countries. Tomatoes are an example. Though people today associate tomatoes with Italian pastas and pizzas, they actually came from Central and South America. (Smithsonianmag.com, 2020)

The teacher then writes a question like: Select the sentence that does not use verb tense correctly. The correct answer would be the following.

A.   When the people of one country take control over an Indigenous population of another, they are said to have colonizing that population.

1. Select a subtype.
   - Sentence structure
   - Verb tense
   - Pronoun usage
   - Modifier placement and formation
   - Agreement
2. Pick a passage with the subtype present.
3. Adjust the passage to be wrong, if desired.
4. Write a correct option (if the passage was made incorrect).
5. Write two or three incorrect options and a NO CHANGE option.

Figure 2.43: Grammar category protocol for creating selected-response language practice items.

The teacher then creates three incorrect alternative choices using other sentences in the passage.

    B.   When they take the Indigenous people's ideas and practices and make them their own, they are said to have appropriated them.

    C.   NO CHANGE

    D.   Tomatoes are an example.

The teacher randomizes the order of the answers, then administers the item to students, and discusses various responses and their rationales with the class.

Mechanics Category

The category of mechanics accounted for 16 percent of the total number of ELA items we analyzed and about 1.4 percent (24 of 1,684) of the total ELA items. Table 2.23 depicts the distribution of mechanics items across the grade levels. Mechanics items have a relatively uneven distribution across the various grade levels, with some grades having high frequencies and some very low. Mechanics items involve three subcategories: punctuation, capitalization, and spelling. We address each briefly.

Punctuation items require students recognize correct usage of punctuation marks and remedy incorrect usages. Punctuation items require students to analyze specific parts of the text and determine how the punctuation should be changed or whether it is accurate as stated. The item in figure 2.44 depicts one manifestation of this type of item.

Capitalization items require students to examine specific instances of capitalization and determine their correctness. The item in figure 2.45 (page 68) shows this.

Table 2.23: Mechanics Category in Short Constructed-Response Language Items

Subcategories	Grade or Test	Percentage of Items*
Punctuation Capitalization Spelling	3	20.00
	4	33.33
	5	20.00
	6	0
	7	40.00
	8	40.00
	9	0
	10	0
	11	25.00
	12 (NAEP)	0
	SAT	9.09
	ACT	14.67

*Percentages indicate how many selected-response language items for a grade or test use the mechanics category.

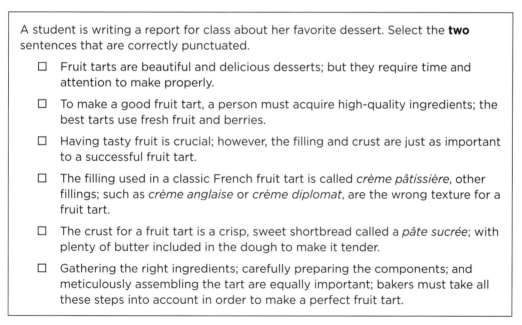

A student is writing a report for class about her favorite dessert. Select the **two** sentences that are correctly punctuated.

☐ Fruit tarts are beautiful and delicious desserts; but they require time and attention to make properly.

☐ To make a good fruit tart, a person must acquire high-quality ingredients; the best tarts use fresh fruit and berries.

☐ Having tasty fruit is crucial; however, the filling and crust are just as important to a successful fruit tart.

☐ The filling used in a classic French fruit tart is called *crème pâtissière*, other fillings; such as *crème anglaise* or *crème diplomat*, are the wrong texture for a fruit tart.

☐ The crust for a fruit tart is a crisp, sweet shortbread called a *pâte sucrée*; with plenty of butter included in the dough to make it tender.

☐ Gathering the right ingredients; carefully preparing the components; and meticulously assembling the tart are equally important; bakers must take all these steps into account in order to make a perfect fruit tart.

Figure 2.44: Example of language mechanics punctuation item.

Read the paragraph and complete the task that follows.

On <u>summer</u> vacation this year, we went to Greece. We spent two days in Athens, and we saw a lot of ancient ruins, including the <u>Acropolis</u>. Next, we took a flight to the <u>Island</u> of Corfu. Corfu had a lot of important history, and it was even mentioned by <u>Thucydides</u>. He was a famous Greek historian.

Choose the underlined word that is incorrectly capitalized.

    A. summer

    B. Acropolis

    C. Island

    D. Thucydides

Figure 2.45: Example of language mechanics capitalization item.

Spelling items require students to examine the spelling of specific words. These spelling items require students to recognize specific spelling errors in a passage as opposed to providing students with options from which to select correct spelling. The item in figure 2.46 depicts a typical spelling item.

Click on the **two** sentences that contain errors in spelling.

The venue could not accommodate more than 100 people, so the bride trimmed the guest list.

The company established its headquarters in a brand new skyscraper in New York.

Though he worked in the hospitalety industry, he was often rude to others.

The longer commute turned out to be a major inconvenience.

A talented makeup artist can turn a handsome actor into a grotesk monster.

The murderous cult operated behind the façade of a suburban utopia.

Figure 2.46: Example of language mechanics spelling item.

Figure 2.47 shows the general protocol for constructing a selected-response mechanics item.

To illustrate how teachers might use this protocol, consider a high school teacher who wishes to construct a mechanics item for the subcategory of capitalization. The teacher selects a passage and underlines several words, but does not adjust any of the capitalization to be incorrect, as in the following paragraph:

> Maybe he would turn up, they thought as the weeks wore on, maybe they should wait at least until <u>Easter</u>. His sister was heading to <u>North</u> Carolina from Texas to spend what they expected would be a somber <u>holiday</u> with the family. (Los Angeles Times, 2015)

The teacher then writes a question like: Select the underlined word that is incorrectly capitalized. The correct answer is the following.

    A. NO INCORRECT CAPITALIZATION

1. Select a subtype
   - Punctuation
   - Capitalization
   - Spelling
2. Pick a passage with the subtype present.
3. Adjust the passage to be wrong, if desired.
4. Write a correct option (if the passage was made incorrect).
5. Write two or three incorrect options and a NO CHANGE option.

Figure 2.47: Mechanics category protocol for creating selected-response language practice items.

The teacher then creates three alternative choices using the underlined words in the passage.

   B. Easter

   C. North

   D. holiday

The teacher randomizes the order of the answers, then administers the item to students, and discusses various responses and their rationales with the class.

Extended Constructed-Response Writing Items

Extended constructed-response items measure students' writing abilities. Typically the expectation for students' responses to these items is that they produce extended text, and educators judge their answers on the extent to which the text they produce includes certain characteristics, some dealing with content and some with the quality of writing. Table 2.24 (page 70) depicts the distribution of extended constructed-response items.

Extended constructed-response items represent about 8 percent of ELA items we analyzed. This notwithstanding, they cover a major area of interest in terms of students' ELA skills—the ability to write extended text. Stated differently, even though there are relatively few extended constructed-response items in large-scale ELA assessments, they are important since students' scores are commonly interpreted as a measure of their abilities to write. There are five types of frames that we identified in our study: narrative, analytic, informative, argumentative, and comparative. Table 2.25 (page 70) depicts the distribution of these five types of items across the grade levels. We consider each of the five types of extended constructed-response items separately.

Table 2.24: Writing Frames in Extended Constructed-Response Items

Frame	Number of Items	Percentage of Items	Most Common Stems
Narrative	51	39.23	Write a narrative story about a topic. Write a narrative from a particular perspective or point of view. Continue the story or write a narrative about what happens after the events in a text.
Analytic	34	26.15	Analyze, explain, or describe how an element functions in the text.
Informative	17	13.08	Describe, explain, or explore information.
Argumentative	14	10.77	Argue for or against a topic. Take and defend a position or stance on a topic. Try to convince someone of an opinion.
Comparative	14	10.77	Compare and contrast information, details, versions, or arguments.
Total	130	100	

Table 2.25: Extended Constructed-Response Writing Items by Grade

	3	4	5	6	7	8	9	10	11	12 (NAEP)	SAT	ACT	Total
Narrative	3	6	7	5	5	8	6	4	5	2	0	0	51
Analytic	3	2	1	5	3	3	5	3	8	0	1	0	34
Informative	2	6	2	0	2	1	0	1	2	1	0	0	17
Argumentative	1	2	1	0	0	3	0	0	3	3	0	1	14
Comparative	1	3	2	4	1	0	2	1	0	0	0	0	14
Total	10	19	13	14	11	15	13	9	18	6	1	1	130
Percentage of Items*	8	15	10	11	8	12	10	7	14	5	1	1	

*Totals do not sum to 100 percent due to rounding.

Narrative Frame

The narrative frame is the most common type of extended constructed-response item and perhaps the most well known. Table 2.26 shows how this frame is distributed across the grade levels. As the distribution depicts, the narrative frame is addressed throughout the grade levels and even in NAEP. However, it is not addressed in the SAT or ACT. The items in figures 2.48–2.50 (page 72) depict typical examples of the narrative frame in extended constructed-response items.

Table 2.26: Narrative Frame in Extended Constructed-Response Writing Items

Most Common Stems	Grade or Test	Percentage of Items*
Write a narrative story about [Topic]. Write a narrative from [Perspective]. Continue the story or write a narrative about what happens after the events in [Text].	3	30.00
	4	31.58
	5	53.85
	6	35.71
	7	45.45
	8	53.33
	9	46.15
	10	44.44
	11	27.78
	12 (NAEP)	33.33
	SAT	0
	ACT	0

*Percentages indicate how many extended constructed-response writing items for a grade or test use the narrative frame.

---

7. How would the story be different if it were told from the uncle's point of view?

Consider how descriptions of the events and characters might change depending on the point of view of the person telling the story.

Retell the story from the uncle's point of view. Include specific details about the events and characters from the story to show this point of view.

Figure 2.48: Grade 4 extended constructed-response item using the narrative frame.

Notice there are three scenarios for these items.

- Write a story.
- Write a narrative from a specific character's perspective.
- Continue a story that has already been started.

These are important distinctions in that writing a story from beginning to end is substantially different from writing a narrative from a specific perspective, which in turn is distinct from continuing a provided story. For example, when continuing a story, students do not compose their own introductions but must connect their writing to the provided first part of the narrative, whereas when writing a complete story, students must create all components of the narrative, but are not constrained by the content or structure of an existing text. Figure 2.51 (page 73) shows the protocol for designing an extended constructed-response item using the narrative frame.

Life at Sea Narrative Performance Task

Part 2

You will now review your notes and sources, and plan, draft, revise, and edit your writing. You may use your notes and refer to the sources. Read your assignment and the information about how your writing will be scored; then begin your work.

Your Assignment:

Your school is publishing a collection of fictional short stories about life at sea. Your assignment is to write a story that is several paragraphs long to include in the collection. For your story, imagine that you are a sailor on board a British Royal Navy sailing ship in the early 19th century. In your story, tell about an exciting encounter you have during your voyage.

The collection of stories will be read by parents, teachers, and the other students in your school. When writing your story, find ways to use information and details from the sources you read on the history of sailing to improve your story. Make sure you develop your character(s), the setting, and the plot. Use details, dialogue, and description where appropriate.

Narrative Story Scoring:

Your story will be scored using the following:

1. **Organization/purpose:** How effective was your plot, and did you maintain a logical sequence of events from beginning to end? How well did you establish and develop a setting, narrative, characters, and point of view? How well did you use a variety of transitions? How effective were your opening and closing for your audience and purpose?

2. **Development/elaboration:** How well did you develop your narrative using description, details, and dialogue? How well did you use relevant details or information from the sources in your story?

3. **Conventions:** How well did you follow the rules of grammar usage, punctuation, capitalization, and spelling?

Now begin work on your story. Manage your time carefully so that you can

- plan your multi-paragraph story.

- write your multi-paragraph story.

- revise and edit the final draft of your multi-paragraph story.

Figure 2.49: Grade 6 extended constructed-response item using the narrative frame.

8. Based on the excerpt from *The Hound of the Baskervilles*, what might happen next? Continue the story by writing a chapter following the ones you read, using details from the novel to develop the plot. Include Watson as one of the characters, and involve at least one other character introduced so far: Dr. James Mortimer, Sir Henry Baskerville, or Sherlock Holmes. Be sure to include dialogue between the characters as well as descriptions of the events and setting.

Figure 2.50: Grade 9 extended constructed-response item using the narrative frame.

To illustrate this process, consider the following example. A fourth-grade teacher provides students with a news article about an Australian family who discovered a koala in their Christmas tree. The article is written as a third-person description of the event with quotes from some of the family members. The teacher has the class read the article, then gives them the following prompt asking for a first-person retelling of the story that includes

1. Pick an appropriate passage (if using the following second or third stem).
2. Write an item using one of the following stems.
   - Write a narrative story about [Topic].
   - After reading the provided text, write a narrative from [Perspective or Point of View].
   - After reading the provided text, continue the story or write a narrative about what happens after the events in [Text].
3. If desired, add special instructions related to:
   - Format
   - Details
   - Audience

Figure 2.51: Narrative frame protocol for creating extended constructed-response writing practice items.

specific details: Retell the story from the koala's point of view, including how the koala ended up in the tree inside the house, and how it reacted to what happened afterward.

Analytic Frame

As its name implies, the analytic frame requires students to analyze content. Table 2.27 depicts the distribution of items using the analytic frame across the grade levels. Analytic items are well represented across the grade levels but not in NAEP or ACT. The items in figures 2.52–2.54 (page 74) depict typical examples of analytic items.

Table 2.27: Analytic Frame in Extended Constructed-Response Writing Items

Most Common Stems	Grade or Test	Percentage of Items*
Analyze how [Textual Element] functions in the text. Explain how [Textual Element] functions in the text. Describe how [Textual Element] functions in the text.	3	30.00
	4	10.53
	5	7.69
	6	35.71
	7	27.27
	8	20.00
	9	38.46
	10	33.33
	11	44.44
	12 (NAEP)	0
	SAT	100
	ACT	0

*Percentages indicate how many extended constructed-response writing items for a grade or test use the analytic frame.

> **3.** The passages from *Hard Times* and *Pride and Prejudice* both describe the setting in great detail. Write an essay explaining how each description relates to themes explored in the rest of each passage. Be sure to use details from **both** stories.

Figure 2.52: Grade 5 extended constructed-response item using the analytic frame.

> **28.** You have learned about commercial space flight by reading three articles, "Billionaires Blast Off," "Space: A Travel Guide," and "Financing the Final Frontier."
>
> Write an essay analyzing how each source uses explanations, examples, and descriptions to help accomplish its purpose. Use evidence from each source to support your response.

Figure 2.53: Grade 7 extended constructed-response item using the analytic frame.

> You have read a passage from William Shakespeare's play *Hamlet* and have watched a clip from the movie *Rosencrantz & Guildenstern Are Dead*, a film featuring two minor characters from *Hamlet* set around the fringes of the play. Though they cover a similar set of events, the stories of the play and film are told from entirely different perspectives and convey different ideas and themes.
>
> Write an essay in which you examine the significance of the points of view from which the stories of the play and film are told. How are the characters and events depicted in each piece? What do these depictions suggest about the nature of the world the characters inhabit? Remember to use relevant and sufficient evidence from each source, citing specific details to support your argument.

Figure 2.54: Grade 11 extended constructed-response item using the analytic frame.

As these examples represent, analytic items can take several forms, but in general they require students to consider multiple sources of information, generate an inference from this information, and then support their inferences. Figure 2.55 shows the protocol for designing an extended constructed-response item using the analytic frame.

> 1. Pick an appropriate passage (or set of passages).
> 2. Write an item using one of the following stems.
>   - Analyze how [Textual Element] functions in the text.
>   - Explain how [Textual Element] functions in the text.
>   - Describe how [Textual Element] functions in the text.
> 3. Add specific questions to answer, if desired.
> 4. Add a prompt for evidence like the following, if desired.
>   - Support your response with evidence from the (each) source.

Figure 2.55: Analytic frame protocol for creating extended constructed-response writing practice items.

To illustrate this process, consider the following example. An eighth-grade teacher provides students with two articles on archaeology. The articles use descriptions and examples to explain characteristics and techniques of archaeology and how the field has changed over time. The teacher has the class read the articles, then gives them the following task and prompt for evidence: Analyze how each article uses examples to support its ideas about the field of archaeology. Support your response with evidence from each source.

Informational Frame

Table 2.28 depicts the distribution of informational extended constructed-response items across the grade levels. Informational items have a presence at most of the grade levels except grades 6 and 9, but do not appear on the SAT or ACT. Extended constructed-response items that focus on information require students to explain or describe content. The items in figures 2.56 and 2.57 (pages 76–77) depict how this manifests on various test items.

Table 2.28: Informational Frame in Extended Constructed-Response Writing Items

Most Common Stems	Grade or Test	Percentage of Items*
Describe [Information or Topic]. Explain [Information or Topic]. Explore [Information or Topic].	3	20.00
	4	31.58
	5	15.38
	6	0
	7	18.18
	8	6.67
	9	0
	10	1.11
	11	11.11
	12 (NAEP)	16.67
	SAT	0
	ACT	0

*Percentages indicate how many extended constructed-response writing items for a grade or test use the informational frame.

Within items using the informational frame, teachers provide students with information (sometimes from multiple sources) and then ask them to describe or explain that information, usually with specific directions in terms of how to present the information. Figure 2.58 (page 77) shows the protocol for designing an extended constructed-response item using the informational frame.

To illustrate this process, consider the following example. A high school teacher wants her students to learn about the negative effects of certain types of food on teenagers' health, so she provides them with two articles on the subject. After the class reads the articles, the teacher gives them the following prompt: Explain how various types of food and drink can negatively affect teenagers' health. The teacher also asks students to address specific details

Star Fruit Informational Performance Task

Part 2

You will review your notes and sources, and plan, draft, revise, and edit your writing. You may use your notes and look back at the sources. Read the assignment and the information about how your writing will be scored; then begin your work.

Your Assignment:

Your teacher is creating a bulletin board display in the school lunch room to show what your class has learned about different types of fruits and vegetables. You decide to write an informational article on star fruit. Your article will be read by other students, teachers, and parents.

Using at least two sources, develop a main idea about star fruit. Choose the most important and relevant information from the sources to support your main idea. Then, write an informational article that is several paragraphs long. Clearly organize your article and support your main idea with details from the sources. Use your own words except when quoting directly from the sources. Be sure to include the source title or number when using details from the sources.

REMEMBER: A well-written informational article

- has a clear main idea.

- is well-organized and focused on the topic.

- has an introduction and conclusion.

- uses logical transitions.

- uses relevant details from the sources to support your main idea.

- puts the information from the sources in your own words, except when using direct quotations from the sources.

- gives the title or number of the source for the details or facts you included.

- develops ideas clearly.

- uses clear language.

- follows rules of writing (spelling, punctuation, and grammar usage).

Now begin work on your informational article. Manage your time carefully so that you can

1. plan your informational article.

2. write your informational article.

3. revise and edit the final draft of your article.

Word-processing tools and spell check are available to you.

For Part 2, you are being asked to write an informational article that is several paragraphs long. Type your response in the box below. The box will get bigger as you type.

Figure 2.56: Grade 3 extended constructed-response item using the informational frame.

by adding information on what types of food and drink can be harmful, what effects they can have, and how differences between adults and adolescents can influence these effects. Finally, the teacher includes the following prompt for evidence: Support your response with specific evidence from each source.

Associated Texts: "Sanitation Voted Top Medical Milestone of Last 150 Years," "A Brief History of Sewers," and "Innovations in Sanitation"

Though more mundane than the invention of vaccines or antibiotics, improvements in sanitation have been among the most significant medical advances of the last several centuries. Write an essay that includes references to **all three** articles to explain the importance of advances in sanitation to public health. Your essay should

- describe public health problems caused by a lack of sanitation before advancements were made
- discuss the kinds of solutions various scientists and officials attempted to improve sanitation
- explain how understanding of problems caused by unsanitary conditions has changed over time
- suggest how future improvements in sanitation may further improve public health

Figure 2.57: Grade 11 extended constructed-response item using the informational frame.

1. Select an appropriate topic.
2. Pick an appropriate passage (or set of passages, if desired).
3. Write an item using one of the following stems.
   - Describe [Information or Topic].
   - Explain [Information or Topic].
   - Explore [Information or Topic].
4. Add specific details to include or address, if desired.
5. Add a prompt for evidence like the following, if desired.
   - Support your response with evidence from the (each) source.

Figure 2.58: Informational frame protocol for creating extended constructed-response writing practice items.

Argument Frame

Educators widely recognize the argument frame, often described as *persuasive writing*. Table 2.29 (page 78) depicts the distribution of such items across the grade levels. As table 2.29 shows, argument frame items have an uneven distribution. They appear at some grade levels but not at others. They have a strong presence on NAEP and the ACT, but do not appear on the SAT. Extended constructed-response items that feature the argument frame require students to design and write a coherent argument or some part of an argument. Argument items take three different forms, as the sample items in figures 2.59–2.61 (pages 79–81) exemplify.

Table 2.29: Argument Frame in Extended Constructed-Response Writing Items

Most Common Stems	Grade or Test	Percentage of Items*
Argue for or against [Topic]. Take and defend a position or stance on [Topic]. Try to convince someone that [Opinion].	3	10.00
	4	10.53
	5	7.69
	6	0
	7	0
	8	20.00
	9	0
	10	0
	11	16.67
	12 (NAEP)	50.00
	SAT	0
	ACT	100

*Percentages indicate how many extended constructed-response writing items for a grade or test use the argument frame.

Electric Scooters Opinion Performance Task

Part 2

You will now review your notes and sources, and plan, draft, revise, and edit your writing. You may use your notes and look back at the sources. Read the assignment and the information about how your writing will be scored; then begin your work.

Your Assignment:

When your class returns from a research trip to the library, your classmates begin to share what they learned about different types of transportation options. They also begin to discuss a rule that prohibits people from riding electric scooters on sidewalks. Some students agree with the rule, while other students disagree with the rule. Your teacher asks you to write a paper explaining your opinion about the rule.

In your paper, you will take a side as to whether you agree with the rule prohibiting people from riding electric scooters on sidewalks, or whether you disagree with the rule. Your paper will be read by your teacher and your classmates. Make sure you clearly state your opinion and write several paragraphs supporting your opinion with reasons and details from the sources. Develop your ideas clearly and use your own words, except when quoting directly from the sources. Be sure to include the source title or number when using details or facts from the sources.

REMEMBER: A well-written opinion paper

- states a clear opinion.
- is well-organized and focused on the topic.
- has an introduction and conclusion.
- uses logical transitions.
- uses details or facts from the sources to support your opinion.
- puts the information from the sources in your own words, except when directly quoting from the sources.
- includes the title or number of the source for the details or facts you included.
- develops ideas clearly.
- uses clear language.
- follows rules of writing (spelling, punctuation, and grammar usage).

Now begin work on your opinion paper. Manage your time carefully so that you can

1. plan your opinion paper.
2. write your opinion paper.
3. revise and edit the final draft of your opinion paper.

Word-processing tools and spell check are available to you.

For Part 2, you are being asked to write an opinion paper that is several paragraphs long. Type your response in the box below. The box will get bigger as you type.

Figure 2.59: Grade 5 extended constructed-response item using the argument frame.

Historic Places Argumentative Performance Task

Part 2

You will now review your notes and sources, and plan, draft, revise, and edit your writing. You may use your notes and refer to the sources. Read your assignment and the information about how your writing will be scored; then begin your work.

Your Assignment:

As part of a local history blog your social studies class is creating, you have been tasked with writing an essay about whether or not a local landmark should be added to the National Register of Historic Places. Your essay will be posted online and will be read by students, teachers, and parents who visit the blog.

Your assignment is to use the sources you have read to write a multi-paragraph argumentative essay in either support of or opposition to placing the landmark on the National Register. Make sure you establish an argumentative claim, address potential counterarguments, and support your claim with information from the sources you have read. Develop your ideas clearly and use your own words, except when quoting directly from the sources. Be sure to reference the sources by title or number when using details or facts directly from the sources.

Figure 2.60: Grade 8 extended constructed-response item using the argument frame.

continued →

Argumentative Essay Scoring:

Your argumentative essay will be scored using the following:

1. **Organization/purpose:** How well did you state your claim, address opposing claims, and maintain your claim with a logical progression of ideas from beginning to end? How smoothly did your ideas flow from beginning to end using effective transitions? How effective were your introduction and conclusion?

2. **Evidence/elaboration:** How well did you integrate relevant and specific information from the sources? How well did you elaborate your ideas? How well did you clearly state ideas in your own words using precise language appropriate for your audience and purpose? How well did you reference the sources you used by title or number?

3. **Conventions:** How well did you follow the rules of grammar usage, punctuation, capitalization, and spelling?

Now begin work on your argumentative essay. Manage your time carefully so that you can

- plan your multi-paragraph argumentative essay.

- write your multi-paragraph argumentative essay.

- revise and edit the final draft of your multi-paragraph argumentative essay.

Word-processing tools and spell check are available to you.

Remember to check your notes and your prewriting/planning as you write and then revise and edit your argumentative essay.

Fully Booked

"You'll never know until you try." These days, parents sign their kids up for all sorts of extracurricular activities, from youth soccer to piano lessons to computer programming summer camps. With so many different options available, many parents feel their children might miss out on something they enjoy or have ability in if they aren't exposed to every possible opportunity. Is this the best way to ensure children are able to discover their interests and talents? Does a busy schedule keep kids engaged and energized, or does it inevitably lead to burnout and exhaustion? Given parents' continuing penchant for packing their kids' calendars, it is worth reflecting on this issue.

Read each of the following perspectives. Each reflects a particular point of view on the issue of parents engaging their children in a large number of extracurricular activities.

Perspective One

It's good for parents to engage their children in lots of different activities, even ones the children might be reluctant to try. Kids don't have enough experience to know what they will or won't enjoy, so it's up to parents to provide them with the opportunity to find out.

Perspective Two

Parents should only sign their children up for activities the children are excited about. Forcing kids to do things they don't enjoy only makes them unhappy and stressed and takes their attention and energy away from activities they like.

Perspective Three

Parents should only commit their children to a limited number of activities. Between school, sports, music, and other activities, many kids are overbooked, and they don't have enough unstructured time to develop and pursue their own interests.

Essay Task

Write a persuasive essay about the trend of parents filling much of their children's time with structured extracurricular activities. In your essay, be sure to:

- State your own perspective on the issue, and analyze the relationship between your perspective and at least one of the given perspectives

- Develop and support your ideas with reasoning and examples

- Organize your ideas clearly and logically

- Communicate your ideas effectively in standard written English

Your perspective may fully align with any of the perspectives given, integrate or agree with elements of any of them, or be completely different.

Figure 2.61: High school extended constructed-response item using the argument frame.

One type of argument frame requires students to argue for or against something (see figure 2.59). The second type of argument frame item requires students to take and defend a specific position regarding a topic (see figure 2.60). The third type of item asks students to convince someone of something regarding a specific topic (see figure 2.61). Figure 2.62 shows the protocol for designing extended constructed-response items using the argument frame.

1. Select an appropriate topic or issue.
2. Write an item using one of the following stems.
    - Argue for or against [Topic].
    - Take and defend a position or stance on [Topic].
    - Try to convince someone that [Opinion].
3. If desired, add special instructions related to:
    - Audience
    - Specific issues or objections
    - Types of evidence or sources
4. Add specific details to include or address, if desired.

Figure 2.62: Argument frame protocol for creating extended constructed-response writing practice items.

To illustrate this process, consider the following example. A fifth-grade teacher provides students with two articles on plastic pollution. One article describes a study that identifies the top plastic-polluting companies around the world and explains issues around plastic pollution. The other article identifies ways in which certain businesses are trying to reduce plastic waste. After reading the articles, the class receives the following prompt: Take and defend a position on whether companies are doing enough to reduce plastic pollution. The teacher adds the following instructions related to specific issues within the topic and a prompt for evidence: Include information on why plastic pollution is a problem and the obstacles to reducing plastic pollution. Support your response with specific evidence from each source.

Comparative Frame

The comparative frame in extended constructed-response items has broad application because almost any set of topics lends itself to comparison. Table 2.30 depicts the distribution of comparative frame items across the grade levels. As table 2.30 shows, comparative items appear up through grade 10 but not at grade 11 or on the NAEP, SAT, and ACT. Comparative items require students to compare information and details, usually from multiple resources. Figures 2.63 and 2.64 depict typical comparative items.

Table 2.30: Comparative Frame in Extended Constructed-Response Writing Items

Most Common Stems	Grade or Test	Percentage of Items*
Compare and contrast [Information, Details, Versions, or Arguments].	3	10.00
	4	15.79
	5	15.38
	6	28.57
	7	9.09
	8	0
	9	15.38
	10	11.11
	11	0
	12 (NAEP)	0
	SAT	0
	ACT	0

*Percentages indicate how many extended constructed-response writing items for a grade or test use the comparative frame.

---

9. You have read "The Golem" and have listened to *Golem*. Write an essay that compares the two different versions of the folktale. Be sure to include details from **both** versions in your essay.

Figure 2.63: Grade 4 extended constructed-response item using the comparative frame.

---

22. You have read three texts that claim cities would benefit from more public parks. Write an essay that compares the evidence each source uses to support this claim. Be sure to cite evidence from all three sources to support your response.

Figure 2.64: Grade 6 extended constructed-response item using the comparative frame.

Notice that in the first example, for fourth grade, students are asked to compare two different versions of a story. In contrast, the second example, for sixth grade, asks students to compare and contrast a specific textual element: evidence used to support a common claim across three texts.

Figure 2.65 shows the protocol for designing an extended constructed-response item using the comparative frame.

1. Pick an appropriate passage (or set of passages).
2. Select what to compare (for example, information, details, versions, or arguments).
3. Write an item using the following stem.
   • Compare and contrast [Information, Details, Versions, or Arguments].
4. Add a prompt for evidence like the following, if desired.
   • Support your response with evidence from the (each) source.

Figure 2.65: Comparative frame protocol for creating extended constructed-response writing practice items.

To illustrate this process, consider the following example. A seventh-grade teacher has the class watch two performances of *The Nutcracker*, one featuring the original dances and costumes, and another with updated and more culturally sensitive choreography and costumes. The teacher decides to have the class focus on how each version portrays various cultures. She has her students write an essay about the two versions using the following prompt: Compare how various cultures and traditions are portrayed in the two performances of *The Nutcracker* we watched. The teacher also adds a prompt for evidence: Support your response with evidence from each version.

Summary

In this chapter, we examined the four different types of ELA items: selected-response reading, short constructed-response reading, selected-response language, and extended constructed-response writing. For each type, we identified the distinct frames that structure the items. We also discussed the frequency with which the various item types and frames occurred in the large-scale assessments we studied, and we suggested protocols for teachers to use in constructing items for each frame. Using the data presented in this chapter and the recommendations for item creation, teachers will be able to anticipate the ways large-scale external assessments will measure their students' ELA knowledge and help them prepare accordingly.

CHAPTER 3

Analysis of Mathematics Assessment Items

Perhaps more than any other quality, the defining feature of mathematics items is their diversity, in terms of both format and content. An item assessing a student's multiplication skills might be presented in terms of an equation, a word problem, or even a graphical array, and over the course of his or her K–12 experience, that student may study basic arithmetic, algebra, geometry, trigonometry, statistics, and more. In addition to this inter-item diversity, we also encountered significant intra-item diversity. Many mathematics items involve multiple parts, themselves having distinct formats and focusing on different content.

These considerations informed two choices during the course of our analysis. First, when we deemed the multiple parts of an item to be sufficiently distinct from one another, we treated them as separate items. Second, we decided to focus our analysis primarily on mathematical content rather than item format. Because some items did not explicitly identify the skills or disciplines students should draw on, we categorized items by those properties that were evident to students. For example, an item requiring students to use trigonometry to identify the measures of angles in a triangle, but which did not identify the use of trigonometry as a necessary approach for solving the problem, was placed in the triangles category rather than the trigonometry category. When an item required students to utilize multiple skills to solve a problem, we categorized the item by the most prominent knowledge or skill being assessed.

One of the main distinctions between mathematics and ELA is that ELA has a relatively small set of frames that cover the vast majority of items we analyzed, and mathematics centers primarily on topics, rather than frames. Specifically, 80 percent of the ELA items analyzed dealt with reading, and all those items are described in six frames.

Mathematics items, by contrast, must be described by a larger number of major categories and subcategories.

Major Categories

After analyzing 2,629 mathematics items, we found nine major categories of mathematics content, as table 3.1 shows. Each of these general categories includes subcategories according to the content it addresses. We consider each of the major categories individually and explain the similarities shared by items in its subcategories as well as their distribution within the major category. For the sake of brevity, we provide an example from only the most prominent subcategory within each major category.

Table 3.1: General Math Topical Categories

Content Category	Number of Items	Percentage of Total Items
Expressions, Equations, Inequalities, and Functions (EEIF)	676	25.71
Operations	620	23.58
Geometry	528	20.08
Quantity and Number	386	14.68
Ratios and Proportional Relationships	170	6.47
Data Displays	88	3.35
Statistics	83	3.16
Measurement	49	1.86
Trigonometry	29	1.10
Total	2,629	100

Expressions, Equations, Inequalities, and Functions

The category of expressions, equations, inequalities, and functions (EEIF) included 25.71 percent of the items we analyzed, making it the largest mathematics category. Table 3.2 lists subcategories for this category. The subcategories in this category generally deal with mathematical statements of equality or inequality. Additionally, one of the subcategories deals with mathematical expressions, which are components of mathematical statements of equality and inequality.

Table 3.2: Subcategories for Expressions, Equations, Inequalities, and Functions (EEIF)

Subcategories	Number of Items	Percentage of Total Items
Equations	320	12.17
Expressions	88	3.35
Functions	221	8.41
Inequalities	47	1.79
Total	676	25.71

The largest subcategory for the general area is equations. It accounted for 12.17 percent of the mathematics items we analyzed. Figure 3.1 presents a sample equation item. Equation items provide students with information (represented by the equation) and ask them to solve the equation or demonstrate understanding of its structure or what it represents in context. In this item, the teacher provides students with an equation and asks them to calculate d for a given value of h. There is also an element of rounding in this particular item, as the term *closest to* indicates.

$d = 371 - 15.1h$

A train is traveling from Salt Lake City, UT to Denver, CO. The formula above shows the relationship between the train's distance from Denver, d, and h, the hours since departure.

At which of the following times will the train's distance from Denver be closest to 340 miles?

    A) 1 hour

    B) 2 hours

    C) 3 hours

    D) 4 hours

Figure 3.1: Example of an equation item.

Operations

The general category of operations deals with basic arithmetic operations. It accounted for 23.58 percent of the items analyzed and encompasses the subcategories table 3.3 (page 88) shows. The common characteristic for each of the operations item subcategories is that all deal with the basic operations of addition, subtraction, multiplication, and division. With the exception of the operation not specified subcategory, the items in this major category are unidimensional—they typically relate to a single operation instead of requiring students to execute or choose among multiple operations.

Table 3.3: Subcategories for Operations

Subcategories	Number of Items	Percentage of Total Items
Addition	40	1.52
Area Model	2	0.08
Division	32	1.22
Multiples and Factors	23	0.87
Multiplication	67	2.55
Subtraction	17	0.65
Operation Not Specified	439	16.70
Total	620	23.58

Operation not specified is also the most prominent subcategory within the operations category. By itself, this subcategory accounts for 16.70 percent of the mathematics items we analyzed. Figure 3.2 provides an example of an operation not specified item. Operation not specified items provide students with a problem that involves a number of possible operations. It is up to students to determine which type of operations they should execute to solve the problem and in what order. In this particular item, students must determine the total amount of money Naomi makes using multiplication, then determine how much she has left after purchasing the game console using subtraction.

Naomi is saving up to buy a $400 video game console by working during the summer.

- The job pays her $12 for every 1 hour worked.
- Naomi works exactly 15 hours each week.

If she works for 3 weeks and buys the game console, how money will she have left over?

Figure 3.2: Example of an operation not specified item.

Geometry

The major category of geometry deals with shapes and their characteristics. Geometry accounted for 20.08 percent of the mathematics items we analyzed. Table 3.4 depicts the geometry subcategories. While the eight subcategories address different topics within geometry, they all involve relationships among lines, angles, and shapes. These eight subcategories within the geometry category are relatively evenly distributed with the topic of area and perimeter accounting for 3.92 percent of the mathematics items we analyzed.

Table 3.4: Subcategories for Geometry

Subcategories	Number of Items	Percentage of Items
2-D and 3-D Shapes	56	2.13
Area and Perimeter	103	3.92
Circles	33	1.26
Construction	16	0.61
Lines and Angles	76	2.89
Transformations	77	2.93
Triangles	72	2.74
Volume	95	3.61
Total	528	20.08

Figure 3.3 (page 90) depicts a typical area or perimeter item. In these types of items, the teacher presents students with visual or verbal representations of 2-D geometric figures, sometimes in the abstract (as in figure 3.3) and sometimes in the context of real-world situations. Then students must determine the area, perimeter, or both properties of the figures to solve the problem.

Quantity and Number

The general category of quantity and number addresses fifteen different subcategories, which together account for 14.68 percent of the mathematics items we analyzed (see table 3.5, page 90). The quantity and number category is fairly heterogeneous in that there are so many subcategories, each with a relatively low frequency of items. The focus on the various ways to express quantities binds them together. Of the fifteen subcategories, equivalence had the most items, accounting for 4.15 percent of the mathematics items we analyzed.

Figure 3.4 (page 91) depicts a typical equivalence item. Equivalence items provide students with quantities or numbers in various forms and ask them to determine whether the given values are equivalent or to generate an equivalent value in a particular form. This particular item asks students to select three fractions equivalent to one-fourth.

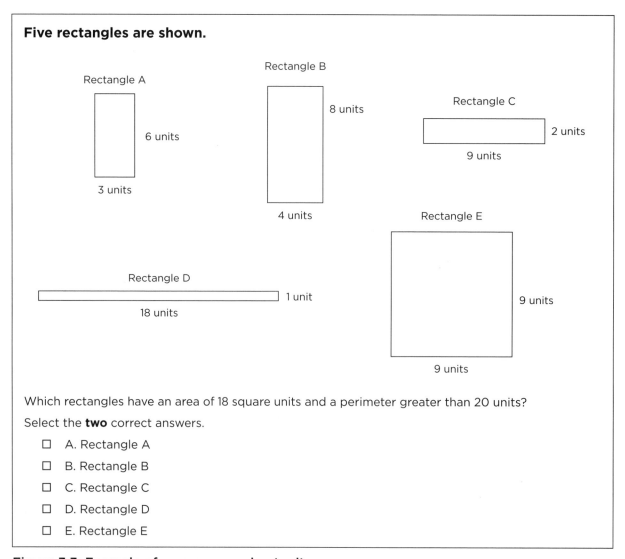

Five rectangles are shown.

Which rectangles have an area of 18 square units and a perimeter greater than 20 units?

Select the **two** correct answers.

☐   A. Rectangle A

☐   B. Rectangle B

☐   C. Rectangle C

☐   D. Rectangle D

☐   E. Rectangle E

Figure 3.3: Example of an area or perimeter item.

Table 3.5: Subcategories for Quantity and Number

Subcategories	Number of Items	Percentage of Total Items
Absolute Value	5	0.19
Comparison	58	2.21
Complex and Imaginary Numbers	13	0.49
Coordinate Plane	42	1.60
Decimals	1	0.04

Equivalence	109	4.15
Exponents, Radicals, and Scientific Notation	31	1.18
Fractions	24	0.91
Matrices	1	0.04
Negative Numbers	9	0.34
Number Lines	20	0.76
Percentages	24	0.91
Place Value	30	1.14
Rational and Irrational Numbers	9	0.34
Rounding and Estimation	10	0.38
Total	386	14.68

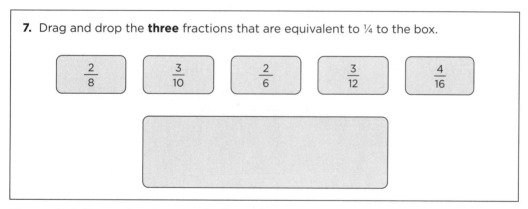

7. Drag and drop the **three** fractions that are equivalent to ¼ to the box.

Figure 3.4: Example of an equivalence item.

Ratios and Proportional Relationships

The major category of ratios and proportional relationships accounted for 6.47 percent of all the items we analyzed. Table 3.6 (page 92) lists the distribution of the various subcategories in this category. The commonality among these subcategories is that they deal with relationships between quantities that are relative or proportional. The subcategory with the greatest number of items is rate and ratio, accounting for 3.77 percent of the mathematics items we analyzed.

Table 3.6: Subcategories for Ratios and Proportional Relationships

Subcategories	Number of Items	Percentage of Total Items
Constant of Proportionality	4	0.15
Proportional Relationships	18	0.68
Rate and Ratio	99	3.77
Scaling	12	0.46
Number Patterns	37	1.41
Total	170	6.47

Figure 3.5 depicts a rate and ratio item. As figure 3.5 indicates, rate and ratio items provide students with quantities in a relationship and ask them to identify proportional relationships, calculate a rate, or use a rate to calculate other quantities. This particular item asks students to calculate a unit rate of production per hour and use it to determine the time required to produce a certain number of items.

A car factory makes 1,700 cars every 5 hours. The factory makes cars for 12 hours each workday. Enter the **fewest** number of workdays the factory will need to make 32,640 cars.

Figure 3.5: Example of a rate and ratio item.

Data Displays

The major category of data displays accounted for 3.35 percent of the items we analyzed. Table 3.7 depicts the subcategories within this category. The eleven subcategories focus on different types of data displays, but all deal with ways of displaying relationships and quantities. Since the eleven subcategories of data display items altogether only account for 3.35 percent of the mathematics items, there are no subcategories with a major role in the mathematics assessments. Additionally, these subcategories are fairly evenly distributed in terms of their frequencies. The subcategory with the highest frequency (0.65 percent) is two-way tables.

Figure 3.6 depicts a two-way table item. As you can see, two-way table items ask students to create or interpret two-way tables. This particular item asks students to identify category counts and relative frequency in a two-way table.

Table 3.7: Subcategories for Data Displays

Subcategories	Number of Items	Percentage of Total Items
Bar Graph	14	0.53
Box Plot	6	0.23
Circle Graph	2	0.08
Dot Plot	3	0.11
Frequency Table	2	0.08
Histogram	7	0.27
Line Plot	13	0.49
Multiple Types	4	0.15
Pictograph	6	0.23
Scatterplot	14	0.53
Two-Way Table	17	0.65
Total	88	3.35

The table shows the results of a survey of students in two different classrooms. The students in each classroom were asked about which toppings they would prefer to have on the pizza provided for an upcoming school event.

Pizza Topping Survey

	Sausage	Pepperoni
Classroom A	14	22
Classroom B	18	9

Based on the results of the survey, which of these statements are true?

Select **all** that apply.

- ○ A. A total of 63 students were surveyed.
- ○ B. A total of 32 students from classroom B were surveyed.
- ○ C. Of the students surveyed from Classroom A, 22 prefer to have pepperoni pizza.
- ○ D. Of the students surveyed from Classroom B, 18 prefer to have pepperoni pizza.
- ○ E. A greater percentage of the students surveyed prefer to have sausage rather than pepperoni on their pizza.

Figure 3.6: Example of a two-way table item.

Statistics

The major category of statistics accounts for 3.16 percent of the mathematics items analyzed. Table 3.8 depicts the subcategories. The general category of statistics is certainly a broad one involving data analysis with elements like making inferences about populations and accounting for errors in sampling. The subcategories in table 3.8 account for the foundational tools of this type of analysis. The subcategory with the most items is measures of center and variance accounting for 1.33 percent of the mathematics items analyzed.

Table 3.8: Subcategories for Statistics

Subcategories	Number of Items	Percentage of Total Items
Correlation Coefficient	1	0.04
Measures of Center and Variance	35	1.33
Probability	26	0.99
Statistical Investigation	21	0.80
Total	83	3.16

Figure 3.7 depicts a typical central tendency item. These types of items ask students to calculate measures of center and variance or reason with these concepts. This particular item asks students to predict the effect of a new data point on various measures of center and variance of a data set.

Alfonso played 15 games on his university's basketball team. His lowest number of points scored in a game was 24. His highest number of points scored was 38. In the sixteenth game, he scored 18 points. Select whether the value of each statistic for his points scored per game increased, decreased, or could not be determined when the last game's points were added.

	Standard Deviation	Median	Mean
Increased	☐	☐	☐
Decreased	☐	☐	☐
Could Not Be Determined	☐	☐	☐

Figure 3.7: Example of a central tendency item.

Measurement

The major category of measurement accounts for 1.86 percent of the items we analyzed. Table 3.9 depicts the subcategories in this category. Measurement is a very broad and diverse aspect of mathematics. The subcategories table 3.9 lists, while not comprehensive in their treatment of the topic, do address foundational concepts. Of the five subcategories of items, units and conversions is the most prominent, accounting for 0.91 percent of the items we analyzed.

Table 3.9: Subcategories for Measurement

Subcategories	Number of Items	Percentage of Total Items
Estimates	1	0.04
Money	1	0.04
Time	9	0.34
Tools	14	0.53
Units and Conversions	24	0.91
Total	49	1.86

Figure 3.8 depicts a sample units and conversions item. These types of items ask students to demonstrate understanding of various units of measure and convert between units. This particular item involves a straightforward conversion from feet to inches.

A tree is 14 feet tall.

How tall is the tree in <u>inches</u>?

inches

Source: U.S. Department of Education, Institute of Education Sciences, National Center for Education Statistics, National Assessment of Educational Progress (NAEP), 2017 Mathematics Assessment. Item 2017-4M9 #14 M230301.

Figure 3.8: Example of a units and conversions item.

Trigonometry

The major category of trigonometry accounts for 1.1 percent of the items we analyzed. Since there were only twenty-nine items within this category, we did not identify subcategories. Figure 3.9 (page 96) depicts a sample trigonometry item. As is evident, trigonometry items ask students to calculate and reason with trigonometric functions. This item asks students to determine the period of a given secant function.

55. What is the period of the function $f(x) = \sec(2x)$?

    A. π

    B. 2π

    C. 4π

    D. $\dfrac{\pi}{2}$

    E. $\dfrac{2}{\pi}$

Figure 3.9: Example of a trigonometry item.

Even though we did not articulate trigonometry subcategories based on our analysis, we noted key topics and recommend teachers provide students with experience solving trigonometry items in the following areas.

- Right triangles

- Angles on the coordinate plane

- Trigonometric expressions, equations, and functions

- Angle of elevation problems

- Graphs of trigonometric equations and functions

Grade-Level Emphases

The distribution of the major categories and subcategories of mathematics topics is certainly informative. However, it would be a mistake to focus on these categories equally at each grade level. This is because our study also disclosed that each grade level emphasizes different topics and subtopics. For example, even though EEIF problems are the predominant item type in general, at some grade levels they represent a relatively small proportion of the items. In other words, tests might emphasize topics and subtopics at one grade level but not another. Knowing this can make preparing students for external assessments easier because educators can narrow the field enough to have adequate time to focus on specific item types.

For each grade level we analyzed, we attempted to articulate those subcategories most crucial to students' success. Our criterion in identifying these particular item types was that the item type accounted for 2 percent or higher of the items at that grade level. We refer to such item types as *prominent subcategories*. We begin with grade 3 items.

Grade 3

Table 3.10 depicts the distribution of prominent subcategories for grade 3.

Table 3.10: Prominent Subcategories for Grade 3

Content Category	Subcategory	Percentage of Grade 3 Items*
Data Displays	Bar Graph	3.50
	Two-Way Table	2.10
Expressions, Equations, Inequalities, and Functions (EEIF)	Expressions	3.85
Geometry	2-D and 3-D Shapes	2.10
	Area and Perimeter	11.54
Measurement	Time	2.80
	Tools	2.80
Operations	Addition	2.10
	Multiplication	6.29
	Operation Not Specified	31.82
Quantity and Number	Comparison	3.85
	Equivalence	4.20
	Fractions	6.99
	Number Lines	3.85
	Total	87.79

*Percentages indicate how many of the total items for grade 3 fall into the designated subcategory.

Fourteen subcategories embedded in six major categories account for almost 88 percent of the items we analyzed at grade 3. Over 50 percent of the items are found within the three most frequent subcategories.

- Operation not specified (operations): 31.82 percent

- Area and perimeter (geometry): 11.54 percent

- Fractions (quantity and number): 6.99 percent

Figures 3.10–3.12 (pages 98–99) depict a third-grade example for each of the three most frequent subcategories. Appendix A (page 187) presents sample items for all the subcategories in table 3.10.

A shuttle van from a hotel to the airport is 36 minutes each way. How many minutes does the van take to go to the airport and back?

 A. 36

 B. 38

 C. 40

 D. 72

Figure 3.10: Grade 3 example of an operation not specified (operations) item.

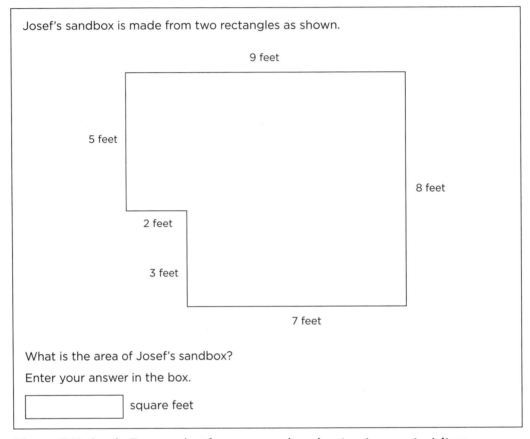

Josef's sandbox is made from two rectangles as shown.

What is the area of Josef's sandbox?

Enter your answer in the box.

_____ square feet

Figure 3.11: Grade 3 example of an area and perimeter (geometry) item.

Grade 4

Table 3.11 depicts the distribution of prominent subcategories for grade 4.

Twelve subcategories embedded in three major categories account for 84.09 percent of the items we analyzed at grade 4. Over 50 percent of the items are found within the three most frequent subcategories.

- Operation not specified (operations): 34.71 percent

- Comparison (quantity and number): 9.24 percent

- Equivalence (quantity and number): 6.69 percent

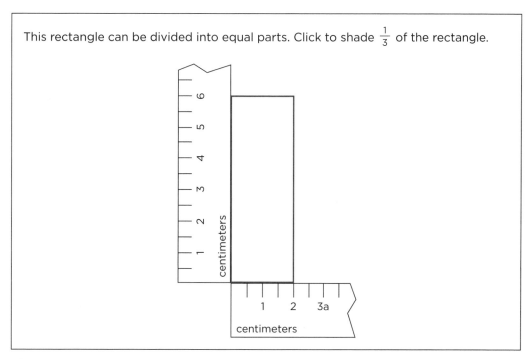

This rectangle can be divided into equal parts. Click to shade $\frac{1}{3}$ of the rectangle.

Figure 3.12: Grade 3 example of a fractions (quantity and number) item.

Table 3.11: Prominent Subcategories for Grade 4

Content Category	Subcategory	Percentage of Grade 4 Items*
Geometry	2-D and 3-D Shapes	2.55
	Area and Perimeter	3.82
	Lines and Angles	4.78
Operations	Addition	5.73
	Division	2.55
	Multiples and Factors	2.87
	Multiplication	5.10
	Subtraction	2.23
	Operation Not Specified	34.71
Quantity and Number	Comparison	9.24
	Equivalence	6.69
	Place Value	3.82
	Total	84.09

*Percentages indicate how many of the total items for grade 4 fall into the designated subcategory.

Figures 3.13–3.15 depict a fourth-grade example for each of the three most frequent subcategories. Appendix A (page 187) presents sample items for all the subcategories in table 3.11.

A car is 16 feet long. A tractor trailer is 4 times the length of a car. Which equation shows the relationship between the lengths of the car and the tractor trailer?

    A. 4 × 16 = 64

    B. 4 + 16 = 20

    C. 4 × 4 = 16

    D. 16 + 16 + 16 + 16 + 16 = 80

Figure 3.13: Grade 4 example of an operation not specified (operations) item.

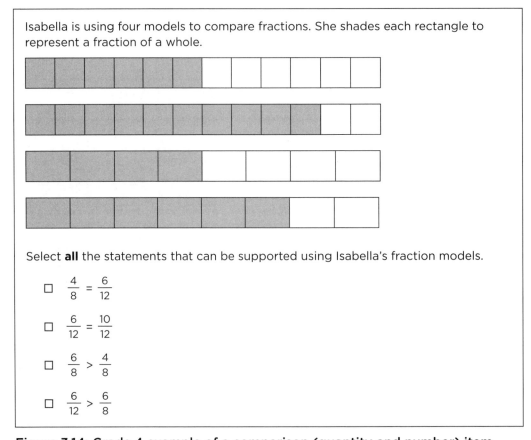

Isabella is using four models to compare fractions. She shades each rectangle to represent a fraction of a whole.

Select **all** the statements that can be supported using Isabella's fraction models.

☐ $\frac{4}{8} = \frac{6}{12}$

☐ $\frac{6}{12} = \frac{10}{12}$

☐ $\frac{6}{8} > \frac{4}{8}$

☐ $\frac{6}{12} > \frac{6}{8}$

Figure 3.14: Grade 4 example of a comparison (quantity and number) item.

Chris changed the mixed number $5\frac{1}{4}$ to a fraction. First, Chris changed the whole number 5 to the fraction $\frac{5}{4}$. Then he added the two fractions together. His work is shown.

$$5\frac{1}{4} = 5 + \frac{1}{4}$$

$$= \frac{5}{4} + \frac{1}{4}$$

$$= \frac{6}{4}$$

Explain the error in Chris's reasoning. Find the correct equivalent fraction. Describe another method you can use to change the mixed number $5\frac{1}{4}$ to a fraction.

Figure 3.15: Grade 4 example of an equivalence (quantity and number) item.

Grade 5

Table 3.12 depicts the distribution of prominent subcategories for grade 5.

Table 3.12: Prominent Subcategories for Grade 5

Content Category	Subcategory	Percentage of Grade 5 Items*
Expressions, Equations, Inequalities, and Functions (EEIF)	Expressions	3.70
Geometry	Volume	10.74
	Area and Perimeter	4.07
	2-D and 3-D Shapes	3.33
Operations	Operation Not Specified	31.85
	Multiplication	10.00
	Addition	3.33
	Division	2.59
Quantity and Number	Coordinate Plane	5.56
	Equivalence	5.19
	Place Value	4.44
	Comparison	4.07
	Total	88.87

*Percentages indicate how many of the total items for grade 5 fall into the designated subcategory.

Twelve subcategories embedded in four major categories account for 88.87 percent of the items we analyzed at grade 5. Over 50 percent of the items are found within the three most frequent subcategories.

- Operation not specified (operations): 31.85 percent

- Volume (geometry): 10.74 percent

- Multiplication (operations): 10.00 percent

Figures 3.16–3.18 depict a fifth-grade example for each of the three most frequent subcategories. Appendix A (page 187) presents sample items for all the subcategories in table 3.12.

Each pizza sold at Gino's Pies cost $18. The total amount of pizza sales for the week was $6,282. How many pizzas were sold?

    A.   157

    B.   349

    C.   426

    D.   785

Figure 3.16: Grade 5 example of an operation not specified (operations) item.

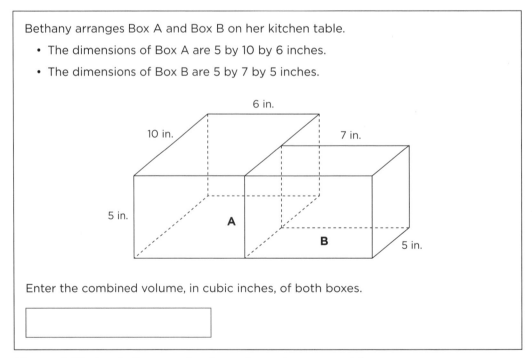

Bethany arranges Box A and Box B on her kitchen table.
- The dimensions of Box A are 5 by 10 by 6 inches.
- The dimensions of Box B are 5 by 7 by 5 inches.

Enter the combined volume, in cubic inches, of both boxes.

Figure 3.17: Grade 5 example of a volume (geometry) item.

14.

What is the value of the expression 3 × 255?

Enter your answer in the box.

Figure 3.18: Grade 5 example of a multiplication (operations) item.

There is a discernable pattern within grades 3, 4, and 5. The major category of operations is certainly important, with the operation not specified subcategory the dominant type of problem students must answer in large-scale assessments, along with multiplication problems. Two types of quantity and number problems are important: comparison and equivalence. Similarly, two types of geometry problems are notable: area and perimeter, and volume. Finally, fractions are dominant, particularly at the third-grade level.

Grade 6

Table 3.13 depicts the distribution of prominent subcategories for grade 6.

Table 3.13: Prominent Subcategories for Grade 6

Content Category	Subcategory	Percentage of Grade 6 Items*
Expressions, Equations, Inequalities, and Functions (EEIF)	Equations	6.56
	Expressions	6.18
Geometry	Area and Perimeter	4.63
	Volume	8.11
Operations	Division	4.63
	Operation Not Specified	17.76
Quantity and Number	Coordinate Plane	5.41
	Equivalence	3.86
	Percentages	2.70
Ratios and Proportional Relationships	Rate and Ratio	9.65
	Number Patterns	2.70
Statistics	Measures of Center and Variance	4.63
	Total	76.82

*Percentages indicate how many of the total items for grade 6 fall into the designated subcategory.

Twelve subcategories embedded in six major categories account for 76.82 percent of the items we analyzed at grade 6. Over 50 percent of the items are found within the eight most frequent subcategories.

- Operation not specified (operations): 17.76 percent

- Rate and ratio (ratios and proportional relationships): 9.65 percent

- Volume (geometry): 8.11 percent

- Equations (EEIF): 6.56 percent

- Expressions (EEIF): 6.18 percent

- Coordinate plane (quantity and number): 5.41 percent

- Measures of center and variance (statistics): 4.63 percent

- Division (operations): 4.63 percent

Figures 3.19–3.21 depict a sixth-grade example for each of the three most frequent subcategories. Appendix A (page 187) presents sample items for all the subcategories in table 3.13.

A large can contains $\frac{21}{24}$ pound of fruit. One serving of fruit weighs $\frac{1}{3}$ pound.
What is the total number of servings of fruit in the can?

   ○ A. $\frac{21}{72}$ serving

   ○ B. $\frac{3}{21}$ serving

   ○ C. $2\frac{15}{24}$ servings

   ○ D. $\frac{21}{27}$ servings

Figure 3.19: Grade 6 example of an operation not specified (operations) item.

16.

The owner of a bakery sells 12 boxes of bagels for $96. What is the cost in dollars per box?

Enter your answer in the box.

Figure 3.20: Grade 6 example of a rate and ratio (ratios and proportional relationships) item.

A right rectangular prism is stacked with identical cubes. The prism's measurements are given in terms of the number of cubes needed to fill the prism.

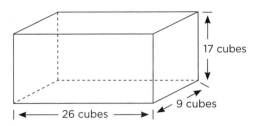

17 cubes

9 cubes

26 cubes

The side length of each cube is ¼ inch. What is the volume, in cubic inches, of the right rectangular prism?

Enter your answer in the space provided. Enter **only** your answer.

Figure 3.21: Grade 6 example of a volume (geometry) item.

Grade 7

Table 3.14 (page 106) depicts the distribution of prominent subcategories for grade 7.

Fifteen subcategories embedded in six major categories account for 86.78 percent of the items we analyzed at grade 7. Over 50 percent of the items are found within the five most frequent subcategories.

- Operation not specified (operations): 18.68 percent

- Rate and ratio (ratios and proportional relationships): 12.45 percent

- Equivalence (quantity and number): 8.79 percent

- Equations (EEIF): 8.42 percent

- Expressions (EEIF): 5.49 percent

Figures 3.22–3.24 (pages 106–107) depict a seventh-grade example for each of the three most frequent subcategories. Appendix A (page 187) presents sample items for all the subcategories in table 3.14.

Table 3.14: Prominent Subcategories for Grade 7

Content Category	Subcategory	Percentage of Grade 7 Items*
Expressions, Equations, Inequalities, and Functions (EEIF)	Equations	8.42
	Expressions	5.49
	Inequalities	2.56
Geometry	2-D and 3-D Shapes	3.66
	Area and Perimeter	3.66
Operations	Operation Not Specified	18.68
Quantity and Number	Coordinate Plane	2.56
	Equivalence	8.79
	Percentages	3.30
Ratios and Proportional Relationships	Proportional Relationships	4.76
	Rate and Ratio	12.45
	Scaling	2.56
Statistics	Measures of Center and Variance	2.93
	Probability	4.40
	Statistical Investigation	2.56
	Total	86.78

*Percentages indicate how many of the total items for grade 7 fall into the designated subcategory.

A carpet installer is putting down carpet in an office building when he realizes that he has run out of carpet.

- He estimates that he has about 950 square feet of floor left on which to install carpet.
- The type of carpet he is installing **only** comes in rolls. (Assume he must buy a whole roll of carpet.)
- Each roll of carpet covers 80 square feet.

How many rolls of carpet does the carpet installer **need** in order to finish flooring the office building? Explain to the installer why he needs this many rolls of carpet.

Figure 3.22: Grade 7 example of an operation not specified (operations) item.

7.

The cost of bulk premium coffee beans at a local market is proportional to their weight. A 12-ounce bag of coffee beans costs $15.

What is the unit rate for premium coffee beans?

  A. $1.12 per ounce

  B. $1.25 per ounce

  C. $0.80 per ounce

  D. $1.15 per ounce

Figure 3.23: Grade 7 example of a rate and ratio (ratios and proportional relationships) item.

Select **all** values equivalent to $-\frac{12}{5}$.

☐ $\frac{-12}{-5}$

☐ $-10\frac{2}{5}$

☐ $2\frac{2}{5}$

☐ $-\frac{-12}{-5}$

☐ $-2\frac{2}{5}$

Figure 3.24: Grade 7 example of an equivalence (quantity and number) item.

Grade 8

Table 3.15 (page 108) depicts the distribution of prominent subcategories for grade 8.

Twelve subcategories embedded in six major categories account for 83.99 percent of the items we analyzed at grade 8. Over 50 percent of the items are found within the four most frequent subcategories.

- Equations (EEIF): 32.99 percent

- Transformations (geometry): 9.86 percent

- Functions (EEIF): 9.18 percent

- Operation not specified (operations): 5.78 percent

Figures 3.25–3.27 (pages 109–110) depict an eighth-grade example for each of the three most frequent subcategories. Appendix A (page 187) presents sample items for all the subcategories in table 3.15.

Table 3.15: Prominent Subcategories for Grade 8

Content Category	Subcategory	Percentage of Grade 8 Items*
Data Displays	Scatterplot	2.04
Expressions, Equations, Inequalities, and Functions (EEIF)	Equations	32.99
	Functions	9.18
	Expressions	2.04
Geometry	Transformations	9.86
	Volume	5.44
	Lines and Angles	2.38
	Triangles	2.38
Operations	Operation Not Specified	5.78
Quantity and Number	Exponents, Radicals, and Scientific Notation	5.44
	Equivalence	2.04
Ratios and Proportional Relationships	Rate and Ratio	4.42
	Total	83.99

*Percentages indicate how many of the total items for grade 8 fall into the designated subcategory.

The cost to rent a moving truck is given by the equation $y = 0.79x + 29.95$, where y is the total cost, in dollars, for driving the truck for a certain number of miles, x.

Part A

In the equation for the cost of renting a moving truck, which statement correctly describes **both** the slope and y-intercept?

A. The slope represents the charge per mile driven, and the y-intercept represents the base cost of renting the truck.

B. The slope represents the charge per mile driven, and the y-intercept represents the total cost after the first mile.

C. The slope represents the base cost of renting the truck, and the y-intercept represents the charge per mile driven.

D. The slope represents the total cost after the first mile, and the y-intercept represents the base cost of renting the truck.

Part B

What is the cost, in dollars, of renting the truck and driving it a total of 40 miles?

    A. $60.76

    B. $61.55

    C. $31.60

    D. $1,198.79

Figure 3.25: Grade 8 example of an equations (EEIF) item.

Rectangle *ABCD* is reflected across the *y*-axis and then translated 2 units right and 3 units up to form *A′B′C′D′*.

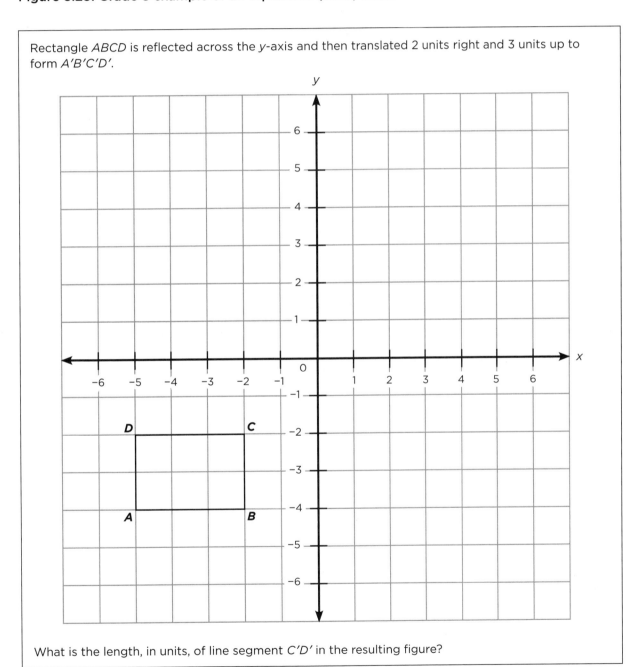

What is the length, in units, of line segment *C′D′* in the resulting figure?

Figure 3.26: Grade 8 example of a transformations (geometry) item.

Biologists at a state wildlife service are tracking the number of an overpopulated rodent species infesting a state park. The biologists use a function that represents the number of a predatory species introduced to the park.

- When the park has no predators, the number of the rodents (r) is 800 per square mile.

- For each predator (p) introduced to the park, the number of rodents decreases by 25 per square mile.

How many predators must be added to a 50-square mile area to reduce the number of rodents to a sustainable 200 rodents per square mile?

Figure 3.27: Grade 8 example of a functions (EEIF) item.

The pattern of item subcategories at the middle school level is different from the pattern at grades 3–5. In grades 6, 7, and 8, EEIF subcategories become very prominent. Geometry subcategories also have more emphasis. The operation not specified subcategory (within operations) remains prominent at the middle school level.

High School

Table 3.16 depicts the distribution of prominent subcategories for high school.

Table 3.16: Prominent Subcategories for High School

Content Category	Subcategory	Percentage of High School Items*
Expressions, Equations, Inequalities, and Functions (EEIF)	Functions	23.07
	Equations	17.30
	Inequalities	3.93
	Expressions	2.58
Geometry	Triangles	7.12
	Lines and Angles	5.89
	Transformations	5.89
	Circles	2.94
	Volume	2.70
	2-D and 3-D Shapes	2.21
Operations	Operation Not Specified	3.44
Quantity and Number	Equivalence	2.33
Ratios and Proportional Relationships	Rate and Ratio	2.82
Trigonometry	Trigonometry	2.94
	Total	85.16

*Percentages indicate how many of the total items for high school fall into the designated subcategory.

It is important to note the items in table 3.16 do not include items from the SAT or ACT. Rather, the items came from assessments like PARCC, Smarter Balanced, and NAEP, which are measures of general mathematics topics at the high school level.

Fourteen subcategories embedded in six major categories account for 85.16 percent of the items we analyzed at the high school level. Over 50 percent of the items are found within the five most frequent subcategories.

- Functions (EEIF): 23.07 percent

- Equations (EEIF): 17.30 percent

- Triangles (geometry): 7.12 percent

- Lines and angles (geometry): 5.89 percent

- Transformations (geometry): 5.89 percent

Figures 3.28–3.30 (page 112) depict a high school example for each of the three most frequent subcategories. Appendix A (page 187) presents sample items for all the subcategories in table 3.16.

x	y
−2	3
−1	0
0	−1
1	0
2	3
3	8

17. The table above shows all the ordered pairs (x, y) that define a relation between the variables x and y. Is y a function of x?

        ◯ Yes   ◯ No

Give a reason for your answer.

Source: U.S. Department of Education, Institute of Education Sciences, National Center for Education Statistics, National Assessment of Educational Progress (NAEP), 2009 Mathematics Assessment. Item 2009-12M2 #7 M1906E1.

Figure 3.28: High school example of a functions (EEIF) item.

A salesperson earns $1,500 per week plus 2% of her sales.

Enter an equation for the salesperson's total earnings, *E*, when she works *x* weeks and has a total of *y* sales, in dollars.

Figure 3.29: High school example of an equations (EEIF) item.

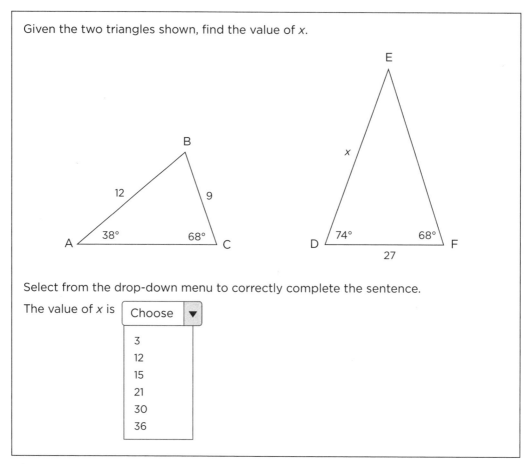

Figure 3.30: High school example of a triangles (geometry) item.

SAT

Table 3.17 depicts the distribution of prominent subcategories on the SAT.

Seven subcategories embedded in four major categories account for 72.43 percent of the items we analyzed from the SAT. Over 50 percent of the items are found within the four most frequent subcategories.

- Equations (EEIF): 34.48 percent

- Expressions (EEIF): 6.90 percent

- Functions (EEIF): 6.90 percent

- Inequalities (EEIF): 6.90 percent

Table 3.17: Prominent Subcategories on the SAT

Content Category	Subcategory	Percentage of SAT Items*
Expressions, Equations, Inequalities, and Functions (EEIF)	Equations	34.48
	Expressions	6.90
	Functions	6.90
	Inequalities	6.90
Operations	Operation Not Specified	6.90
Quantity and Number	Equivalence	3.45
Ratios and Proportional Relationships	Rate and Ratio	6.90
	Total	72.43

*Percentages indicate how many of the total items from the SAT fall into the designated subcategory.

Figures 3.31–3.34 (page 114) depict common formats for SAT items from each of the four most frequent subcategories. In this case, we display four item types because three of these subcategories have the same level of frequency. Appendix A (page 187) presents sample items for all the subcategories in table 3.17.

$h = -2.5t^2 + 47t$

The equation above expresses the approximate height h, in meters, of an arrow t seconds after it is launched straight up from the ground with an initial velocity of 47 meters per second. After approximately how many seconds will the arrow hit the ground?

A) 4.5

B) 8.0

C) 9.5

D) 19.0

Figure 3.31: Example of an equations (EEIF) item based on common SAT formats.

Zhikun opened a bank account that earns 3 percent interest compounded annually. His initial deposit was $1,500, and he uses the expression $1,500(x)^t$ to find the value of the account after t years.

What is the value of x in the expression?

Figure 3.32: Example of an expressions (EEIF) item based on common SAT formats.

For a polynomial $p(x)$, the value of $p(5)$ is -3. Which of the following must be true about $p(x)$?

A) $x - 2$ is a factor of $p(x)$.

B) $x - 3$ is a factor of $p(x)$.

C) $x + 3$ is a factor of $p(x)$.

D) The remainder when $p(x)$ is divided by $x - 5$ is -3.

Figure 3.33: Example of a functions (EEIF) item based on common SAT formats.

Which of the following numbers is **not** a solution of the inequality $7x + 5 \leq 6x + 3$?

A) -1

B) -2

C) -3

D) -5

Figure 3.34: Example of an inequalities (EEIF) item based on common SAT formats.

ACT

Table 3.18 depicts the distribution of prominent subcategories on the ACT.

Table 3.18: Prominent Subcategories on the ACT

Content Category	Subcategory	Percentage of ACT Items*
Expressions, Equations, Inequalities, and Functions (EEIF)	Equations	11.67
	Functions	3.33
Geometry	Area and Perimeter	11.67
	Lines and Angles	5.00
	Volume	3.33
Operations	Multiples and Factors	3.33
	Operation Not Specified	11.67
Quantity and Number	Exponents, Radicals, and Scientific Notation	5.00
	Percentages	5.00
Statistics	Measures of Center and Variance	5.00
	Probability	6.67
Trigonometry	Trigonometry	6.67
	Total	78.34

*Percentages indicate how many of the total items from the ACT fall into the designated subcategory.

Twelve subcategories embedded in six major categories account for 78.34 percent of the items we analyzed from the ACT. Over 50 percent of the items are found within the nine most frequent subcategories.

- Equations (EEIF): 11.67 percent

- Area and perimeter (geometry): 11.67 percent

- Operation not specified (operations): 11.67 percent

- Probability (statistics): 6.67 percent

- Trigonometry: 6.67 percent

- Lines and angles (geometry): 5.00 percent

- Exponents, radicals, and scientific notation (quantity and number): 5.00 percent

- Percentages (quantity and number): 5.00 percent

- Measures of center and variance (statistics): 5.00 percent

Figures 3.35–3.37 (page 116) depict common formats for ACT items for each of the three most frequent subcategories. Appendix A (page 187) presents sample items for all the subcategories in table 3.18.

---

17. In the standard (x, y) coordinate plane, what is the slope of the line given by the equation $2x = 5y - 3$?

    A. $-\dfrac{2}{5}$

    B. $\dfrac{2}{5}$

    C. $\dfrac{5}{2}$

    D.   2

    E.   5

Figure 3.35: Example of an equations (EEIF) item based on common ACT formats.

The Process for Creating Mathematics Assessment Items

Using guidance about the frequency of item subcategories (see the two preceding sections), teachers can create practice items for the most prominent subcategories at their particular grade level. Appendix A (page 187) contains sample items and item-creation templates for each of the mathematics subcategories in the previous sections. In all, there are 110 sets of sample items and templates. Creating assessment items for each subcategory follows a general process.

1. Within the appropriate grade level, find the desired subcategory and read the sample item and item template.

Terrance is a farmer and is calculating the area of one of his trapezoidal fields. The figure below shows his scale drawing of the field with 3 side lengths and the radius of a grain silo given in centimeters. In Terrance's scale drawing, each 1 centimeter represents 1.5 meters.

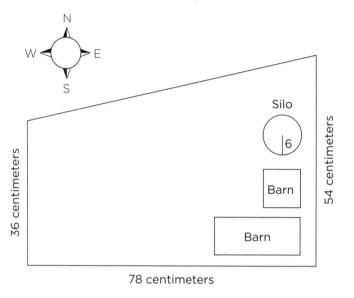

What is the area, in square centimeters, of the scale drawing of the field?

    A. 1,944

    B. 2,106

    C. 2,808

    D. 3,510

    E. 5,616

Figure 3.36: Example of an area and perimeter (geometry) item based on common ACT formats.

---

24. Holly is trying to decide whether to buy a season pass for access to the slopes of a ski resort during the upcoming 25-week ski season. The cost of visiting the resort for a single day is $90, and the cost of the season pass is $550. The season pass will allow Holly to have access to the resort at no additional cost. What is the minimum number of days Holly would need to visit the resort this season in order for the cost of the season pass to be less than the total cost of paying for entry each day she visits?

    A. 4

    B. 6

    C. 7

    D. 22

    E. 25

Figure 3.37: Example of an operation not specified (operations) item based on common ACT formats.

2. Use the template instructions to create elements according to the specifications in the template key and insert the elements into the template.

3. Clearly articulate the correct response, criteria, or both for a correct response.

4. If appropriate, create plausible response alternatives.

The process is fairly straightforward: teachers select a grade level and subcategory, follow the step-by-step template instructions using the template key, and then create a correct response and plausible alternative responses. The template instructions and key provide the details for each item subcategory. Here, we exemplify how teachers can use these instructions to generate practice items by focusing on three common subcategories: operation not specified, equations, and functions.

Operation Not Specified (Operations)

The operation not specified subcategory is found in the major mathematics category of operations, and has a rather large footprint among the mathematics items we analyzed. Table 3.19 depicts the distribution of operation not specified items across the grade levels (or tests). Operation not specified items are very prominent through grade 7, and in grades 3, 4, and 5, they represent over 30 percent of the items. While not equally as prominent at the high school level, they do represent 12 percent of the mathematics items we analyzed in the ACT.

Table 3.19: Distribution of Operation Not Specified Items Across Grade Levels

Grade or Test	Percentage of Items*
3	32
4	35
5	32
6	18
7	19
8	6
High School	3
SAT	7
ACT	12

*Percentages indicate how many of the total items for a grade level or test use this subcategory.

The first part of every template is a sample item. For example, figure 3.38 (page 118) depicts a sample operation not specified item for grade 3.

Appendix A (page 187) has samples of items for the subcategory of operation not specified at various grade levels. To illustrate how a teacher would use the sample items and

> A bakery sold 98 cupcakes. The cupcakes come in boxes. Each box came with 6 chocolate cupcakes, 4 vanilla cupcakes, and 4 red velvet cupcakes.
>
> How many cupcakes were in each box? Show your work.
>
> How many boxes did the bakery sell? Show your work.

Figure 3.38: Sample item for operation not specified at grade 3.

item-creation templates in appendix A (page 187) to create a practice item, assume a third-grade teacher is using the item-creation template for operation not specified that accompanies the sample item in figure 3.38 (which features cupcakes and boxes).

The teacher would examine the item in depth to obtain a sense of what it requires of students. Next the teacher would consider the item-creation template for this item subtype, as figure 3.39 shows.

> [Person A] [Select] [Quantity 1] [Item Type]. The [Item Type] come in [Group A]. Each [Group A] came with [Quantity 2] [Item Subtype A], [Quantity 3] [Item Subtype B], and [Quantity 4] [Item Subtype C].
>
> How many [Item Type] were in each [Group A]? Show your work.
>
> How many [Group A] did [Person A] [Select]? Show your work.

Figure 3.39: Item-creation template for operation not specified at grade 3.

An *item-creation template* represents an abstract schematic of the item subcategory selected. In isolation, an item template will not be very helpful to a teacher creating an assessment item. However, when the teacher uses the template instructions in conjunction with the template key, he or she has all necessary components to create any type of mathematics item presented in this book with great fidelity, relative to the items in the tests we analyzed. Figures 3.40 and 3.41 present the template instructions and template key, respectively, for this operation not specified item at grade 3.

> 1. Choose definitions for [Person A], [Select], [Item Type], [Item Subtype A], [Item Subtype B], [Item Subtype C], and [Group A]. Insert these definitions into the template.
> 2. Create [Quantity 2], [Quantity 3], and [Quantity 4] according to the specifications found in the key. Insert these quantities into the template.
> 3. Create [Quantity 1] according to the specifications found in the key. Insert this quantity into the template.

Figure 3.40: Template instructions for operation not specified item at grade 3.

The template instructions indicate three steps for creating this item subtype. The first step involves choosing definitions for the following elements.

- Person A
- Select

> Person A: A person or other entity (for example, Mr. Zody, bakery, Stephanie)
>
> Select: Any act of selection, acquisition, or designation (for example, bought, sold, picked)
>
> Quantity 1: A two-digit whole number evenly divisible by the sum of [Quantity 2], [Quantity 3], and [Quantity 4]
>
> Quantity 2: A single-digit whole number
>
> Quantity 3: A single-digit whole number
>
> Quantity 4: A single-digit whole number
>
> Item Type: Any type of object (for example, flowers, cupcakes, neckties)
>
> Item Subtype A: A unique variation of [Item Type] (for example, lilies, chocolate cupcakes, striped ties)
>
> Item Subtype B: A unique variation of [Item Type] (for example, roses, vanilla cupcakes, polka-dot ties)
>
> Item Subtype C: A unique variation of [Item Type] (for example, daisies, red velvet cupcakes, plain ties)
>
> Group A: A group of [Item Type] (for example, bouquet, box of cupcakes, package of ties)

Figure 3.41: Template key for operation not specified item at grade 3.

- Item Type
- Item Subtype A
- Item Subtype B
- Item Subtype C
- Group A

Each bracketed element in the instructions represents a decision the teacher must make about what to include in the item; the template key describes each bracketed element, as follows.

- [Person A] represents a person or other entity (for example, Mr. Zody).
- [Select] represents any act of selection, acquisition, or designation (for example, bought).
- [Item Type] represents any type of object (for example, flowers).
- [Item Subtype A] represents a unique variation of [Item Type] (for example, lilies).
- [Item Subtype B] represents a unique variation of [Item Type] (for example, roses).
- [Item Subtype C] represents a unique variation of [Item Type] (for example, daisies).
- [Group A] represents a group of [Item Type] (for example, bouquet).

To keep track of the definitions for elements of an item, we recommend teachers create an element matrix they fill out after they complete each item in the template instructions. This will help teachers keep track of the decisions they have already made and the decisions yet to make. After the teacher completes the first instruction, the element matrix might look like figure 3.42 (page 120).

Element	Definition
Person A	Mr. Zody
Select	Bought
Quantity 1	
Quantity 2	
Quantity 3	
Quantity 4	
Item Type	Flowers
Item Subtype A	Lilies
Item Subtype B	Roses
Item Subtype C	Daisies
Group A	Bouquet

Figure 3.42: Element matrix for operation not specified item at grade 3 after step 1.

The directions note that as teachers make decisions, they should insert their created elements into the template. Thus, after the first step, the template would look like figure 3.43.

Mr. Zody bought [Quantity 1] **flowers**. The **flowers** come in **bouquets**. Each **bouquet** came with [Quantity 2] **lilies**, [Quantity 3] **roses**, and [Quantity 4] **daisies**.

How many **flowers** were in each **bouquet**? Show your work.

How many **bouquets** did **Mr. Zody buy**? Show your work.

Figure 3.43: Item-creation template for operation not specified at grade 3 after step 1.

The second step in the template instructions notes that the teacher should create [Quantity 2], [Quantity 3], and [Quantity 4] according to the specifications in the key. The teacher then inserts these quantities into the template. The template key notes the following.

- [Quantity 2] is a single-digit whole number.

- [Quantity 3] is a single-digit whole number.

- [Quantity 4] is a single-digit whole number.

Let's assume the teacher selects the quantities 3, 7, and 9, respectively. The element matrix now looks like figure 3.44.

Element	Definition
Person A	Mr. Zody
Select	Bought
Quantity 1	
Quantity 2	3
Quantity 3	7
Quantity 4	9
Item Type	Flowers
Item Subtype A	Lilies
Item Subtype B	Roses
Item Subtype C	Daisies
Group A	Bouquet

Figure 3.44: Element matrix for operation not specified item at grade 3 after step 2.

The teacher inserts the new elements into the template (see figure 3.45).

Mr. Zody bought [Quantity 1] flowers. The flowers come in bouquets. Each bouquet came with **3** lilies, **7** roses, and **9** daisies.

How many flowers were in each bouquet? Show your work.

How many bouquets did Mr. Zody buy? Show your work.

Figure 3.45: Item-creation template for operation not specified at grade 3 after step 2.

For the third step of the template instructions, the teacher defines [Quantity 1]. The instructions note that this may be any two-digit whole number that is evenly divisible by the sum of [Quantity 2], [Quantity 3], and [Quantity 4]. Figure 3.46 (page 122) depicts the complete element matrix and figure 3.47 (page 122) shows the completed item.

It is important to note that decisions about definitions for abstract elements should be made in the order the template instructions specify. This is because some elements make sense only in the context of other predetermined elements.

Finally, the teacher clearly articulates the correct response or the criteria for the correct response (see figure 3.48, page 122).

The teacher now has a completed item for operation not specified at the third-grade level. Additionally, the process of creating the item provides teachers with an understanding of the working dynamic of this type of item, which will aid greatly in helping students understand the nature of this item type. In chapter 6 (page 169), we describe how teachers can use this deep-level understanding of the item type to engage students in a process in which they can create their own items.

Element	Definition
Person A	Mr. Zody
Select	Bought
Quantity 1	57
Quantity 2	3
Quantity 3	7
Quantity 4	9
Item Type	Flowers
Item Subtype A	Lilies
Item Subtype B	Roses
Item Subtype C	Daisies
Group A	Bouquet

Figure 3.46: Element matrix for operation not specified item at grade 3 after step 3.

Mr. Zody bought 57 flowers. The flowers come in bouquets. Each bouquet came with 3 lilies, 7 roses, and 9 daisies.

How many flowers were in each bouquet? Show your work.

How many bouquets did Mr. Zody buy? Show your work.

Figure 3.47: Item-creation template for operation not specified at grade 3 after step 3.

Mr. Zody bought **57** flowers. The flowers come in bouquets. Each bouquet came with 3 lilies, 7 roses, and 9 daisies.

How many flowers were in each bouquet? Show your work.

How many bouquets did Mr. Zody buy? Show your work.

Correct Responses:

How many flowers were in each bouquet? 19

How many bouquets did Mr. Zody buy? 3

Response Criteria:

The student will provide the correct response and show his or her work in written form or as expressions, equations, or both.

Figure 3.48: Finished operation not specified item at grade 3 with correct responses and response criteria.

Equations (EEIF)

Equations is another item subcategory used extensively in the items we analyzed. Table 3.20 depicts the distribution of equation items across the grade levels, which become very prominent from grade 8 onward. They are particularly prominent in the SAT items we analyzed.

Table 3.20: Distribution of Equation Items Across Grade Levels

Grade or Test	Percentage of Items*
3	1
4	2
5	2
6	7
7	8
8	33
High School	17
SAT	34
ACT	12

*Percentages indicate how many of the total items for a grade level or test use this subcategory.

As before, the first part of every template is a sample item. For example, figure 3.49 depicts a sample equation item for grade 7.

Here are two equations.

$3x - 26 = -11$

$-5(r + 17) = -70$

Solve each equation. Give *only* your solutions.

$x =$

$r =$

Figure 3.49: Sample item for equations at grade 7.

Appendix A (page 187) includes samples for these items in the subcategory of equations at various grade levels. To illustrate how a teacher would use the sample items and item-creation templates in appendix A to create a practice item, assume a seventh-grade teacher is using the item-creation template for equations that accompanies the sample item in figure 3.49 (solving two equations for x and r).

After examining the sample item, the teacher reads the item-creation template (see figure 3.50, page 124), noting the elements he or she will need to define.

Here are two equations.

[Equation 1]

[Equation 2]

Solve each equation. Give *only* your solutions.

[Variable 1] =

[Variable 2] =

Figure 3.50: Item-creation template for equations at grade 7.

Figures 3.51 and 3.52 present the template instructions and template key, respectively, for the equations item at grade 7 template in figure 3.50.

1. Choose separate variables for [Variable 1] and [Variable 2]. Insert them into the template.
2. Select positive or negative integer values for [Variable 1] and [Variable 2].
3. Create two separate equations of the form specified in the key that satisfy the values selected for [Variable 1] and [Variable 2] in step 2. Insert the equations into the template as [Equation 1] and [Equation 2].

Figure 3.51: Template instructions for equations item at grade 7.

Equation 1: An equation of the form $ax + b = c$ where a, b, and c are positive or negative integer constants and x is [Variable 1].

Equation 2: An equation of the form $a(x + b) = c$ where a, b, and c are positive or negative integer constants and x is [Variable 2].

Variable 1: Any variable (for example, x, n, r).

Variable 2: Any variable (for example, x, n, r).

Figure 3.52: Template key for equations item at grade 7.

The teacher next uses the template instructions and template key to define the elements and insert them into the template. The first step is to choose separate variables for [Variable 1] and [Variable 2] and insert them into the template. The template key says [Variable 1] and [Variable 2] should simply be different variables. Assume the teacher chooses x for [Variable 1] and r for [Variable 2]. The teacher then inserts them into the template (see figure 3.53).

Next the template instructions direct the teacher to select positive or negative integer values for [Variable 1] and [Variable 2]. Assume the teacher selects the positive integer +5 for variable x and the negative integer −3 for the variable r. However, the template instructions do not indicate that the teacher should enter them into the item template at this time, so the teacher keeps track of his or her definitions relative to this instruction using an element matrix (see figure 3.54).

Here are two equations.

[Equation 1]

[Equation 2]

Solve each equation. Give only your solutions.

x =

r =

Figure 3.53: Item-creation template for equations at grade 7 after step 1.

Element	Definition
Equation 1	
Equation 2	
Variable 1	$x = 5$
Variable 2	$r = -3$

Figure 3.54: Element matrix for equations item at grade 7 after step 2.

Next the teacher creates two separate equations of the form the key specifies to satisfy the values he or she selects for [Variable 1] and [Variable 2] in step 2.

As the template key (see figure 3.52) shows, [Equation 1] should take the form $ax + b = c$ where x is [Variable 1]. The teacher has already defined [Variable 1] as x with a value of 5. Therefore, the following equation is true: $a(5) + b = c$. The teacher has several ways to identify values for a, b, and c that satisfy the equation. One efficient method would be to assign values to the variables a and b according to the specifications in the template key and then solve the equation to determine the necessary value for c. In this case, the teacher starts by assigning the value of 3 to a, and the value of -26 to b, producing the equation: $3(5) - 26 = c$. Carrying out the specified operations, the value of $c = -11$. Since students will be solving for x, the teacher changes the 5 back to x, leaving integers for a, b, and c. Therefore, [Equation 1] is $3x - 26 = -11$.

The teacher follows the same process for [Equation 2], which according to the template key has the form $a(x + b) = c$. In this abstract form, x is [Variable 2], which the teacher already defined as r. Therefore the equation is $a(r + b) = c$. The teacher selects the following integers for constants a and b, respectively: -5 and 17. The teacher has also already defined r as -3. Inserting these into the equation produces: $-5(-3 + 17) = c$. Carrying out these operations, it is clear that c must be defined as -70 for [Equation 2] to work. [Equation 2] then is defined as $-5(r + 17) = -70$.

Figure 3.55 shows the complete element matrix and figure 3.56 the completed item. Since the teacher defined the values of x and r during step 2, he or she can use that information to fill in the correct responses (see figure 3.54).

Element	Definition
Equation 1	$3x - 26 = -11$
Equation 2	$-5(r + 17) = -70$
Variable 1	$x = 5$
Variable 2	$r = -3$

Figure 3.55: Element matrix for equations item at grade 7 after step 3.

Here are two equations.

$3x - 26 = -11$

$-5(r + 17) = -70$

Solve each equation. Give *only* your solutions.

$x =$

$r =$

Correct Responses:

$x = 5$

$r = -3$

Figure 3.56: Finished equations item at grade 7 with correct responses.

The teacher now has a completed equations item at the seventh-grade level. Additionally, the process of creating the item provides teachers with an understanding of the working dynamic of this item type.

Functions (EEIF)

Functions is another item subcategory used extensively in the items we analyzed. Table 3.21 depicts the distribution of function items across the grade levels. Function items are very prominent at the high school level, although they don't have a major presence on the SAT or ACT in terms of the items we analyzed.

Appendix A (page 187) includes sample items for the subcategory of functions at various grade levels. To illustrate how a teacher would use the sample items and item-creation templates in appendix A to create a practice item, assume a high school teacher is using the item-creation template for functions that accompanies the sample item in figure 3.57.

As before, the first part of every template is a sample item. For example, figure 3.57 depicts a sample function item for high school.

After examining the sample item, the teacher reads the item-creation template (see figure 3.58, page 128), noting the elements he or she will need to define.

Table 3.21: Distribution of Function Items Across Grade Levels

Grade or Test	Percentage of Items*
3	0
4	0
5	0
6	0
7	0
8	9
High School	23
SAT	7
ACT	3

*Percentages indicate how many of the total items for a grade level or test use this subcategory.

In a certain region, a viral infection is spreading at the rate the table shows.

Days	Number of People Infected (millions)
0	2
2	2.08
5	2.21

Write an exponential function, $V(d)$, that you can use to model the spread of the infection after d days.

Enter your function in the space provided.

$V(d) =$

Figure 3.57: Sample item for functions at high school.

Figures 3.59 (page 128) and 3.60 (page 129) present the template instructions and template key, respectively, for this high school function item.

The teacher next uses the template instructions and template key to define the elements and insert them into the template. The first step is to create a setting in which some object or entity is undergoing a measurable exponential change. Further, the template key explains the following.

- [Setting] is the scenario in which an object or other entity is exponentially changing in magnitude at a measurable rate.

In [Setting], [Object] [Change] at the rate the table shows.

[Unit A]	[Unit B]
0	[Quantity 3]
[Quantity 1]	[Quantity 4]
[Quantity 2]	[Quantity 5]

Write an exponential function, *[Function Variable]([Argument Variable])*, you can use to model the [Change] of the [Object] after *[Argument Variable]* [Unit A].

Enter your function in the space provided.

[Function Variable]([Argument Variable]) =

Figure 3.58: Item-creation template for high school function item.

1. Create a setting in which some object or entity is undergoing a measurable exponential change in magnitude. Insert the setting, the object or entity, and a verb describing the exponential change into the template as [Setting], [Object], and [Change].

2. Identify the independent variable [Unit A] and dependent variable [Unit B] by which the change in magnitude of the object is measured. Insert them into the template.

3. Select nonsequential values for [Quantity 1] and [Quantity 2] according to the specifications in the key. Insert them into the template.

4. Select a value for [Quantity 3] as an initial magnitude of [Object]. Insert it into the template.

5. Choose variables for [Function Variable] and [Argument Variable]. Insert them into the template.

6. Create a function that defines an exponential change in magnitude for [Object].

7. Use the function to calculate values for [Quantity 4] and [Quantity 5]. Insert those values into the template.

Figure 3.59: Template instructions for high school function item.

Setting: The setting for the scenario in which an object or other entity is exponentially changing in magnitude at a measurable rate

Object: An object or other entity exponentially changing in magnitude at a measurable rate (for example, viral infection, nuclear reaction, rodent population)

Change: An exponential change in magnitude of [Object] in either the positive or negative direction (for example, spread, increase, grow)

Function Variable: Any variable you use to represent a function (for example, f, h, g)

Argument Variable: Any variable you use to represent the argument of a function (for example, x, n, j)

Unit A: The independent variable in relation to which the exponential change in magnitude of [Object] is measured (for example, days, seconds, weeks)

Unit B: The dependent variable by which the exponential change in magnitude of [Object] is measured (for example, people, fission events, rodents)

Quantity 1: Any whole number

> Quantity 2: Any whole number greater than [Quantity 1]
>
> Quantity 3: Any whole number or decimal value indicating the initial magnitude of [Object]
>
> Quantity 4: Any whole number or decimal value indicating an exponential change in magnitude from [Quantity 3]
>
> Quantity 5: Any whole number or decimal value indicating an exponential change in magnitude from [Quantity 4] that displays the same rate of change as that between [Quantity 3] and [Quantity 4]

Figure 3.60: Template key for high school function item.

- [Object] is an object or other entity exponentially changing in magnitude at a measurable rate (for example, rodent population).

- [Change] is an exponential change in magnitude of the object in either the positive or negative direction (for example, growth).

Following these instructions, the teacher defines the setting as *a certain city*, the object as *rodent population*, and the change as *growth*. The teacher keeps track of these definitions in an element matrix (see figure 3.61), and inserts them into the template (see figure 3.62, page 130).

Element	Definition
Setting	A certain city
Object	Rodent population
Change	Growth
Function Variable	
Argument Variable	
Unit A	
Unit B	
Quantity 1	
Quantity 2	
Quantity 3	
Quantity 4	
Quantity 5	

Figure 3.61: Element matrix for high school function item after step 1.

The second step directs the teacher to identify the independent variable [Unit A] and dependent variable [Unit B] by which the change in magnitude of the object is measured. The template key notes that [Unit A] is the independent variable in relation to which the exponential change in magnitude of [Object] is measured (for example, days, seconds, weeks). For [Unit A] the teacher selects *weeks*. It is now the independent variable in the item. The template key notes that [Unit B] is the dependent variable by which the

In **a certain city, the rodent population is growing** at the rate the table shows.

[Unit A]	[Unit B]
0	[Quantity 3]
[Quantity 1]	[Quantity 4]
[Quantity 2]	[Quantity 5]

Write an exponential function, *[Function Variable]([Argument Variable])*, you can use to model the **growth** of the **rodent population** after *[Argument Variable]* [Unit A].

Enter your function in the space provided.

[Function Variable]([Argument Variable]) =

Figure 3.62: Item-creation template for high school function item after step 1.

exponential change in magnitude of [Object] is measured (for example, people, fission events, rodents). For [Unit B], the teacher selects *rodents (measured in millions)*. This is the dependent variable in the function. The teacher enters these definitions in the element matrix and template (see figure 3.63 and figure 3.64).

Element	Definition
Setting	A certain city
Object	Rodent population
Change	Growth
Function Variable	
Argument Variable	
Unit A	Weeks
Unit B	Rodents (measured in millions)
Quantity 1	
Quantity 2	
Quantity 3	
Quantity 4	
Quantity 5	

Figure 3.63: Element matrix for high school function item after step 2.

The third step directs the teacher to select nonsequential values for [Quantity 1] and [Quantity 2] according to the specifications in the key. The template key notes [Quantity 1] is any whole number and [Quantity 2] is any whole number greater than [Quantity 1]. The teacher selects 2 and 5, respectively. The teacher then enters these definitions in the element matrix and template (see figure 3.65 and figure 3.66, page 132).

In a certain city, the rodent population is growing at the rate the table shows.

Weeks	Rodents (measured in millions)
0	[Quantity 3]
[Quantity 1]	[Quantity 4]
[Quantity 2]	[Quantity 5]

Write an exponential function, *[Function Variable]([Argument Variable])*, you can use to model the growth of the rodent population after *[Argument Variable]* **weeks**.

Enter your function in the space provided.

[Function Variable]([Argument Variable]) =

Figure 3.64: Item-creation template for high school function item after step 2.

Element	Definition
Setting	A certain city
Object	Rodent population
Change	Growth
Function Variable	
Argument Variable	
Unit A	Weeks
Unit B	Rodents (measured in millions)
Quantity 1	2
Quantity 2	5
Quantity 3	
Quantity 4	
Quantity 5	

Figure 3.65: Element matrix for high school function item after step 3.

For the fourth step, the teacher should select a value for [Quantity 3] as an initial magnitude of the object. The teacher selects 2 for [Quantity 3]. The teacher then enters this definition in the element matrix and template (see figure 3.67, page 132, and figure 3.68, page 133).

In a certain city, the rodent population is growing at the rate the table shows.

Weeks	Rodents (measured in millions)
0	[Quantity 3]
2	[Quantity 4]
5	[Quantity 5]

Write an exponential function, *[Function Variable]([Argument Variable])*, you can use to model the growth of the rodent population after *[Argument Variable]* weeks.

Enter your function in the space provided.

[Function Variable]([Argument Variable]) =

Figure 3.66: Item-creation template for high school function item after step 3.

Element	Definition
Setting	A certain city
Object	Rodent population
Change	Growth
Function Variable	
Argument Variable	
Unit A	Weeks
Unit B	Rodents (measured in millions)
Quantity 1	2
Quantity 2	5
Quantity 3	2
Quantity 4	
Quantity 5	

Figure 3.67: Element matrix for high school function item after step 4.

The fifth step directs the teacher to choose variables for the function and argument variables. The template key notes the function variable is any variable the teacher uses to represent a function (for example, *f, h, g*). The teacher selects the variable *f*. The template key notes the argument variable is any variable the teacher uses to represent the argument of a function (for example, *x, n, j*). The teacher selects *n* for the argument variable. The teacher then enters these definitions in the element matrix and template (see figure 3.69 and figure 3.70, page 134).

In a certain city, the rodent population is growing at the rate the table shows.

Weeks	Rodents (measured in millions)
0	**2**
2	[Quantity 4]
5	[Quantity 5]

Write an exponential function, *[Function Variable]([Argument Variable])*, you can use to model the growth of the rodent population after *[Argument Variable]* weeks.

Enter your function in the space provided.

[Function Variable]([Argument Variable]) =

Figure 3.68: Item-creation template for high school function item after step 4.

Element	Definition
Setting	A certain city
Object	Rodent population
Change	Growth
Function Variable	*f*
Argument Variable	*n*
Unit A	Weeks
Unit B	Rodents (measured in millions)
Quantity 1	2
Quantity 2	5
Quantity 3	2
Quantity 4	
Quantity 5	

Figure 3.69: Element matrix for high school function item after step 5.

The sixth step involves creating a function that defines an exponential change in magnitude for the object, which in this case is the rodent population. This step is completely under the control of the teacher creating the item. To do this, the teacher refers to the general form of an exponential function, which is: $f(x) = b^x$. In this general form, x is the argument of the function. The argument of a function is the variable term or expression on which a function operates. In this case, the argument is number of weeks. The teacher has provided two values thus far: 2 weeks and 5 weeks. What the student answering the item must determine is b in the general formula or the *base*. In this sixth step of the instructions,

In a certain city, the rodent population is growing at the rate the table shows.

Weeks	Rodents (measured in millions)
0	2
2	[Quantity 4]
5	[Quantity 5]

Write an exponential function, **f(n)**, you can use to model the growth of the rodent population after **n** weeks.

Enter your function in the space provided.

f(n) =

Figure 3.70: Item-creation template for high school function item after step 5.

the teacher fills in a base to form a complete equation for the exponential relationship: $f(n) = 2(1 + 0.02)^n$. In the seventh step, the teacher computes the two values of the argument he or she specified and fills them in as [Quantity 4] and [Quantity 5]. In this case, those values would be 2.08 and 2.21, respectively.

Figure 3.71 shows the complete element matrix and figure 3.72 shows the completed item. Since the teacher defined the function $f(n) = 2(1 + 0.02)^n$ during step 6, he or she can use that information to fill in the correct response, as figure 3.72 shows.

Element	Definition
Setting	A certain city
Object	Rodent population
Change	Growth
Function Variable	f
Argument Variable	n
Unit A	Weeks
Unit B	Rodents (measured in millions)
Quantity 1	2
Quantity 2	5
Quantity 3	2
Quantity 4	2.08
Quantity 5	2.21

Figure 3.71: Element matrix for high school function item after steps 6 and 7.

In a certain city, the rodent population is growing at the rate the table shows.

Weeks	Rodents (measured in millions)
0	2
2	2.08
5	2.21

Write an exponential function, $f(n)$, you can use to model the growth of the rodent population after n weeks.

Enter your function in the space provided.

$f(n) =$

Correct Response(s):

$f(n) = 2(1 + 0.02)^n$ or another equivalent function

Figure 3.72: Finished high school function item with correct response.

The teacher now has a completed item for functions at the high school level. Additionally, the process of creating the item provides teachers with an understanding of the working dynamic of this type of item.

Summary

In this chapter, we identified the different types of mathematics frames students are likely to encounter on large-scale assessments. Unlike ELA, where item type and format largely inform the frames to use, mathematics items are primarily structured in terms of the content they address. We identified nine major categories of mathematics content, with each category encompassing a number of more specific subcategories. We presented the relative frequency of each frame across the large-scale assessments we examined and proposed a strategy for teachers to create their own mathematics items using these frames. In this case, the strategy involves using the templates and instructions appendix A (page 187) of this book presents. Using the data and recommendations in this chapter, teachers can prepare their students for both the mathematics content they are most likely to encounter on large-scale assessments and the specific ways in which tests are likely to assess that content.

CHAPTER 4

Analysis of Science Assessment Items

Our analysis of science assessment items included the ACT, NAEP, TIMSS, and PISA, as well as thirty-nine state tests. This comprised a wider variety of tests than our ELA and mathematics analyses. We also analyzed more science items than we did with ELA or mathematics individually. Specifically, we analyzed 4,491 science items as compared to 1,684 ELA items and 2,629 mathematics items for a total of 8,804 items across all three subject areas. Some of the state tests we analyzed addressed grade bands rather than individual grades. To accurately account for the data from these tests in our analysis, we likewise used grade bands to display our results, rather than the individual grades used for our analyses of ELA and mathematics items. Table 4.1 shows the distribution of science items across three grade-level bands.

Table 4.1: Distribution of Science Items Across Grade Bands

Grade	Number of Items
3–5	1,222
6–8	1,377
High School	1,892
Total	4,491

A substantial number of the state-assessment items we analyzed came from subject tests at the high school level. Table 4.2 (page 138) shows how these high school items were distributed across various science subjects.

Table 4.2: Distribution of High School Items Across Science Subjects

Science Subject	Number of Items
General Science	315
Biology	680
Chemistry	268
Physical Science	63
Physics	160
Earth Science	130
Living Environment	85
Technology and Engineering	55
Total	1,756

We also examined a number of national and international science tests; table 4.3 shows the distribution of items across those tests at various grade levels.

Table 4.3: Distribution of Science Items Across National and International Tests

Grade, Test, or Both	Number of Items
Grade 4 NAEP	35
Grade 4 TIMSS	72
Grade 8 NAEP	17
Grade 8 TIMSS	91
Grade 12 NAEP	38
ACT	80
PISA	18
Total	351

Figure 4.1 depicts the conceptual framework of our analysis of the 4,491 science items. It also serves as an organizer for providing students with exposure to the item types they will encounter on science tests.

As figure 4.1 depicts, science items fell into two broad categories: items that require declarative knowledge about science and items that do not require declarative knowledge about science. This bivariate classification is interesting by definition. More specifically, while the majority of the science items we analyzed assess students' understanding of science concepts, generalizations, and principles, some do not. Items in this second category require students to read and understand novel information about science, analyze and interpret data, or utilize mathematics skills and procedures within the context of science. We first consider the items that require declarative science knowledge.

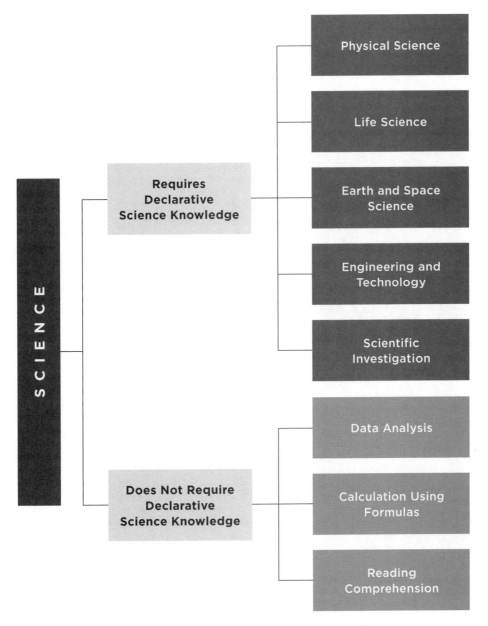

Figure 4.1: Conceptual framework for science assessment items.

Items Requiring Declarative Science Knowledge

Unsurprisingly, a vast majority of science items we analyzed required knowledge of specific science concepts, generalizations, and principles. Science items should determine how much science information students know. For the most part, these items require students to have internalized science information and then recognize or recall that information to answer the items. Figure 4.2 (page 140) depicts an example of this type of item. To answer this fourth-grade item, students must have an understanding of the relationship between latitude and climate.

2. The diagram below shows four places on Earth. Places 1, 2, 3, 4 are all at sea level.

Which place has the coldest winters?

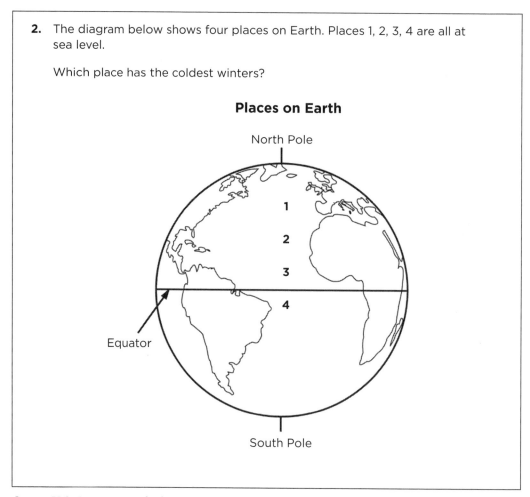

Source: U.S. Department of Education, Institute of Education Sciences, National Center for Education Statistics, National Assessment of Educational Progress (NAEP), 2009 Science Assessment, item 2009-4S7 #15 K085101.

Figure 4.2: Sample grade 4 science item requiring declarative science knowledge.

As table 4.4 shows, these types of items are quite frequent on state tests across three grade-level bands. Table 4.5 shows the distribution of these types of items on national and international tests.

Table 4.4: Distribution of Items Requiring Declarative Science Knowledge Across Grade-Level Bands

Grade Band	Number of Items	Percentage of Grade Band Items
3–5	919	82.42
6–8	1,105	87.08
High School	1,573	89.58

Table 4.5: Distribution of Items Requiring Declarative Science Knowledge Across National and International Tests

Grade, Test, or Both	Number of Items	Percentage of Test
Grade 4 NAEP	31	88.57
Grade 4 TIMSS	72	100
Grade 8 NAEP	13	76.47
Grade 8 TIMSS	85	93.41
Grade 12 NAEP	37	97.37
ACT	10	12.5
PISA	8	44.44

Items requiring declarative science knowledge can be organized by content into the five categories table 4.6 shows. Here, we consider each of the five content categories briefly.

Table 4.6: Categories of Items Requiring Declarative Science Knowledge

Category	Percentage of All Items Analyzed
Earth and Space Science	19.31
Physical Science	29.95
Life Science	32.91
Engineering and Technology	1.31
Scientific Investigation	2.32

Earth and Space Science

The category of earth and space science involves topics such as solar energy, celestial motion, and earth systems. We address specific topics at various grade levels later in this chapter. Figure 4.3 (page 142) depicts a typical earth and space science item. This fifth-grade item requires students to understand the relationship between the position of the sun in the sky and shadows from objects.

Table 4.7 (page 142) shows earth and space science items distributed across the grade bands on state tests. Earth and space science items are fairly evenly distributed across grades 3–8, but their frequency at the high school level drops significantly. Table 4.8 (page 142) depicts the distribution of earth and space science items on national and international tests. Earth and space science items are represented in all the national and international tests we examined and were particularly prominent on the NAEP.

3. A student takes a picture of the shadow of a house at four different times during one day. The following pictures are not in order of the time the student took them.

Identify the correct order of the pictures according to the time of day when the student took each picture. Write the number of each picture in one of the boxes to show this order.

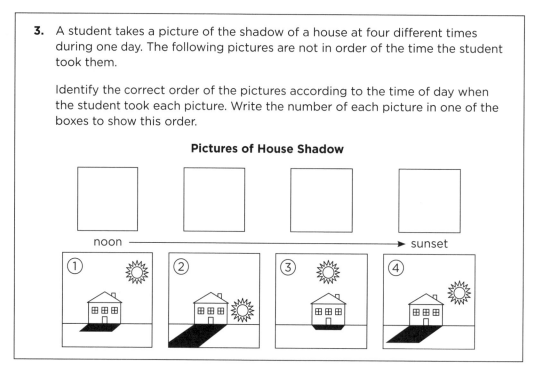

Source: Missouri Department of Elementary and Secondary Education, 2018. Used with permission.

Figure 4.3: Sample grade 5 earth and space science item.

Table 4.7: Distribution of Earth and Space Science Items Across Grade Bands

Grade Band	Number of Items	Percentage of Grade Band Items
3–5	249	22.33
6–8	335	26.40
High School	215	12.24

Table 4.8: Distribution of Earth and Space Science Items Across National and International Tests

Grade, Test, or Both	Number of Items	Percentage of Test
Grade 4 NAEP	11	31.43
Grade 4 TIMSS	15	20.83
Grade 8 NAEP	8	47.06
Grade 8 TIMSS	21	23.08
Grade 12 NAEP	10	26.32
ACT	1	1.25
PISA	3	16.67

Physical Science

The category of physical science involves topics such as matter, energy, and motion. Again, we address specific topics at various grade levels later in this chapter. Figure 4.4 depicts a typical physical science item. To answer this item, students must understand various types of energy and the specific meaning of the type the picture portrays.

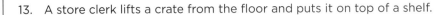

13. A store clerk lifts a crate from the floor and puts it on top of a shelf.

What type of energy has been transferred to the crate as a result of the clerk placing the box on the shelf?

   - ○ A. heat energy
   - ○ B. kinetic energy
   - ○ C. potential energy
   - ○ D. electrical energy

Figure 4.4: Sample grade 8 physical science item.

Table 4.9 shows the physical science items distributed across the grade bands on state tests. Physical science items are fairly evenly distributed across the grade bands. Table 4.10 (page 144) depicts the distribution of physical science items on national and international tests. Physical science items have a varying presence in national and international tests, except for the PISA.

Table 4.9: Distribution of Physical Science Items Across Grade Bands

Grade Band	Number of Items	Percentage of Grade Band Items
3–5	302	27.09
6–8	375	29.55
High School	567	32.29

Table 4.10: Distribution of Physical Science Items Across National and International Tests

Grade, Test, or Both	Number of Items	Percentage of Test
Grade 4 NAEP	10	28.57
Grade 4 TIMSS	27	37.50
Grade 8 NAEP	2	11.76
Grade 8 TIMSS	40	43.96
Grade 12 NAEP	14	36.84
ACT	6	7.50
PISA	0	0

Life Science

The category of life science involves topics such as organism traits, genetic variation, and natural selection. Figure 4.5 depicts a typical life science item. To answer this question, students must understand how an animal's behavior can help it survive—in this case, an electric eel's use of electricity to stun its prey.

An animal's behavior can help it survive. Electric eels can generate electrical pulses capable of stunning other creatures. How might this behavior help electric eels survive?

   A.   The electric pulse will heat up the water, so electric eels will have more comfortable surroundings.

   B.   The stunned creatures will be unable to reproduce, so electric eels will not have to compete with their offspring for resources.

   C.   The stunned creatures will leave the area, so electric eels will have enough space in their habitat to survive.

   D.   The stunned creatures will make easier prey, so electric eels will get enough food to survive.

Figure 4.5: Sample grade 4 life science item.

Table 4.11 shows life science items distributed across the grade bands on state tests. Life science items are found across the grade levels and are particularly prominent at the high school level. Table 4.12 depicts the distribution of life science items on national and international tests. Life science items were found on all the national and international tests we analyzed except for the ACT.

Table 4.11: Distribution of Life Science Items Across Grade Bands

Grade Band	Number of Items	Percentage of Grade Band Items
3–5	318	28.52
6–8	345	27.19
High School	740	42.14

Table 4.12: Distribution of Life Science Items Across National and International Tests

Grade, Test, or Both	Number of Items	Percentage of Test
Grade 4 NAEP	5	14.29
Grade 4 TIMSS	29	40.28
Grade 8 NAEP	3	17.65
Grade 8 TIMSS	23	25.27
Grade 12 NAEP	13	34.21
ACT	0	0
PISA	2	11.11

Engineering and Technology

The category of engineering and technology involves topics such as design issues within engineering, troubleshooting, and testing possible solutions to problems. Figure 4.6 depicts a typical engineering and technology item. To answer this item, students must understand terminology associated with the process of developing a complex product.

12. During the engineering design process, steps are often repeated to help arrive at the best possible solution.

A company that produces airplane engines creates one design and tests it, then modifies the design based on the results and tests the new model. Each of these repeated processes is called a(n)

    A. prototype.

    B. iteration.

    C. concept.

    D. production.

Figure 4.6: Sample high school engineering and technology item.

Table 4.13 shows engineering and technology items distributed across the grade bands on state tests. Engineering and technology items are not frequently used in tests across the grade levels. Table 4.14 depicts the distribution of engineering and technology items on national and international tests. Engineering and technology items were found only on the PISA.

Table 4.13: Distribution of Engineering and Technology Items Across Grade Bands

Grade Band	Number of Items	Percentage of Grade Band Items
3–5	19	1.70
6–8	19	1.50
High School	20	1.14

Table 4.14: Distribution of Engineering and Technology Items Across National and International Tests

Grade, Test, or Both	Number of Items	Percentage of Test
Grade 4 NAEP	0	0
Grade 4 TIMSS	0	0
Grade 8 NAEP	0	0
Grade 8 TIMSS	0	0
Grade 12 NAEP	0	0
ACT	0	0
PISA	1	5.56

Scientific Investigation

The category of scientific investigation involves topics such as setting up experiments, generating hypotheses, and revising hypotheses. Figure 4.7 depicts a typical scientific investigation item. To answer this item students must understand the distinction between independent variables, dependent variables, and elements that should be constant in an experiment.

Table 4.15 shows scientific investigation items distributed across the grade bands on state tests. As was the case with engineering and technology items, scientific investigation items were not frequently used on the tests we analyzed. Table 4.16 depicts the distribution of scientific investigation items on national and international tests. Scientific investigation items were found in the majority of the national and state tests, although they did not represent a significant number of items except on the NAEP at grade 4. Interestingly, the NAEP at grades 8 and 12 did not include any such items.

7

A company that makes hand warmers wants to know which filling material stays warm for the longest time once it has been activated. Design an experiment to determine the best material to use.

Click on the boxes in the table to identify the independent variable, the dependent variable, and the factors that are held constant in your experiment. Be sure to complete each row.

Table 1. Hand Warmer Experiment Setup

Factor	Experiment Setup
Hand warmer size	▼
Hand warmer exterior material	▼
Hand warmer filling material	▼
Amount of time remaining warm	▼
Outside temperature	▼

Figure 4.7: Sample grade 8 scientific investigation item.

Table 4.15: Distribution of Scientific Investigation Items Across Grade Bands

Grade Band	Number of Items	Percentage of Grade Band Items
3–5	31	2.78
6–8	31	2.44
High School	31	1.77

Table 4.16: Distribution of Scientific Investigation Items Across National and International Tests

Grade, Test, or Both	Number of Items	Percentage of Test
Grade 4 NAEP	5	14.29
Grade 4 TIMSS	1	1.39
Grade 8 NAEP	0	0
Grade 8 TIMSS	1	1.10
Grade 12 NAEP	0	0
ACT	3	3.75
PISA	2	11.11

The Process for Creating Declarative Science Knowledge Assessment Items

As the previous discussion illustrates, the vast majority of science items are very straightforward; they require students to recognize or recall science information (that is, declarative science knowledge). When creating practice items for science, teachers should be cognizant of the declarative science knowledge students must know. This focus on content is similar to the approach taken with mathematics, but while the wide range of procedures and skills required to answer mathematics problems entails the use of very specific templates in creating practice items, the more direct inquiries typical of large-scale science tests are best replicated through detailed attention to the topics being assessed.

To this end, analysts at Marzano Resources identified the critical science content across the grade levels. More specifically, they analyzed various science standards documents to identify a set of essential topics known as the *Critical Concepts* (Simms, 2016). The development of the Critical Concepts also included similar analyses of standards in mathematics, ELA, social studies, technology, cognitive skills, and metacognitive skills.

Our analysis of assessment items revealed that the science items that require declarative knowledge fall into five categories: earth and space science (ESS), physical science (PS), life science (LS), engineering and technology (ET), and scientific investigation (SI). When the topics from the Critical Concepts are sorted into these five categories, the result is a list of the specific science topics most often used as the basis for generating science items on the tests we analyzed. We present a complete listing of these science topics in appendix B (page 335) of this book. To demonstrate how a teacher might use them to generate practice items for declarative science knowledge, consider table 4.17.

Table 4.17: Fourth-Grade Science Topics

Science Category	Expectation for Student Knowledge	Critical Concepts Topic
Earth and Space Science	**GF1—Model patterns of Earth's features** (for example, chart the locations of a specific landform on a map, such as mountain ranges, coral reefs, volcanoes, or ocean ridges, to form conclusions about where this landform tends to develop).	Earth Features
Earth and Space Science	**EC1—Identify factors that contribute to weathering and erosion** (for example, explain how weathering and erosion are caused by water, ice, wind, and vegetation and identify factors that increase the effect and rate of weathering and erosion).	Factors Contributing to Weathering and Erosion
Earth and Space Science	**EC2—Use patterns in rock formations to explain how a landscape has changed over time** (for example, analyze specific rock formations and explain how weathering and erosion have contributed to their formation and changed the landscape over time).	Rock Formations and Earth Changes

Science Category	Expectation for Student Knowledge	Critical Concepts Topic
Earth and Space Science	**EH1—Explain how fossils can be used to describe how a landscape has changed over time** (for example, determine the habitat an organism preserved in a fossil would likely live in, describe the location of where the fossil was found, and explain how disparities between the fossil and its location provide evidence that the landscape changed over time).	Investigating Landscape Changes Through Fossils
Earth and Space Science	**NH1—Explain how to reduce the impacts of a natural hazard caused by Earth processes** (for example, describe the effects of earthquakes on humans, identify multiple methods that could lessen these effects, and compare their effectiveness).	Natural Hazards from Earth Processes
Earth and Space Science	**NR1—Describe how different methods of energy production use natural resources** (for example, explain how different energy sources rely on renewable and nonrenewable resources for power).	Producing Energy from Natural Resources
Earth and Space Science	**NR2—Describe the impacts of different methods of energy production on the environment** (for example, describe the impact renewable and nonrenewable energy sources can have on the environment by analyzing the effects of their production and consumption).	Environmental Impacts of Energy Production
Physical Science	**E1—Explain how energy converts between different forms** (for example, use the law of conservation of energy to explain how energy changes form and identify how energy changes in a real-world scenario).	Energy Conversion
Physical Science	**E2—Explain that energy can travel over a distance** (for example, observe instances of sound, light, heat, or electricity traveling across a distance to explain how energy can be transferred from place to place).	Energy Transfer
Physical Science	**M1—Explain the relationship between the speed and energy of an object** (for example, relate the concept of energy as ability to do work to comparisons of objects of the same mass moving at different speeds).	Energy and Speed of Objects
Physical Science	**M2—Explain how energy is transferred when objects collide** (for example, make predictions about the outcomes of various collisions as the speed, mass, and angle of the objects involved in the collision change and explain how energy is transferred between the objects as well as to their surroundings as heat or sound).	Collisions and Energy Transfer
Physical Science	**LV1—Explain how vision is a product of light reflecting off objects and entering the eye** (for example, diagram how light moves from a luminous object, reflects off an object, and enters the eye; explain how the reflected light travels through the eye to hit the retina; and describe how the information from both eyes is turned into an image by the brain).	Light, Vision, and the Eye

continued →

Science Category	Expectation for Student Knowledge	Critical Concepts Topic
Physical Science	**W1—Identify patterns related to a wave's amplitude and wavelength** (for example, model waves to determine how changes to period, amplitude, frequency, wavelength, and speed affect movement and explain how the disturbances that cause waves determine amplitude and wavelength).	Wave Properties
Physical Science	**W2—Explain how waves can cause objects to move** (for example, compare the movement of particles within transverse, longitudinal, and ocean waves to explain how particles within a wave oscillate but do not travel over a distance).	Wave Motion
Physical Science	**IT1—Explain how patterns can be used to transfer information** (for example, analyze a method of communication that uses patterns to transfer information over a distance, such as Morse code and the mechanics of the technology that sends and receives Morse code).	Information Transfer
Life Science	**PN1—Explain how specific plant structures contribute to a plant's survival, growth, or reproduction** (for example, describe the internal and external structures of a specific plant and explain how they are adapted to the organism's habitat, such as by explaining how a cactus's lack of leaves, waxy external coating, thick stem, and long roots help it to survive in the desert).	Plant Structures
Life Science	**AN1—Explain how specific animal structures contribute to an animal's survival, growth, or reproduction** (for example, explain how a camel's eyelashes, nostrils, humps, hooves, and coloration help it to survive in the desert).	Animal Structures
Life Science	**AN2—Explain how animals' response to stimuli support their survival, growth, or reproduction** (for example, explain how an animal responds to danger by running away, becoming very still, or preparing to fight).	Animal Behaviors

Source: Marzano Resources, n.d.

Table 4.17 presents the eighteen fourth-grade science topics that fall into three of the five science categories for declarative knowledge: physical science, earth and space science, and life science. (Note that for the engineering and technology and the scientific investigation categories, content is organized by grade bands, with fourth-grade content as part of the grades 3–5 band; see appendix B, page 335, for details.) Table 4.17 also includes a statement of the core content a student should know or be able to do in addressing each topic. What is particularly useful about the Critical Concepts topics is that each has an associated proficiency scale like the one figure 4.8 shows.

Figure 4.8 shows the proficiency scale that defines the learning progression for the fourth-grade Critical Concepts topic of energy transfer (listed in the ninth row of table 4.17). Educators can use proficiency scales such as this one in a wide variety of ways, including classroom assessment, instruction, student feedback, and student goal setting, to name a few. These uses are chronicled in a number of books, including *Formative Assessment and Standards-Based Grading* (Marzano, 2010), *The New Art and Science of*

4.0	In addition to score 3.0 performance, the student demonstrates in-depth inferences and applications that go beyond what was taught.
3.5	In addition to score 3.0 performance, partial success at score 4.0 content
3.0	The student will: **ET—Explain that energy can travel over a distance** (for example, observe instances of sound, light, heat, or electricity traveling across a distance to explain how energy can be transferred from place to place).
2.5	No major errors or omissions regarding score 2.0 content, and partial success at score 3.0 content
2.0	**ET—**The student will recognize or recall specific vocabulary (for example, *chemical energy, circuit, electrical energy, heat, sound energy, thermal energy*) and perform basic processes such as: • Explain how energy can be transferred from place to place by sound (for example, the vibrations of sound energy can travel through a medium, such as air or water). • Explain how energy can be transferred from place to place by light (for example, light energy travels in straight lines using waves of energy, which can be absorbed by other materials). • Explain how energy can be transferred from place to place by heat (for example, heat energy in an object transfers to colder objects or an object's surroundings). • Explain how energy can be transferred from place to place by electrical currents (for example, electrical circuits rely on the movement of electrical energy). • State that energy transfer is never completely efficient.
1.5	Partial success at score 2.0 content, and major errors or omissions regarding score 3.0 content
1.0	With help, partial success at score 2.0 content and score 3.0 content
0.5	With help, partial success at score 2.0 content but not at score 3.0 content
0.0	Even with help, no success

Source: Marzano Resources, n.d.

Figure 4.8: Proficiency scale for Critical Concepts topic of energy transfer.

Teaching (Marzano, 2017), *The New Art and Science of Classroom Assessment* (Marzano, Norford, & Ruyle, 2019), *A Teacher's Guide to Standards-Based Learning* (Heflebower, Hoegh, Warrick, & Flygare, 2019), and *A Handbook for Developing and Using Proficiency Scales in the Classroom* (Hoegh, 2020).

For the purposes of item construction, teachers start by examining the content at the 3.0 level of the proficiency scale (the 3.0 content for each of the Critical Concepts science topics is provided in appendix B, page 335). In this case, the 3.0 content is the general statement that students will be able to explain that energy can travel over a distance. In addition to this general statement, the scale provides an example regarding what that explanation might entail. In this case, those explanations might focus on how the student could use sound, light, heat, or electricity to demonstrate how energy is transferred over distance. Certainly, with this information, teachers could create selected-response or short constructed-response science items regarding this fourth-grade expectation.

At the 2.0 level, the proficiency scale provides even more content specificity for teachers. Some of that detail involves terminology important to this topic such as *chemical energy*, *circuit*, *electrical energy*, *heat*, *sound energy*, and *thermal energy*. Additionally, the 2.0 content provides guidance about the specific details teachers could use to exemplify the score 3.0 expectations.

- Students can explain how energy can be transferred from place to place by sound (for example, the vibrations of sound energy can travel through a medium, such as air or water).

- Students can explain how energy can be transferred from place to place by light (for example, light energy travels in straight lines using waves of energy, which can be absorbed by other materials).

- Students can explain how energy can be transferred from place to place by heat (for example, heat energy in an object transfers to colder objects or an object's surroundings).

- Students can explain how energy can be transferred from place to place by electrical currents (for example, electrical circuits rely on the movement of electrical energy).

- Students can explain that energy transfer is never completely efficient.

This level of detail makes it easy to create short constructed-response items like the following.

> We know that energy from heat can be transferred. Describe an example of this, paying particular attention to those things that can decrease or increase the transfer of this type of energy.

Teachers can also construct selected-response items using the detailed information in the score 2.0 content. The following item is generated from this proficiency scale.

> You grab a hot frying pan on the stove, and it burns your hand. This is an example of:
>
> A. Percolation
> B. Energy transfer
> C. Refraction
> D. Erosion

In general, the process for designing items for declarative science knowledge is very straightforward. It involves the following steps.

1. Using the guidelines and information in appendix B (page 335), identify the specific science content on which the item will focus. (If available, use the Critical Concept proficiency scale for this content.)

2. Determine if a short constructed-response item or a selected-response item better serves the content.

3. Design the selected item.

Suppose a third-grade class is working on a unit about climate and weather. The teacher would like to create an item to assess students' knowledge of climates around the world. Using appendix B (page 335), the teacher locates the earth and space science topic, World Climates. The 3.0 statement for this topic asks students to describe different climates around the world, but the teacher would like to assess a simpler level of content with this particular item. Using the corresponding Critical Concepts proficiency scale, the teacher selects a 2.0 element asking students to locate where a given type of climate occurs on Earth. Because of the simpler nature of this content, the teacher decides a selected-response item will be appropriate. She creates the following item.

Draw a line from each type of climate to the region where it commonly occurs.

Tropical	North Africa
Dry	Antarctica
Temperate	Central America
Continental	Mediterranean
Polar	Eastern Europe

Items Not Requiring Declarative Science Knowledge

In the science tests we analyzed, there were a number of items that did not rely greatly on the test taker's knowledge of science information. Figure 4.9 (page 154) provides an example of such an item.

Considering this item at face value as an assessment of science, you might determine it involves understanding the relationship between bacterial growth and time. But on closer scrutiny it becomes clear that a student might know very little about the relationship and be able to correctly answer the item simply by reading the provided graph. In general, these types of items require students to apply data-analysis processes (8.80 percent of all science items analyzed), use a mathematics formula (1.49 percent of all science items analyzed), or simply read and comprehend information presented to them (3.92 percent of all items analyzed). As table 4.18 (page 154) shows, these item types are present, but infrequent, on state tests across three grade-level bands.

Table 4.19 (page 155) shows the distribution of these types of items on national and international tests. As these data indicate, ACT and PISA employ rather large percentages of these types of items.

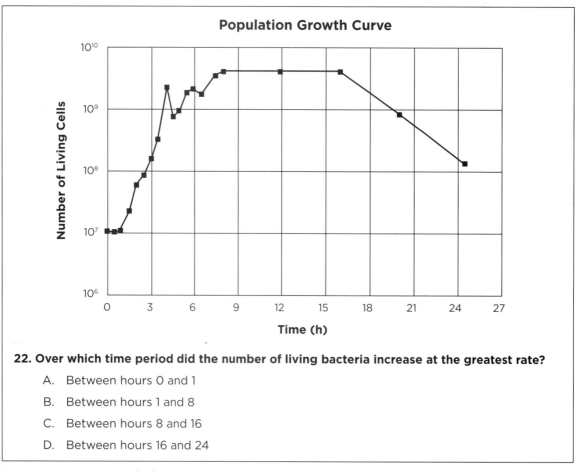

22. Over which time period did the number of living bacteria increase at the greatest rate?

A.   Between hours 0 and 1

B.   Between hours 1 and 8

C.   Between hours 8 and 16

D.   Between hours 16 and 24

Source: U.S. Department of Education, Institute of Education Sciences, National Center for Education Statistics, National Assessment of Educational Progress (NAEP), 2009 Science Assessment, item 2009-12S10 #4 K141501.

Figure 4.9: Sample grade 12 science item not requiring declarative science knowledge.

Table 4.18: Distribution of Items Not Requiring Declarative Science Knowledge Across Grade Bands

Grade Band	Number of Items	Percentage of Grade Band Items
3–5	196	17.58
6–8	164	12.92
High School	183	10.42

Data Analysis

Data analysis items require students to interpret or create various data sets and displays, including graphs, tables, maps, and charts involving both quantitative and qualitative data. Consider the example in figure 4.10. To answer data analysis science items, students must be able to describe a set of relationships a data display depicts. This is a defining characteristic of virtually all these types of science items.

Table 4.19: Distribution of Items Not Requiring Declarative Science Knowledge Across National and International Tests

Grade, Test, or Both	Number of Items	Percentage of Test
Grade 4 NAEP	4	11.43
Grade 4 TIMSS	0	0
Grade 8 NAEP	4	23.53
Grade 8 TIMSS	6	6.59
Grade 12 NAEP	1	2.63
ACT	70	87.50
PISA	10	55.56

Question refers to the following information.

Most soils are a mixture of particles of different sizes. Water moves through soil at different rates, depending largely on how much of each size particle makes up the soil. The table below shows the percentage of each size particle in five different soils (A, B, C, D, E) and the rate at which water moves through each of the soils.

RATE OF WATER MOVING THROUGH DIFFERENT SOILS

Soil	Percentage Largest Particles (%)	Percentage Medium-Sized Particles (%)	Percentage Smallest Particles (%)	Rate of Water Draining Through Soil (cm/hr)
A	100	0	0	21
B	85	10	5	6.1
C	40	40	20	1.3
D	20	65	15	0.69
E	0	0	100	0.05

6. Describe the relationship between the size of soil particles and the rate at which water moves through the soil. Use the data in the table to support your answer.

_____

_____

_____

_____

_____

Source: U.S. Department of Education, Institute of Education Sciences, National Center for Education Statistics, National Assessment of Educational Progress (NAEP), 2011 Science Assessment. Item 2011-8S11 #K111801.

Figure 4.10: Sample grade 8 data analysis science item.

Table 4.20 shows data analysis science items distributed across the grade bands. Data analysis science items have a relatively even distribution across the grade-level bands, with the emphasis becoming slightly smaller at the higher grade levels. Table 4.21 depicts the distribution of data analysis science items on national and international tests. These types of items have a rather large presence in ACT and PISA.

Table 4.20: Distribution of Data Analysis Science Items Across Grade Bands

Grade Band	Number of Items	Percentage of Grade Band Items
3–5	113	10.13
6–8	110	8.67
High School	106	6.04

Table 4.21: Distribution of Data Analysis Science Items Across National and International Tests

Grade, Test, or Both	Number of Items	Percentage of Test
Grade 4 NAEP	0	0
Grade 4 TIMSS	0	0
Grade 8 NAEP	4	23.53
Grade 8 TIMSS	6	6.59
Grade 12 NAEP	1	2.63
ACT	46	57.50
PISA	9	50.00

Items of this type provide students with a data display and require them to describe the relationships implied. In the item in figure 4.10, students must analyze the relationship between particle size of soil and rate of water drainage. They don't have to actually have any prior knowledge of these relationships, but they must be able to read the table, discern the relationships, and describe what events will occur because of these relationships.

Data displays can take many forms. In chapter 3 (page 85), we note that the mathematics topic of data display has many subcategories. Thus, there are many types of display tools students can use to represent relationships: tables, bar graphs, line graphs, and so on. Using the list of data display types in table 3.7 (page 93) as a resource, science teachers can use the following process to create data display practice items.

1. Select the science relationship that will be the focus of the item.

2. Select the type of data display that best depicts the relationship.

3. Fill in the display with data that demonstrate the desired relationship.

4. Determine if a short constructed-response item or a selected-response item better serves the relationship.

5. Design the selected item.

Suppose a middle school science class is studying ecosystem changes. The teacher wants the class to analyze a set of data about the relationship between the wolf and elk populations in a particular area over time. The teacher decides to use a table to depict the relationship, and fills it with data showing the size of each population each year over a ten-year span. The teacher decides because he would like his students to describe the relationship in detail, a short constructed-response item will be most appropriate. He creates the data display shown in figure 4.11, which shows the size of the wolf and elk populations in a wildlife refuge each year from 2004 to 2013. Then, he writes the following prompt.

Describe the relationship between the size of the wolf population and the size of the elk population in the wildlife refuge. Use the data in the table to support your answer.

Year	Number of Wolves	Number of Elk
2004	15	8,010
2005	16	7,850
2006	30	6,090
2007	60	5,510
2008	81	4,630
2009	84	4,380
2010	90	4,100
2011	85	4,250
2012	82	4,610
2013	63	5,360

Source: Adapted from Koshmrl, 2018.

Figure 4.11: Sample middle school data display.

Calculation Using Formulas

Items classified as calculation using formulas ask students to calculate solutions or use other mathematical concepts as they relate to science content, like the item figure 4.12 (page 158) depicts. To answer this seventh-grade item, students must perform a fairly straightforward set of calculations using the formula distance (d) = speed (s) × time (t). The difference between this item type and the data analysis items we described previously is that, with calculation items, students must perform some type of calculation.

Typically, these calculations are based on a common science formula or equation, such as the following.

- Acceleration = change in velocity over change in time

- Force = mass × acceleration

Use the equation to solve the problem.

distance (d) = speed (s) × time (t)

How far would a car traveling at a speed of 75 miles per hour go in 3 hours?

- A.   25 miles
- B.   78 miles
- C.   225 miles
- D.   250 miles

Figure 4.12: Sample grade 7 calculation science item.

Table 4.22 depicts the calculation science items distributed across the grade bands. The emphasis on this item type increases slightly through the grade levels, but had a miniscule presence overall. Only one item of this type appeared in the national and international tests we analyzed.

Table 4.22: Distribution of Calculation Science Items Across Grade Bands

Grade Band	Number of Items	Percentage of Grade Band Items
3–5	9	0.81
6–8	24	1.89
High School	33	1.88

To create practice items of this type, teachers can follow the following steps.

1. Select the science formula on which the item will focus.

2. Identify the science context for the formula.

3. Determine if a short constructed-response or a selected-response item better serves the formula.

4. Design the selected item.

Suppose a high school physics class is studying electricity. The teacher wants students to practice using Ohm's law to calculate electric current through a circuit. Because the problem involves a straightforward calculation, the teacher decides a selected-response item is appropriate. The teacher creates the following item.

Use the equation to solve the problem.

$$\text{Current (I) in amps} = \frac{\text{Voltage (E) in volts}}{\text{Resistance (R) in ohms}}$$

A circuit used to illuminate a lamp has 12 volts of voltage from a battery and 3 ohms of resistance from the lamp. What is the amount of current in the circuit, in amps?

    A. 3 amps

    B. 4 amps

    C. 6 amps

    D. 12 amps

Reading Comprehension

Items involving reading comprehension require students understand and interpret what a text presents. To illustrate, consider the item in figure 4.13. In this item, students first read about an explicit relationship between science concepts. In this case, that relationship is between levels of phosphorus in bodies of water and algae growth. Another important component of the relationship is that some algae can produce dangerous toxins. Based on an understanding of this relationship, students must determine which conclusions are valid regarding the outcomes of such a relationship.

---

2. Fertilizers used for farming can affect nearby sources of water. Many fertilizers use phosphorus, and runoff from farms can raise the levels of phosphorus in lakes and rivers and feed the rapid growth of algae. Some of these algae can release toxins that are harmful to humans and animals.

Based on this information, which change will most likely be a direct result of increased phosphorus pollution?

    A. Massive amounts of rain will dilute phosphorus levels, so there will be no change.

    B. Algae will be undernourished and die off, leading to imbalanced ecosystems.

    C. Water levels will rise and cause flooding that could be dangerous to humans and animals.

    D. The growth of toxic algae will increase, making more water unsafe for humans and animals.

Figure 4.13: Sample grade 7 comprehension science item.

Table 4.23 (page 160) shows the comprehension science items distributed across the grade bands. These item types are most prominent at the lower grade levels. Table 4.24 (page 160) shows the distribution of these types of items across national and international tests we analyzed. These items can be found in NAEP at the fourth grade, as well as in PISA and ACT.

Table 4.23: Distribution of Comprehension Science Items Across Grade Bands

Grade Band	Number of Items	Percentage of Grade Band Items
3–5	74	6.64
6–8	30	2.36
High School	44	2.51

Table 4.24: Distribution of Comprehension Science Items Across National and International Tests

Grade, Test, or Both	Number of Items	Percentage of Test
Grade 4 NAEP	4	11.43
Grade 4 TIMSS	0	0
Grade 8 NAEP	0	0
Grade 8 TIMSS	0	0
Grade 12 NAEP	0	0
ACT	23	28.75
PISA	1	5.56

Science teachers can use the following process to create comprehension practice items.

1. Identify the relationship between science concepts that will be the focus of the item.

2. Write a description of a specific example of how these concepts might interact.

3. Based on your description, determine what conclusions students should infer regarding the effects of the relationship.

4. Determine if a short constructed-response or a selected-response item better serves the relationship.

5. Design the selected item.

Suppose a fourth-grade class is learning about how organisms adapt to their environments. The teacher wants students to explore the relationship between an animal's physical features and the conditions in its natural habitat. The teacher determines that, given the relationship between advantageous traits and environment, students should infer which physical features are more or less likely among animals in a given habitat. In order to present a list of features, the teacher decides on a selected-response format. The teacher then creates the following item.

Animals develop adaptations to help them survive and thrive in their natural environment. The Sahara in North Africa is extremely hot and dry. Average high air temperatures are more than 100 degrees Fahrenheit, and the ground can reach temperatures of more than 175 degrees Fahrenheit. The driest parts of the Sahara can go years without rainfall. Despite these conditions, some animals have adapted to survive in this desert region.

Based on this information, which of the following features would an animal that lived in the Sahara be *least* likely to have?

A.   Dark fur to absorb more heat

B.   Large ears to make it easier to lose heat

C.   Fur to protect paw pads from hot surfaces

D.   The ability to retain water for long periods

Summary

In this chapter, we examined the assessment-item frames for science. Science items fall into two major categories: those that require declarative scientific knowledge, and those that do not. Within the category of items that require scientific knowledge, the items break down into five content categories: (1) earth and space science, (2) physical science, (3) life science, (4) engineering and technology, and (5) scientific investigation. Among items that do not require declarative scientific knowledge, three subcategories emerge, with a focus on skills over content: data analysis, calculation using formulas, and reading comprehension. We presented data on the frequency of each item frame within our analyzed assessments and suggested strategies for teachers to create and use science items that match these frames. For items requiring declarative science knowledge, we propose the use of topics identified in Marzano Resources' Critical Concepts and provided in appendix B (page 335) of this book. For items not requiring the declarative science knowledge, we advise teachers select the desired scientific context for the item and use the item type and format appropriate to that context. Teachers can use the data and strategies to create science items to measure students' knowledge while also providing exposure to the types of items used in large-scale assessments.

CHAPTER 5

The Issue of Test Preparation

In the previous three chapters, we detailed the results of our analysis of thousands of test items, showing how items in each of the major subject areas fit into discernable frames, and how those frames are distributed across tests and grade levels. We recommended that teachers use these frames to create practice assessment items, thereby familiarizing their students with the format of items they will encounter on large-scale external assessments while practicing important content. In chapters 5 and 6, we consider some of the broader implications and applications of this approach.

Schools and districts using our recommendations thus far should consider questions about test preparation that might arise from parents, community members, or even educators within the school or district. Various constituent groups might pose questions about *teaching to the test*. These are valid and reasonable questions, and we recommend you address them outright. The rather considerable amount of research and recommendations from testing experts should inform answers about the nature and efficacy of test preparation.

Three Forms of Test Preparation

Most forms of test preparation fall into three broad categories: (1) instruction in the relevant subject matter, (2) test familiarization, and (3) test-taking tricks. The first type naturally constitutes the bulk of preparation students receive in the course of normal schooling, with curriculum designers possibly supplementing it with tutoring or independent study. The second encompasses areas such as exposure to the structure and directions of the test and different item formats as well as basic test-taking skills like pacing and knowing when to guess. The third refers to strategies designed to exploit flaws in the design of the test or individual items. This last type of preparation is often called *coaching*, but as testing specialist Donald E. Powers (2017) noted, educators use that term in ways that cover the whole spectrum of test-preparation activities, so we will avoid it here to minimize confusion.

In the testing literature, there has been significant discussion about the effects of test preparation on test validity. If test preparation produces a score that does not reflect the student's true understanding of the content, then preparation is a threat to the test's validity.

Validity is generally thought of as "the extent to which an assessment measures what it purports to measure" (Marzano, 2018, p. 7), though measurement experts have noted that validity is ultimately a function of the interpretation and use of test scores rather than a characteristic of the test itself (American Educational Research Association, American Psychological Association, & National Council on Measurement in Education, 2014). In the case of the first type of test preparation, subject-matter instruction, any resulting increases in test scores would reflect increased knowledge and ability in the subject being tested, and would therefore not pose a threat to validity.

On its face, the second type of preparation, familiarizing students with the assessment, might seem to impair the validity of score interpretations, as examinees who receive this form of instruction might improve their scores without any commensurate increase in the ability the test is supposed to measure. However, as Thomas M. Haladyna and Steven M. Downing (2004), Samuel Messick (1982), Donald E. Powers (1985, 2017), and other assessment experts (for example, ACT, 2017) have argued, unfamiliarity with an assessment and the anxiety and confusion that could result are artificial impediments to students' ability to demonstrate their true level of knowledge and skill in the domain being assessed. Providing all students with a baseline of exposure to and practice with an assessment and its various item formats could improve scores *and* enhance the validity of score interpretations by raising scores that would otherwise be inaccurately low indicators of students' abilities.

The third method of preparation also has the potential to raise scores, but in a way that would undermine the validity of their interpretations and uses. The distinction between test-taking *skills* and *tricks* might seem unclear, as both involve the use of strategies external to pure content knowledge. To illustrate the difference, take the example of two types of guessing on a multiple-choice assessment. A student, Jim, has enough knowledge of the subject to narrow down each answer to two choices. Having been familiarized with the test beforehand, Jim knows he will not be penalized for guessing, so he chooses one of these two options for each question. In this scenario, Jim would almost certainly achieve a lower score than a student who had mastered the relevant material, but would also very likely outperform a student without any knowledge of the topic who guessed randomly. Assuming the results came out in this way (and the test properly covered the relevant material), it would be valid to interpret the students' scores as indicating that Jim was the second-most proficient in the given subject.

In contrast, assume instead that Jim had no knowledge of the topic but was still able to narrow down the answer choices because he knew that the longest answer choice was most likely to be correct. He still might achieve the second-highest score, but it would no longer be valid to use the scores to claim that Jim was any more proficient in the subject being tested than the student who guessed randomly (see Haladyna, 2016, for further discussion of guessing).

Most test-preparation resources involve aspects of all three methods. Even those offering "beat-the-test" tricks emphasize that knowledge and ability in the area being tested are the most important factor in achieving high scores (for example, Martin, 2015). Thus, practice with the relevant academic skills and concepts forms the core of most test preparation. In addition, test-preparation programs offer detailed breakdowns of the structure and content of the assessment, including such information as descriptions of the item types test-takers will encounter and the skills they assess; the number and proportion of each item type and skill likely to appear on the test; and tips for approaching each content area and the items it contains. Beyond offering students a greater sense of familiarity with the assessment, preparation programs use these breakdowns to advise students what to prioritize in their study and practice.

Support for Test Preparation From Testing Companies and Experts

Despite claims from some of the commercial test-preparation companies that the major testing companies do not want students to learn strategies and tips for test taking (for example, Cheng, 2017b), officially sanctioned preparation resources are now replete with the same strategies that third-party commercial organizations recommend. For example, the College Board partnered with the online learning organization Khan Academy to create *Official SAT Practice*, a free online SAT preparation program (College Board, 2018a). These test-preparation resources often present general test-taking tips and subject-specific guidance.

General test-taking tips include pacing advice on the amount of time to spend on each question and section, the recommendation to skip harder questions initially to focus on answering a greater number of easier ones, and the reminder to at least guess on every question (provided there are no penalties for incorrect answers). For individual items, test-preparation programs offer advice on how to eliminate incorrect answer choices. Resources remind students that test creators often design wrong answers to be plausible. In the case of mathematics, the answers might represent the results of the most common errors teachers expect students to make; in reading, the wrong answers might contain related ideas but be too broad or too specific to properly answer the question. In the parlance of some of the commercial test-preparation companies, this is how the assessment is "designed to trick you" (Cheng, 2017a), whereas resources from the testing companies characterize these distractors as "the kind of mistakes that are frequently made by students who are rushing or trying to cut corners" (Khan Academy, n.d.).

Other test-taking tips are more subject specific. For reading, test-prep resources often advise examinees to first skim the passage and look at the questions to see what elements to pay particular attention to in a full read-through. To protect against plausible distractors, test developers advise students to formulate their own answers before going through the choices. To avoid errors, resources widely recommend plugging in numbers for variables rather than using pure algebraic reasoning to solve mathematics questions when the student might not know the proper procedure for solving the problem, and writing out work on multistep problems rather than relying on mental computation (Cheng, 2017a; Kaplan, n.d.; Khan Academy, n.d.).

These strategies can sometimes be difficult to parse in terms of whether they fall into the category of familiarizing students with the assessment and enabling them to demonstrate what they know, or teaching them tricks for exploiting the test format and thereby artificially raising scores. For example, answering every question accrues points, regardless of whether the examinee knows the answer or can even narrow the choices down. This would not reflect increased knowledge or ability in the domain an assessment seeks to measure. Yet to the extent educators universally recommend this strategy, a student who did not employ it would likely receive a lower score than many of his or her peers with an equivalent level of ability. For this reason, assessment experts typically include it under acceptable test-familiarization strategies rather than tricks that would undermine the validity of score interpretations and uses.

Certain resources contain explicitly format-based tips that would constitute more obvious threats to validity. These include suggestions like the following (Martin, 2015).

- Choose *all of the above* or *none of the above* if either is a choice.

- Do not repeat answer choices consecutively.

- Eliminate answer choices with incongruous content or structure.

- Choose the longest answer.

However, these sorts of tricks are notably absent from most of the recommendations from major test-preparation organizations, perhaps in part because developers of large-scale standardized assessments have pre-empted such strategies through careful test and item design (Rodriguez, 2016).

In the interest of reducing irrelevant sources of difficulty and ensuring students are on relatively equal footing, most assessment specialists recommend at least some level of test preparation for large-scale standardized assessments (Powers, 2017). For example, test-development coauthors Haladyna and Downing (2004) noted that in order to reduce threats to validity posed by students' unfamiliarity with a test, "All students should receive ethical test preparation and the extensiveness of this ethical test preparation should be uniform" (p. 21). Ethical test preparation refers to the first two types of preparation we described earlier in this chapter: instruction in the relevant subject matter and test familiarization. While the proliferation of commercial test-preparation programs has increased the amount of test preparation some students receive, a patchwork of private tutors cannot provide the uniformity of preparation necessary to ensure fair tests.

Testing giants such as ACT and the College Board have taken steps to equalize access to preparation by providing test-preparation materials, many of them free, with the stated goal of "leveling the playing field" (College Board, 2018a). While asserting that any claims of massive score increases due solely to short-term test preparation courses are likely overblown, they acknowledged that test preparation "can be helpful" as "students who are familiar with the assessment, have taken practice tests, understand the instructions and have engaged in thoughtful review and preparation tend to be less anxious and more successful than those who haven't" (ACT, 2017) and that "the more you practice, the more familiar you'll be with the test format and content on test day" (College Board, 2018b).

In effect, by making more resources available to all prospective examinees, the testing companies aim to reduce the potential threats to validity that testing experts have noted can result from unequal access to test preparation. In this book, we operationalize that recommendation. Specifically, we believe all K–12 students should receive the same amount and type of ethical test preparation. Such preparation should include a focus on the content on which they will be tested and the aspects of the test items they must be aware of and negotiate to render the test a valid measure of their knowledge and skills. Chapter 6 (page 169) details our recommended approach.

Summary

In this chapter, we addressed questions of ethics and validity that will likely accompany any effort around test preparation, such as the strategies proposed in this book. We outlined the three major forms of test preparation and explained why assessment experts generally regard the first two, subject-matter instruction and test familiarization, as valid and ethical forms of test preparation. We defined the concept of assessment validity and described how test familiarization could increase the validity of test scores and interpretations by removing irrelevant sources of difficulty that could impair test-takers' ability to demonstrate their knowledge. We also discussed how the major testing companies have endorsed ethical test preparation and worked to make resources for this sort of preparation more widely available to students, in accordance with the recommendations from testing experts. In the next chapter, we explain how schools and districts can follow this guidance to engage in uniform ethical test preparation by systematizing and deepening their use of practice assessment items.

CHAPTER 6

A Systemic Approach to Ethical Test Preparation

Providing students with experience answering items they will likely encounter in large-scale assessments has value and is an obvious function of practice items teachers create for ELA, mathematics, and science. However, if a school or district wishes to maximize such practice, it must engage students in activities that more thoroughly develop students' strategic knowledge of specific content and sharpen their ability to solve problems in general. In this chapter, we describe a school- or district-level comprehensive approach. While executing the recommendations in this chapter at the school level is a powerful intervention, executing them at the district level can dramatically alter and enhance the effects of curriculum, instruction, and assessment. Regardless of the level of effort, educators in a school or district must begin with a thorough analysis of each item's schema.

The Importance of Schema

In psychology and cognitive science, a *schema* is defined as a pattern of thought one uses to organize information or accomplish a specific task. In the context of reading and understanding a text, the concept of a schema has historically referred to the overall mental model or mental picture of what the particular text is referring to. The following paragraph depicts the importance of schemata when reading text.

> If the cord around the milk loosened it could drop, perhaps injuring pedestrians. A break in the clothesline would likewise cause a fall. Alternatively, a jam in either pulley would leave the milk stuck in the middle or high winds could cause it to sway and possibly spill. It is clear that the best solution would involve ground travel, in which the least number of things could go wrong.

Even though you recognize every word in this paragraph, you probably don't understand it. While specific phrases and sentences make sense, it's difficult to understand what is being described. This is because the typical reader cannot access an overall mental model or mental picture for this passage. Stated differently, the typical reader has no schema for this passage. However, once the reader observes the picture in figure 6.1, then the passage becomes understandable.

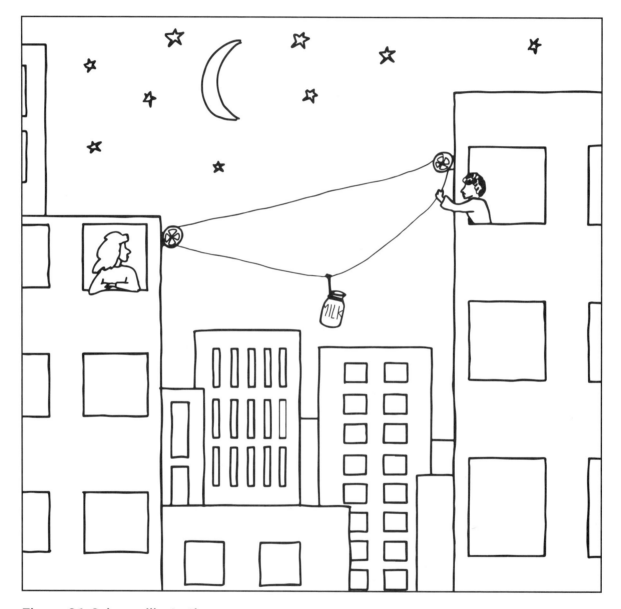

Figure 6.1: Schema illustration.

While this passage and its schema-generating picture are contrived, they make an important point. To understand something you read, hear, or see, you need a schema you can access. This process is constantly being enacted without conscious thought. When you open a webpage in a browser, you have a general idea of its format and how to navigate it even before seeing it. The schema for a webpage includes information such as "will have icons and pictures" and "if I click on specific icons, they will take me to different web-pages." In effect, you have a schema for webpages that allows access to the information on a webpage. If you had never seen a webpage before (that is, did not have a schema for a webpage), you would have great difficulty accessing and understanding the information on the webpage even though you might readily understand that information if you encountered it in traditional text, such as a short article.

This same phenomenon is true for test items. In the introduction (page 1), we explained that many items on state and national assessments have format characteristics students must understand if they are to demonstrate what they know relative to the academic content. The mental representations of those characteristics constitute a student's schema for a given item type. Building on the discussion in the introduction, one can conclude if students have not developed the schemata for the items they will encounter on assessments, they may very well know the content a particular item is designed to assess but be unable to correctly answer the item simply because they do not have a schema for the particular item type.

If students encounter a test item with a format they have never experienced before, the lack of a schema for that format will inhibit their ability to answer the item correctly, even though the students might be proficient on the content the item is designed to assess. This is particularly true for K–12 students who do not have the years of experience that adults have deciphering text in different formats. On the other hand, if students encounter an item for which they have a schema, they will more likely be able to display their understanding of the content or focus of the item. For example, when students are faced with the task of answering a selected-response item that employs the function frame in ELA, they will perform better if they can immediately decipher what the item requires of them. Again, students will perform better if they have a schema for the function item.

Guidance for Articulating Item Schema

We believe providing students with schemata for specific item types is a critical aspect of what testing experts have referred to as *ethical test preparation* (Haladyna & Downing, 2004; see chapter 5, page 163). Certainly, ethical test preparation involves ensuring students have effective instruction on the content on which they will be tested. In addition, ethical test preparation must involve an emphasis on developing students' schemata for the types of items teachers will use to assess their knowledge. Consequently, it is up to schools and districts to provide students with the information necessary to create these schemata. To this end, teachers at the school or district level should analyze the practice items they will present to students and answer the following questions for each item.

- What will I present to students in the item?

- What am I asking students to do in the item?

- What should I directly teach students?

We consider these questions for sample items in ELA, mathematics, and science.

ELA

In chapter 2 (page 23), we described six frame types for selected-response items involving reading. Each of these frames has unique answers to the three questions designed to establish a student's schema for an item. Consider the function item figure 6.2 depicts.

Part A:

Chicago
By Carl Sandburg

1	Hog Butcher for the World,
2	Tool Maker, Stacker of Wheat,
3	Player with Railroads and the Nation's Freight Handler;
4	Stormy, husky, brawling,
5	City of the Big Shoulders:
6	They tell me you are wicked and I believe them, for I have seen your painted women under the
7	gas lamps luring the farm boys.
8	And they tell me you are crooked and I answer: Yes, it is true I have seen the gunman kill and
9	go free to kill again.
10	And they tell me you are brutal and my reply is: On the faces of women and children I have
11	seen the marks of wanton hunger.
12	And having answered so I turn once more to those who sneer at this my city, and I give them
13	back the sneer and say to them:
14	Come and show me another city with lifted head singing so proud to be alive and coarse and
15	strong and cunning.
16	Flinging magnetic curses amid the toil of piling job on job, here is a tall bold slugger set vivid
17	against the little soft cities;
18	Fierce as a dog with tongue lapping for action, cunning as a savage pitted against the
19	wilderness,
20	Bareheaded,
21	Shoveling,
22	Wrecking,
23	Planning,
24	Building, breaking, rebuilding,
25	Under the smoke, dust all over his mouth, laughing with white teeth,
26	Under the terrible burden of destiny laughing as a young man laughs,
27	Laughing even as an ignorant fighter laughs who has never lost a battle,
28	Bragging and laughing that under his wrist is the pulse, and under his ribs the heart of the people,
29	Laughing!
30	Laughing the stormy, husky, brawling laughter of Youth, half-naked, sweating, proud to be Hog Butcher, Tool Maker, Stacker of Wheat, Player with Railroads and Freight Handler to the Nation.

Source: Sandburg, 1914.

How does the poet's use of personification affect the tone of the poem?

- A. It creates a tone of innocence and naiveté by comparing Chicago to a farm boy.
- B. It conveys a tone of sadness and desperation by comparing Chicago to hungry women and children.
- C. It emphasizes a tone of ferocity and violence by comparing Chicago to a dog.
- D. It reinforces a tone of confidence and energy by comparing Chicago to a laughing young man.

Part B:

Which lines from the poem provide the best evidence for the answer to Part A?

- A. "Under the terrible burden of destiny laughing as a young man laughs, / Laughing even as an ignorant fighter laughs who has never lost a battle" (lines 26–27)
- B. "Fierce as a dog with tongue lapping for action" (line 18)
- C. "And having answered so I turn once more to those who sneer at this my city, and I give them back the sneer" (lines 12–13)
- D. "And they tell me you are brutal and my reply is: On the faces of women and children I have seen the marks of wanton hunger." (lines 10–11)

Figure 6.2: Function frame item example.

The first question teachers should ask is, "What will I present to students in the item?" The item in figure 6.2 has some distinct characteristics relative to its physical format, the first of which is the passage has numbered lines. This should signal to students they will probably have to refer back to the passage in their answers. The teacher should point out such features and their implications to students. Another feature of this item is the two parts, A and B, with the answer to part B being dependent on the answer to part A. Again, teachers should highlight this component of the item's structure for students.

The second question is, "What am I asking students to do in the item?" To answer this question, it is useful for educators to mentally walk through the serial thinking students must engage in to answer the item. A summary of that thinking might be as follows.

- Read the passage, making note of the numbered lines.
- Read item A, making note of the literary element it highlights.
- Determine the function of the literary element.
- Examine the alternatives for item A and select the one that represents your determination of the literary element's function.
- Read item B, making note of what type of evidence it requests.
- Go back to the passage and identify the line that fulfills the requirement of the requested evidence.

While this step-by-step accounting of the cognitive process required to answer the item is very granular, it discloses what students have to know and be able to do to answer the item. This is useful when answering the third question, "What should I directly teach students?"

The quintessential aspect of this question in terms of developing students' schema for a particular item type is that direct instruction is required.

The first consideration to this end should be the actual academic content that is the focus of the item. For example, in the case of the preceding ELA function item, a teacher might determine students need direct instruction regarding the fact that passages frequently have certain sentences, paragraphs, and so on that influence the message of the passage. In chapter 2 (page 23), you saw some of these elements.

- The overall structure of a section of text

- The actions or attitudes of a character

- A specific sentence

- A specific event

- The artistic choices of an author

- The apparent point of view expressed in a text

- The description of specific characteristics of a person, place, thing, event, or concept

- Photographs, pictures, or images in a text

- Dialogues of conversations

- Interactions described within a text

A teacher might determine students should receive direct instruction as to the nature of these elements and how each fulfills a certain function in texts.

To answer the third question, teachers would also identify elements of the item format students should receive direct instruction about. For example, a teacher might decide students need to be made aware of the intricacies of two-part items. Specifically, teachers might determine students need direct instruction regarding the fact that part B items require them to identify the lines in the text that represent specific evidence for their answer. Teachers might also decide students need to be made aware that the convention of numbering lines (or paragraphs) in a text typically signals that the item will ask readers to refer back to specific parts of the text. Consequently, as they read, students should look for parts of the text that play an important role in the meaning of the text.

Finally, we recommend that if possible, teachers provide students with an explicit strategy for addressing specific items they encounter in tests. For selected-response function frames, that explicit strategy might have steps like the following.

1. Before you read the passage, look at the questions about the passage and try to determine what type of item it is. If it is a function item, then go to step 2.

2. Read the passage and pay attention to the line numbers (or paragraph numbers), particularly for parts of the text you think might be serving a particular function in the text.

3. When you are done, read item A. It will ask you to identify the function of a specific part of what you read. Go back and find that part of the passage and try to answer the question without looking at the alternatives.

4. After you have come up with your answer, look through the alternatives and select the one that is closest to your answer. If you don't see your answer reflected in the alternatives, look over each alternative and determine which one is the most probable answer. You might have to go back and look at the passage again.

5. Next consider item B. It will ask you to identify the specific part of the text that provides evidence for your answer in item A. Try to identify the part of the text that provides evidence for your answer without looking at the alternatives. If you don't see your answer reflected in the alternatives, look over each alternative and determine which one is the most probable answer. You might have to go back and look at the passage again.

It's important to note that steps such as these are not designed to provide an exact answer for students. Rather, they are designed to provide students with a framework that allows them to discern what an item requires of them, much like the picture in figure 6.1 (page 170) allows the reader to understand a paragraph that otherwise makes little sense.

Mathematics

To illustrate the process of articulating an item schema in mathematics, consider the units and conversions item in figure 6.3 (page 176).

Again, the first question a teacher would ask to articulate this item's schema is, "What will I present to students in the item?" In this type of mathematics item, the teacher usually presents students with a set of measurements (5 quarts, 5 pints, 5 gallons, 1 gallon and 1 pint, and 1 gallon and 5 pints). The measurements are represented using different units (pints, quarts, and gallons). The teacher asks students to perform an operation (comparison) with the measurements that would be made easier by representing the measurements in the same unit. The ratio between relevant measurement units is often provided in symbolic form (2 pints = 1 quart; 4 quarts = 1 gallon), verbal form (There are 2 pints in a quart and there are 4 quarts in a gallon), or both.

The second question is, "What am I asking students to do in the item?" Based on the information teachers provide them, students must perform an operation on measurements having dissimilar units. In this case, the teacher asks students to compare measurements given in pints and gallons to a measurement given in quarts. Because the operation would be easier to perform on measurements represented in similar units, the item implicitly requires students to convert the provided measurements to the same unit. Since the ratios between unit types are provided in the item, students do not need to recall this information from memory.

2 pints = 1 quart

4 quarts = 1 gallon

There are 2 pints in a quart and there are 4 quarts in a gallon.

Which of the following measures are less than 5 quarts and which are more than 5 quarts?

Make one selection for each measure to show your answer.

Measures	Less than 5 Quarts	More than 5 Quarts
5 pints	○	○
5 gallons	○	○
1 gallon and 1 pint	○	○
1 gallon and 5 pints	○	○

Clear Answer

Source: U.S. Department of Education, Institute of Education Sciences, National Center for Education Statistics, National Assessment of Educational Progress (NAEP), 2017 Mathematics Assessment. Item 2017-8M3 #5 M3838MS.

Figure 6.3: Sample item for units and conversions at grade 8.

The third question is, "What should I directly teach students?" To effectively answer items like this, students must understand the basic nature of the required computation. Specifically, students must understand the defining characteristic of these types of items is the ratio relationship between measurement units. In this item, that is the ratio between pints and quarts and between quarts and gallons. The same measurement represented in a particular unit can also be represented by a different number of related units. Measurements can be converted between unit types using certain calculations that utilize the set ratio between them. Once measurements are represented in terms of the same unit, operations involving them are more easily performed.

Again, we recommend teachers provide students with an explicit strategy such as the following.

1.   Read the item and determine what it requires you to do. If it is a units and conversions item, use the following steps.

2.   Identify the operation required by the item.

3.   Identify the measurements involved in the operation and the units in which they are represented.

4.   Determine which measurements will need to be converted to which units in order to more easily perform the required operation.

5.   Identify the ratios between the relevant units.

6.   Use these ratios to convert the measurements to the same unit.

7.   Perform the required operation.

Again, it is important to remember steps like these are not designed to lead students to a precise answer; they are to provide students with an approach to determining what the teacher requires of them to answer the item.

Science

To illustrate the process of articulating an item schema in science, consider the item in figure 6.4 (page 178).

The first question in the process is, "What will I present to students in the item?" In this case, the teacher presents students with a partial periodic table with several elements highlighted. The teacher also presents the names and chemical symbols of these elements in an accompanying table. The teacher provides students four possible elements as the alternative choices in the item.

The second question is, "What am I asking students to do in the item?" To answer this science item, students must select the correct answer among the four elements the teacher provides in the alternatives. This selection process requires students to recall how the periodic table is organized, identify the positions of the elements listed as alternatives relative to the position of argon, and select the element in the position that indicates the most similarity in chemical properties between it and argon (helium).

The third question is, "What should I directly teach students?" In answer to this question, a teacher might decide to teach students about the organization of elements in the periodic table and what the relative position of elements can indicate about their chemical properties.

Finally, the teacher might provide students with the following strategy to help them with science items of this nature.

1. Read the item and determine what it requires you to do. If it requires you to apply a science concept, use the following steps.

2. Determine which scientific concept or principle applies to the situation presented in the item.

3. Answer the item to yourself first without looking at the possible answers the teacher provides.

4. Next look at the alternatives the teacher provides, and if you see the same answer as yours, mark that answer as correct.

5. If you don't see your answer reflected in the alternatives, look over each alternative and determine which one is the most probable answer to the question.

Periodic Table of the Elements

GROUP 1A (1)	IIA (2)	IIIA (3)	IVA (4)	VA (5)	VIA (6)	VIIA (7)	VIIIA (8)			II (1)	III (2)	IIIB (3)	IVB (4)	VB (5)	VIB (6)	VIIB (7)	VIIIB (8)
1 H 1.0079																	2 He 4.0026
3 Li 6.941	4 Be 9.012											5 B 10.811	6 C 12.011	7 N 14.007	8 O 16.00	9 F 19.00	10 Ne 20.179
11 Na 22.99	12 Mg 24.30											13 Al 26.98	14 Si 28.09	15 P 30.974	16 S 32.06	17 Cl 35.453	18 Ar 39.948
19 K 39.10	20 Ca 40.08	21 Sc 44.96	22 Ti 47.90	23 V 50.94	24 Cr 52.00	25 Mn 54.938	26 Fe 55.85	27 Co 58.93	28 Ni 58.69	29 Cu 63.559	30 Zn 65.39	31 Ga 69.72	32 Ge 72.59	33 As 74.92	34 Se 78.96	35 Br 79.90	36 Kr 83.80
37 Rb 85.47	38 Sr 87.62	39 Y 88.91	40 Zr 91.22	41 Nb 92.91	42 Mo 95.94	43 Tc (98)	44 Ru 101.1	45 Rh 102.91	46 Pd 106.42	47 Ag 107.87	48 Cd 112.41	49 In 114.82	50 Sn 118.71	51 Sb 121.75	52 Te 127.60	53 I 126.91	54 Xe 131.29

Element	Symbol
Argon	Ar
Chlorine	Cl
Helium	He
Nitrogen	N
Zinc	Zn

4.

Based on its location on the partial periodic table shown above, which element would you predict has chemical properties that are most similar to argon (Ar)?

A. Chlorine (Cl)

B. Helium (He)

C. Nitrogen (N)

D. Zinc (Zn)

Source: U.S. Department of Education, Institute of Education Sciences, National Center for Education Statistics, National Assessment of Educational Progress (NAEP), 2011 Science Assessment. Item 2011-8S11 #4 K156701.

Figure 6.4: Sample grade 8 physical science item.

Deeper Understanding Through Student-Generated Items

Once teachers have articulated the schemata for items for a specific grade level and content area and presented them to students, they should engage students in activities that deepen their knowledge of the content and the characteristics of various item types. The vehicle for such development is *writing to learn*.

Having students write about content they are learning is commonly referred to as *writing to learn*. According to researchers Steve Graham, Sharlene A. Kiuhara, and Meade MacKay (2020), the interest in writing as a tool for learning started in the later part of the 20th century: "educators in English and the humanities in the 1960s and 1970s began to encourage students to use writing as a tool for learning in all content areas" (p. 180).

This early interest in writing as a tool for learning (as opposed to simply a tool for communication) was based on a seemingly logical connection between writing about a topic and understanding that topic better. It was theorist and researcher James Britton (1982) who galvanized and popularized the premise that the very act of writing about a topic makes one better understand the topic. Graham and his colleagues (2020) describe in their meta-analysis:

> [Britton] claimed that writers do not know exactly what they will say when they begin to convert an idea into written text, and that the semantics and syntax of language shape this process, resulting in new learning about an idea at the "point of utterance." (p. 181)

Over the decades, there have been many studies on the effects of writing to learn, and those studies were synthesized in two high-visibility meta-analyses, one in 2004 (Bangert-Drowns, Hurley, & Wilkinson) and one in 2007 (Graham & Perin). A third meta-analysis by Graham and his colleagues (2020) involved fifty-six studies, spanning grades K–12; this study examined the effects of writing to learn on multiple subject areas. Graham and his colleagues (2020) found writing to learn reliably enhanced learning, and it "was equally effective at improving learning in science, social studies, and mathematics" (p. 179).

The findings from this latest meta-analytic synthesis of the research solidify the efficacy of writing about content as a tool for better understanding the content (Graham et al., 2020). We take this one step further and assert that writing about specific types of items and content helps deepen the writer's understanding of both.

The writing-to-learn process, when applied to practice items, starts after teachers present students with the explicit strategy associated with a specific type of item. For example, assume a teacher has provided students with the strategy for the ELA function frame previously described (page 174), along with some direct instruction about the nature of literary elements that perform a function.

The teacher would then ask students to create their own version of the item. This is the foundational writing-to-learn activity. Recall Britton's (1982) assertion about the power of writing. When students write their own items, they deepen their understanding of the content "at the point of utterance" (as cited in Graham et al., 2020, p. 181).

Before students individually write their own example items, they should discuss in small groups of two or three how they might go about this. This helps individual students formulate their own thinking and get new ideas from their group partners. After this small-group discussion, students should then work individually to write their own sample items. This might take some time and some students might require help from the teacher or other students who are more comfortable with the process.

Immediately after students create their own version of the item, they individually record their thoughts about this item type in a journal. They should refer to item types by their name, like *function frame*, and then write their reactions to them (see figure 6.5).

Function frame

- How does [Textual Element] do [Literary Element]?

- [Textual Element] = character actions, thoughts, or words; a sentence; an event; a point of view; a picture; a literary device

- [Literary Element] = an important or main idea; an argument or purpose of the passage; the whole plot; the structure of the passage

---

Figure 6.5: Student journal notes.

Each time students encounter a practice item for which they have previously written their own version, they deepen their knowledge base by adding to what they have written in their journal. To facilitate this, the teacher provides writing prompts like the following.

- What new insights do you have about this type of item?

- What makes this type of item easier?

- What makes this type of item harder?

Figure 6.6 depicts an entry a student might make in his or her journal as a result of these prompts.

Follow this same pattern for mathematics and science. The teacher first presents students with specific mathematics and science frames, along with direct instruction to help students develop a schema for the item and a strategy for addressing such items on tests. Students create their own versions of the frames. As they encounter these frames in practice sessions, they write about their growing understanding of those frames in their writing-to-learn journals.

> New Insights
> - Other ways of saying "How does [Textual Element] do [Literary Element]?":
>   + How does [Textual Element] affect [Literary Element]?
>   + How does [Textual Element] influence [Literary Element]?
>   + How does [Textual Element] contribute to [Literary Element]?
> - Part B usually asks for evidence or support for answer to Part A
> - Easier:
>   + Look for line or paragraph numbers (will often refer to these in the answer)
>   + Often helps to figure out the main idea of the passage
> - Harder:
>   + Can't answer Part B correctly if answer to Part A is wrong

Figure 6.6: Augmented student journal notes.

A Schoolwide or Districtwide Approach

An individual teacher can certainly select item frames to use with his or her students and employ the previously described schema-development techniques. However, a much more powerful strategy is to approach the recommendations in this book using a schoolwide or (better yet) districtwide effort. We believe it is the responsibility of schools and districts as educational organizations to provide students with an awareness of the item schemata they will most likely face in external assessments and the academic content that is the focus of those items. We recommend the following actions as components of a schoolwide or districtwide approach.

Organize Standards Using Item Frames

Educators can use the item frames in this book to organize and focus state or local standards. This is because the item frames' topics typically represent the topics highlighted in state standards. To illustrate, consider the mathematics item frames for the seventh grade reported in table 3.14 (page 106).

If you compare these fifteen subcategories to the state standards, you will probably find a great deal of overlap. To illustrate, consider the alignment between prominent subcategories and Colorado state standards for grade 7 (see table 6.1, page 182).

We found twelve of the fifteen prominent subcategories at this grade level align with evidence outcomes in the Colorado Academic Standards, with some standards encompassing content from more than one subcategory (Colorado Department of Education, 2019). In total, thirty-five of the forty-three standards, or 81 percent, describe knowledge and skills these subcategories represent. Schools and districts should perform this type of analysis using their own standards, and explicitly identify the state standards addressed by each item subtype.

Table 6.1: Alignment of Prominent Subcategories With Colorado Standards for Grade 7

Content Category	Subcategory	Aligned Standards
Expressions, Equations, Inequalities, and Functions (EEIF)	Equations	5
	Expressions	0
	Inequalities	2
Geometry	2-D and 3-D Shapes	1
	Area and Perimeter	1
Operations	Operation Not Specified	6
Quantity and Number	Coordinate Plane	0
	Equivalence	3
	Percentages	0
Ratios and Proportional Relationships	Proportional Relationships	6
	Rate and Ratio	1
	Scaling	1
Statistics	Measures of Center and Variance	2
	Probability	9
	Statistical Investigation	2

Source for standards: Colorado Department of Education, 2019.

Create a Database of Student-Generated Items

As described previously, one of the steps in the writing-to-learn process is for students to write their own examples of specific item types. As students create their examples, the school or district can collect and archive them in a location other students can access. Teachers should vet and edit these student examples so they are accurate and useful exemplars of specific item frames. Over time, the school or district can have students create videos or screencasts describing their insights about specific items or the content within those items. Students might view these student-generated resources to help them better understand a particular type of item or the content it addresses. Teachers might also use the videos and screencasts when they present new frames, review frames, or both for students. For example, if a student created an item for operation not specified, he or she might then record a video or screencast that explains how to successfully solve the problem. Teachers and other students could then use this student's video as a learning tool, and teachers could use it as an example of the operation not specified frame during review or during a subsequent year or semester when they are introducing that frame.

Have Teachers Regularly Introduce and Review Item Frames and the Academic Content They Assess

Once a week or at least every other week, teachers should lead students in a review of previously addressed frames, introduce new frames, or both. If students are using the writing-to-learn process, they make entries in their journal on each of these occasions. For example, at the end of a lesson on inequalities, a teacher might introduce the frame for that type of item. Students would record the frame and some examples of its use in their journals. Then, the teacher might have students revisit the equation frame they'd learned the week before, and create an item using it. Each student would record this new item in their journal. If time permits, students could also meet briefly to exchange and solve each other's items. Such activities reinforce previous learning and strengthen new learning. This provides students with a systematic and systemic review of the critical content that assessments cover and the manner in which it will be assessed. The following vignette depicts how this might manifest in one teacher's classroom.

Suppose a high school ELA teacher is working with her students on how to research and write an informational essay. As one element of the process, the class practiced comparing sources to determine which ones will be the most useful and relevant to address a chosen topic. To reinforce this skill and demonstrate how an external examination might assess it, the teacher had the class work with short constructed-response evidence items, providing students with a topic and descriptions of multiple sources and having them select the most relevant source and explain their choices. Now that the class is preparing to work on constructing an essay itself, the teacher reviews the evidence frame by having students write their own short constructed-response evidence items and reflect on the item type in their journals. The teacher then introduces the extended constructed-response informational frame, which asks students to derive information from sources and present it in a particular way. After providing direct instruction on how to approach these items and how to compose informational essays, the teacher might have students construct their own examples of these items and reflect on the item type in their journals. By following this process, the students learn the necessary academic content (in this case, how to write an informational essay), while also becoming familiar with the ways external examinations assess these skills.

Summary

In this chapter, we explained why and how students should receive direct instruction in and practice with recognizing and articulating the underlying characteristics that constitute the schema of an assessment item. We first suggested how teachers might help their students become familiar with these characteristics by identifying what each item frame presents to students and what it asks them to do, and then determining which of these features to explicitly point out and explain to students. We then proposed students reinforce their knowledge of item schema and the content the items address through the writing-to-learn strategy, namely by writing their own practice items based on the observed schema of each item type in each subject area. To maximize the reach and impact of these exercises, we encourage a systemwide approach in which a school or district determines the correspondence between their standards and the item frames; compiles a central database of student-generated exemplar practice items; and has teachers periodically review previous item frames and introduce new frames and the content they assess. By incorporating direct instruction and practice with item schema into the everyday teaching of academic content, schools and districts will enable their students to overcome the obstacles assessment-item characteristics pose and present a more faithful representation of what they know without having to devote as much time solely to test preparation.

Epilogue

If students know what to expect on large-scale assessments and have the opportunity to learn about both the content and the schemata they will encounter, their performance on such assessments is more likely to accurately reflect what they know and are able to do. In this book, we provide a framework based on an analysis of thousands of large-scale assessment items in three subject areas. Although the primary goal of our analysis was to identify and codify the schemata (that is, the frames, structures, and templates) large-scale assessments use, our analysis also provided guidance about the content educators should focus on.

The applications of the framework presented in this book are varied and complex. An individual teacher who finds this approach compelling might use the frames and templates to design classroom assessment items, thus giving students exposure to the types of items they will encounter on large-scale assessments. Going a step further, that teacher, or a team of teachers, might also adjust the relative emphasis on content topics during instruction to provide students with ample opportunity to learn the content they will encounter on large-scale assessments. At the highest level of implementation, the entire school or district could engage students in systematic activities to develop knowledge of specific content and sharpen general problem-solving abilities.

Admittedly, this book provides an exceptional level of detail, about both the assessment-items analysis and the framework that analysis produced. However, we believe this level of detail provides a firm foundation for educators to implement the ideas presented throughout the book, but particularly in chapter 6 (page 169). The best way for students to learn about text structures and schemata is to practice writing them themselves; this is the foundational premise of countless writer's workshops. An assessment item *is* a text structure, one that is critically important for students to understand and interact effectively with in order to accurately demonstrate their knowledge and skills.

Ultimately, student-generated assessment items serve multiple educational purposes, all positive and productive. First, they provide an opportunity for students to learn about the content and the schema of the item they are creating. Second, teachers can use well-crafted student-generated items in a variety of formal and informal ways to collect information about what students know and are able to do. Finally, given their impact on students' lives and future opportunities, teaching students about the structure of assessment items (by asking them to create them) ensures students are prepared to demonstrate their knowledge and skills as clearly and unequivocally as possible on large-scale assessments. We hope that this book empowers and inspires educators to do just that.

Appendix A:
Mathematics Templates

Appendix A contains mathematics item templates for the most prominent subcategories at each grade level. The test items in our analysis displayed more diversity than can be shown here, but the templates represent the most common formats for items in each subcategory. Each template includes a sample item created using the template, step-by-step instructions, a key describing the properties of elements within the template, and the template itself.

Grade 3

Data Displays

Bar Graph

Sample Item

There are 15 animals in a zoo exhibit. There are 5 different types of animals. The bar graph shows the number of each type of animal.

Part A

How many more giraffes are there than zebras?

Fill in your answer in the box.

```
┌─────────────────┐
│                 │
└─────────────────┘
```

Part B

What is the difference between the number of hippos and the number of giraffes and zebras combined?

Fill in your answer in the box.

```
┌─────────────────┐
│                 │
└─────────────────┘
```

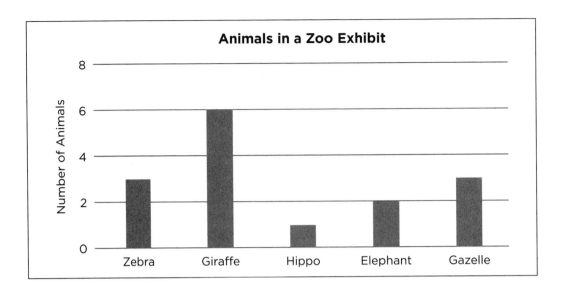

Template Instructions

1. Create a bar graph with three to nine categories (bars) on the horizontal axis. The vertical axis should be marked with a nonconsecutive, single-digit integer scale (that is, with single-digit integers that skip-count in regular intervals). Each bar of the graph should indicate a single-digit integer quantity and at least some of the bars should lie between the marked intervals on the vertical axis (for example, if the vertical axis marks every even integer, then at least some of the bars of the graph should indicate odd quantities). Insert the bar graph into the template in place of the box.

2. Choose a definition for [Item]. Insert it into the graph.

3. Select a different unique variation of [Item] for each bar of the graph. Insert these into the template as category labels for the horizontal axis of the graph.

4. Create a title for the graph. Insert it into the template.

5. Select [Quantity 1] and [Quantity 2]. Insert them into the template.

6. Choose definitions for [Category 1] through [Category 5]. Insert them into the template.

Template Key

Item: Any object or entity with multiple variations that comes in whole-number quantities (for example, animals, people, pastries)

Quantity 1: The sum of all the unique variations of [Item] (that is, the sum of the measures of all the bars on the graph)

Quantity 2: The number of unique variations of [Item] (that is, the number of bars on the graph)

Category 1: Any of the unique variations of [Item] chosen for the bars of the graph; this variation should have a quantity greater than that chosen for [Category 2].

Category 2: Any of the unique variations of [Item] chosen for the bars of the graph; this variation should have a quantity less than that chosen for [Category 1].

Category 3: Any of the unique variations of [Item] chosen for the bars of the graph, different from [Category 4] or [Category 5]

Category 4: Any of the unique variations of [Item] chosen for the bars of the graph, different from [Category 3] or [Category 5]

Category 5: Any of the unique variations of [Item] chosen for the bars of the graph, different from [Category 3] or [Category 4]

Template

There are [Quantity 1] [Item]. There are [Quantity 2] different types of [Item]. The bar graph shows the number of each type of [Item].

Part A

How many more [Category 1] are there than [Category 2]?

Fill in your answer in the box.

Part B

What is the difference between the number of [Category 3] and the number of [Category 4] and [Category 5] combined?

Fill in your answer in the box.

Two-Way Table

Sample Item

Two apartment complexes each have two buildings full of residents. The table displays the number of residents in each building.

	Building 1	Building 2	Total
Stony Brook Apartments	56	77	
Rocky Creek Apartments	84	93	

Part A

What is the total number of residents in the Stony Brook Apartments?

- A.   133
- B.   140
- C.   170
- D.   177

Part B

What is the total number of residents in the Rocky Creek Apartments?

- A.   133
- B.   140
- C.   170
- D.   177

Part C

What is the difference between the number of residents in Building 1 of the Rocky Creek Apartments and the number of residents in Building 1 of the Stony Brook Apartments?

Fill in your answer in the box.

Part D

One unit in the Stony Brook Apartments has 5 residents. Another unit has 7 residents. How many residents are in the rest of the Stony Brook Apartments?

Show the steps you used to solve the problem. Fill in your answer and your work.

Template Instructions

1.   Choose a definition for [Scenario]. Insert it into the template.

2.   Choose definitions for [Category 1] and [Category 2], [Element 1] and [Element 2], [Unit], [Item], and [Quantity 1] through [Quantity 4]. Insert them into the template.

3.   Select [Answer 1] through [Answer 4]. Insert them into the template.

4.   Select [Answer 5] through [Answer 8]. Insert them into the template.

5.   Select [Quantity 5] and [Quantity 6]. Insert them into the template.

Template Key

Scenario: A scenario in which two [Category] each have two [Element] that can be subdivided into smaller [Unit] that themselves contain whole-number quantities of [Item] (for example, two apartment complexes each have two buildings with units full of residents, a football team plays two games of two halves each in which players score points, two ponds each contain two schools of fish that eat bugs).

Categories 1–2: Entities that can each have two [Element] (for example, apartment complexes, football games, ponds)

Elements 1–2: Components of each [Category], each subdivided into smaller [Unit] that contain whole-number quantities of [Item] (for example, apartment buildings, halves of a football game, schools of fish in a pond)

Unit: A smaller subset of each [Element] that can have or produce whole-number quantities of [Item] (for example, unit of an apartment building, football player, fish)

Item: An individual entity contained or produced by [Unit] (for example, apartment residents, points scored, bugs eaten)

Quantities 1–4: One- or two-digit whole numbers

Quantity 5: One- or two-digit whole number less than or equal to [Quantity 1]

Quantity 6: One- or two-digit whole number less than or equal to [Quantity 2]

Answers 1–8: Whole numbers. One of [Answer 1] through [Answer 4] is the answer to Part A. One of [Answer 5] through [Answer 8] is the answer to Part B.

Template

[Scenario]. The table displays the number of [Item] in each [Element].

	[Element 1]	**[Element 2]**	**Total**
[Category 1]	[Quantity 1]	[Quantity 2]	
[Category 2]	[Quantity 3]	[Quantity 4]	

Part A

What is the total number of [Item] in [Category 1]?

A. [Answer 1]

B. [Answer 2]

C. [Answer 3]

D. [Answer 4]

Part B

What is the total number of [Item] in [Category 2]?

A. [Answer 5]

B. [Answer 6]

C. [Answer 7]

D. [Answer 8]

Part C

What is the difference between the number of [Item] in [Element 1] of [Category 2] and the number of [Item] in [Element 1] of [Category 1]?

Fill in your answer in the box.

[ ]

Part D

One [Unit] in [Category 1] has [Quantity 5] [Item]. Another [Unit] has [Quantity 6] [Item]. How many [Item] are in the rest of [Category 1]?

Show the steps you used to solve the problem. Fill in your answer and your work.

Expressions, Equations, Inequalities, and Functions (EEIF)

Expressions

Sample Item

72 cans of soda are put into packs with 6 cans of soda in each pack. Which expression can you use to show the total number of packs made?

A. 72×6

B. $72 \div 6$

C. $6 \div 72$

D. $72 - 6$

Template Instructions

1.   Choose definitions for [Item] and [Group]. Insert them into the template.

2.   Select [Quantity 1] and [Quantity 2]. Insert them into the template.

3.   Choose definitions for [Answer 1] through [Answer 4].

Template Key

Item: Any entity that exists in whole-number quantities (for example, cans of soda, sheep, ships)

Group: A group composed of several of [Item] (for example, pack, herd, fleet)

Quantity 1: A two-digit, whole-number multiple of [Quantity 2]

Quantity 2: A one-digit, whole-number factor of [Quantity 1]

Answers 1–4: Addition, subtraction, multiplication, or division expressions consisting of two values, in which [Quantity 1] and [Quantity 2] are the values. One of the expressions should correctly represent the scenario in the problem.

Template

[Quantity 1] [Item] are put into [Group] with [Quantity 2] [Item] in each [Group]. Which expression can be used to show the total number of [Group] made?

   A.   [Answer 1]

   B.   [Answer 2]

   C.   [Answer 3]

   D.   [Answer 4]

Geometry

2-D and 3-D Shapes

Sample Item

Which shapes are hexagons?

Select the two correct shapes.

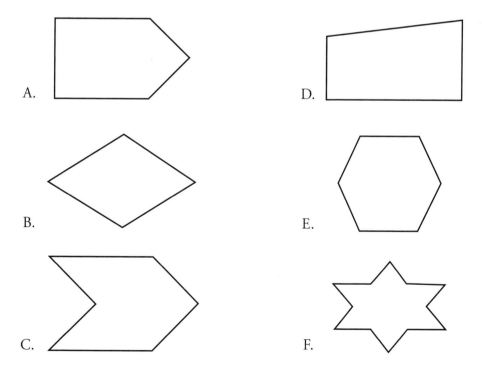

Template Instructions

1. Choose a definition for [Category]. Insert it into the template.

2. Select [Quantity]. Insert it into the template.

3. Create six different regular or irregular polygons, [Quantity] of which are [Category]. Insert each shape into the template in place of one of the boxes.

Template Key

Category: A category of three- to six-sided polygons (for example, triangles, quadrilaterals, pentagons, or hexagons).

Quantity: A whole-number quantity from two to five.

Template

Which shapes are [Category]?

Select the [Quantity] correct shapes.

A.

D.

B.

E.

C.

F.

Area and Perimeter

Sample Item

The side lengths of a shape are shown.

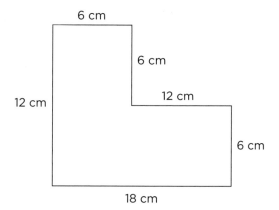

Fill in the perimeter, in centimeters, of the shape.

Template Instructions

1. Create a rectilinear, two-dimensional polygon with more than four sides. Insert it into the template in place of the box.

2. Choose a definition for [Unit]. Insert it into the template.

3. Create an appropriate one- or two-digit integer side length for each side of the polygon and label each side with its length in [Unit].

Template Key

Unit: Any standard unit used to measure length (for example, centimeters, inches, yards).

Template

The side lengths of a shape are shown.

Fill in the perimeter, in [Unit], of the shape.

Measurement

Time

Sample Item

Look at the time on the following clock.

Select the time shown on the clock, to the nearest minute.

    A.   3:06

    B.   2:18

    C.   4:06

    D.   1:18

Template Instructions

1. Create an image of an analog clock face in which the minute hand rests between numerals on the face (that is, the minute hand does not rest at a five-minute interval).

2. Choose definitions for [Time 1] through [Time 4]. Insert them into the template.

Template Key

Times 1–4: Different times in a 12-hour format, to the minute. One of these is the correct time shown on the clock face.

Template

Look at the time on the following clock.

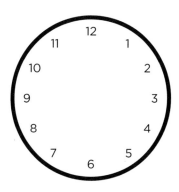

Select the time shown on the clock, to the nearest minute.

A.   [Time 1]

B.   [Time 2]

C.   [Time 3]

D.   [Time 4]

Tools

Sample Item

What is the best estimate of the amount of water in the container?

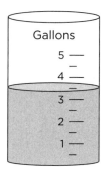

A.   2 gallons

B.   4 gallons

C.   3 gallons

D.   6 gallons

Template Instructions

1.   Create an image of a graduated cylinder or other object that can be used for measuring liquid volume (bottle, bucket, and so on). The object should be marked with tick marks in [Unit] that are labeled at whole-number intervals. It should be filled with water to a level close to one of the whole-number tick marks (that is, the water should be near to, but not exactly level with, the tick mark). Insert the image into the template in place of the box.

2.   Choose a definition for [Unit]. Insert it into the template.

3.   Select [Quantity 1] through [Quantity 4]. Insert them into the template.

Template Key

Unit: A unit of liquid volume (for example, gallons, liters, milliliters).

Quantities 1–4: Whole numbers. One of these is the correct answer.

Template

What is the best estimate of the amount of water in the container?

    A.   [Quantity 1] [Unit]

    B.   [Quantity 2] [Unit]

    C.   [Quantity 3] [Unit]

    D.   [Quantity 4] [Unit]

Operations

Addition

Sample Item

Fill in your answer in the box.

528 + 252 = ⬚

Template Instructions

1.   Select [Quantity 1] and [Quantity 2]. Insert them into the template.

Template Key

Quantity 1: A three-digit whole number.

Quantity 2: A different three-digit whole number than [Quantity 1].

Template

Fill in your answer in the box.

[Quantity 1] + [Quantity 2] = ⬚

Multiplication

Sample Item

What unknown number makes this equation true?

$3 \times 9 =$ ☐

Template Instructions

1.   Select [Quantity 1] and [Quantity 2]. Insert them into the template.

Template Key

Quantities 1–2: Single-digit whole numbers.

Template

What unknown number makes this equation true?

[Quantity 1] × [Quantity 2] = ☐

Operation Not Specified

Sample Item

A bakery sold 98 cupcakes. The cupcakes come in boxes. Each box came with 6 chocolate cupcakes, 4 vanilla cupcakes, and 4 red velvet cupcakes.

How many cupcakes were in each box? Show your work.

How many boxes did the bakery sell? Show your work.

Template Instructions

1.   Choose definitions for [Person A], [Select], [Item Type A], [Item Subtype A], [Item Subtype B], [Item Subtype C], and [Group A]. Insert these definitions into the template.

2.   Create [Quantity 2], [Quantity 3], and [Quantity 4] according to the specifications in the key. Insert these quantities into the template.

3.   Create [Quantity 1] according to the specifications in the key. Insert this quantity into the template.

Template Key

Person A: A person or other entity (for example, Mr. Zody, bakery, Stephanie).

Select: Any act of selection, acquisition, or designation (for example, bought, sold, picked).

Quantity 1: A two-digit whole number evenly divisible by the sum of [Quantity 2], [Quantity 3], and [Quantity 4].

Quantity 2: A single-digit whole number.

Quantity 3: A single-digit whole number.

Quantity 4: A single-digit whole number.

Item Type A: Any type of object (for example, flowers, cupcakes, neckties).

Item Subtype A: A unique variation of [Item Type A] (for example, lilies, chocolate cupcakes, striped ties).

Item Subtype B: A unique variation of [Item Type A] (for example, roses, vanilla cupcakes, polka-dot ties).

Item Subtype C: A unique variation of [Item Type A] (for example, daisies, red velvet cupcakes, plain ties).

Group A: A group of [Item Type A] (for example, bouquet, box of cupcakes, package of ties).

Template

[Person A] [Select] [Quantity 1] [Item Type A]. The [Item Type A] come in [Group A]. Each [Group A] came with [Quantity 2] [Item Subtype A], [Quantity 3] [Item Subtype B], and [Quantity 4] [Item Subtype C].

How many [Item Type A] were in each [Group A]? Show your work.

How many [Group A] did [Person A] [Select]? Show your work.

Quantity and Number

Comparison

Sample Item

Two comparisons are shown.

$$\frac{\square}{\square} < \frac{1}{4}$$

$$\frac{\square}{\square} > \frac{1}{8}$$

Fill in one fraction that makes both comparisons true.

Template Instructions

1. Select [Quantity 1] through [Quantity 3]. Insert them into the template.

Template Key

Quantity 1: A whole number.

Quantity 2: Either 2, 3, 4, 6, or 8. This must be at least two less than [Quantity 3].

Quantity 3: Either 2, 3, 4, 6, or 8.

Template

Two comparisons are shown.

$$\frac{\square}{\square} < \frac{[\text{Quantity 1}]}{[\text{Quantity 2}]}$$

$$\frac{\square}{\square} > \frac{[\text{Quantity 1}]}{[\text{Quantity 3}]}$$

Fill in one fraction that makes both comparisons true.

┌─────────────────────────┐
│   │
└─────────────────────────┘

Equivalence

Sample Item

Which statements are true?

Select the **three** correct answers.

A. $3 \times 7 = 2 \times 9$

B. $45 \div 9 = 25 \div 5$

C. $8 \times 3 = 6 \times 4$

D. $32 \div 8 = 36 \div 9$

E. $2 \times 8 = 3 \times 5$

Template Instructions

1.   Select [Quantity]. Insert it into the template.

2.   Create [Answer 1] through [Answer 5]. Insert them into the template.

Template Key

Quantity: A whole number between two and four.

Answers 1–5: Equations with a single multiplication or division expression on each side. Expressions should contain only one- and two-digit positive integers. Each equation should contain only multiplication or only division expressions and care should be taken that any division expressions produce quotients without remainders. [Quantity] of the equations should be true and the rest should be false.

Template

Which statements are true?

Select the **[Quantity]** correct answers.

A.   [Answer 1]

B.   [Answer 2]

C.   [Answer 3]

D.   [Answer 4]

E.   [Answer 5]

Fractions

Sample Item

A model is divided into 10 equal parts. Which model shows the correct shading of $\frac{7}{10}$?

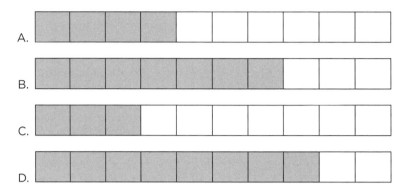

Template Instructions

1. Select [Quantity 1]. Insert it into the template.

2. Select [Quantity 2]. Insert it into the template.

3. Create four different tape diagrams, each divided into [Quantity 1] equal cells. Shade a different number of adjacent cells in each diagram. One of the diagrams should have [Quantity 2] cells shaded. Insert each diagram in place of a box in the template.

Template Key

Quantity 1: A whole number between two and ten.

Quantity 2: A whole number less than or equal to [Quantity 1].

Template

A model is divided into [Quantity 1] equal parts. Which model shows the correct shading of $\frac{[\text{Quantity 2}]}{[\text{Quantity 1}]}$?

A.

B.

C.

D.

Number Lines

Sample Item

Fill in the fraction located at Point *A* on the number line.

Template Instructions

1. Create a number line ranging from zero to one. Tick marks should divide the number line into halves, thirds, fourths, sixths, or eighths. Label one of the tick marks as point A.

Template Key

(Not applicable)

Template

Fill in the fraction located at Point *A* on the number line:

Grade 4

Geometry

2-D and 3-D Shapes

Sample Item

Draw all the lines of symmetry for the shape. If there are no lines of symmetry, write *None*.

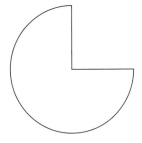

Template Instructions

1. Create a closed two-dimensional figure. Insert the shape into the template in place of the box.

Template Key

(Not applicable)

Template

Draw all the lines of symmetry for the shape. If there are no lines of symmetry, write *None*.

Area and Perimeter

Sample Item

The area of a rectangular field is 136 square meters.

The field has a width of 8 meters, as shown in the diagram.

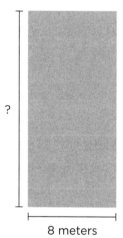

?

8 meters

Fill in the length, in meters, of the field.

Template Instructions

1. Choose definitions for [Object] and [Unit]. Insert them into the template.

2. Select [Quantity 1] and [Quantity 2]. Insert them into the template.

3. Create a rectangle with a labeled width of [Quantity 2] [Unit]. Insert it into the template in place of the box.

Template Key

Object: An object that can exist in the shape of a rectangle (for example, field, TV screen, billboard).

Unit: A unit of length (for example, meters, feet, inches).

Quantity 1: Positive two- or three-digit integer multiple of [Quantity 2].

Quantity 2: Positive one-digit integer factor of [Quantity 1].

Template

The area of a rectangular [Object] is [Quantity 1] square [Unit].

The [Object] has a width of [Quantity 2] [Unit] as shown in the diagram.

Fill in the length, in [Unit], of the [Object].

Lines and Angles

Sample Item

Some angles are shown.

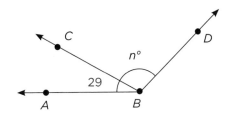

Part A

The measure of angle *ABD* is 135°. Which of these equations could be used to find the measure of angle *CBD*?

A. $29 + n = 135$

B. $n - 29 = 135$

    C. $29 \times n = 135$

    D. $135 \div n = 29$

Part B

Fill in the measure, in degrees, of angle *CBD*.

┌─────────────┐
│   │
└─────────────┘

Template Instructions

1.   Select [Quantity 1] and [Quantity 2]. Insert them into the template.

2.   Create a labeled diagram of an angle, *ABD*, of [Quantity 1]°.

3.   Create a ray, *BC*, to create an angle, *ABC*, of [Quantity 2]° inside angle *ABD*. Label the measure of this angle [Quantity 2]°. Label the measure of angle *CBD n*°.

4.   Insert the complete angle diagram into the template in place of the box.

Template Key

Quantity 1: A positive integer less than or equal to 180.

Quantity 2: A positive integer less than [Quantity 1].

Template

Some angles are shown.

Part A

The measure of angle *ABD* is [Quantity 1]°. Which of these equations could be used to find the measure of angle *CBD*?

    A.   [Quantity 2] + n = [Quantity 1]

    B. n – [Quantity 2] = [Quantity 1]

    C.   [Quantity 2] × n = [Quantity 1]

    D.   [Quantity 1] ÷ n = [Quantity 2]

Part B

Fill in the measure, in degrees, of angle *CBD*.

┌─────────────┐
│   │
└─────────────┘

Operations

Addition

Sample Item

Fill in your answer in the box.

6,378 + 5,017 = ☐

Template Instructions

1.   Select [Quantity 1] and [Quantity 2]. Insert them into the template.

Template Key

Quantity 1: A positive four-digit integer.

Quantity 2: A positive four-digit integer.

Template

Fill in your answer in the box.

[Quantity 1] + [Quantity 2] = ☐

Division

Sample Item

Fill in the missing numbers to complete the division problem.

Enter your answers in the spaces provided.

9,023 ÷ 8 = ☐

Remainder: ☐

Template Instructions

Select [Quantity 1] and [Quantity 2]. Insert them into the template.

Template Key

Quantity 1: A positive four-digit integer not evenly divisible by [Quantity 2].

Quantity 2: A positive single-digit integer.

Template

Fill in the missing numbers to complete the division problem.

Enter your answers in the spaces provided.

[Quantity 1] ÷ [Quantity 2] = [   ]

Remainder = [   ]

Multiples and Factors

Sample Item

Select the **three** choices that are factor pairs for the number 84.

- A.   3 and 28
- B.   4 and 21
- C.   6 and 13
- D.   7 and 12
- E.   8 and 11
- F.   9 and 8

Template Instructions

1. Select [Quantity]. Insert it into the template.
2. Select three correct factor pairs of [Quantity].
3. Create three alternate incorrect factor pairs of [Quantity].
4. Insert the correct factor pairs and the incorrect factor pairs randomly into the template as [Factor 1] through [Factor 12].

Template Key

Quantity: A positive integer under 100, having at least three factor pairs.

Factors 1–12: Pairs of positive integers.

Template

Select the **three** choices that are factor pairs for the number [Quantity].

- A.   [Factor 1] and [Factor 2]
- B.   [Factor 3] and [Factor 4]
- C.   [Factor 5] and [Factor 6]
- D.   [Factor 7] and [Factor 8]
- E.   [Factor 9] and [Factor 10]
- F.   [Factor 11] and [Factor 12]

Multiplication

Sample Item

Part A

Using properties of operations, explain why the expression 5 × (6,000 + 300 + 90 + 7) can or cannot be used to find the value of 6,397 × 5.

Provide your answer and your explanation.

Part B

Write a new expression that can be used to find the value of 6,397 × 5.

Provide your expression in the space provided.

Part C

What is the value of 6,397 × 5?

Fill in your answer in the box.

```
┌─────────────────┐
│                 │
└─────────────────┘
```

Template Instructions

1. Select [Term 1] and [Term 6]. Insert them into the template.

2. Select [Term 2] through [Term 5]. Insert them into the template.

Template Key

Term 1: A positive single-digit integer.

Term 2: A positive four-digit integer with the thousands digit of [Term 6] in the thousands place and zeroes in every other place.

Term 3: A positive three-digit integer with the hundreds digit of [Term 6] in the hundreds place and zeroes in every other place.

Term 4: A positive two-digit integer with the tens digit of [Term 6] in the tens place and a zero in the ones place.

Term 5: The ones digit of [Term 6].

Term 6: A positive four-digit integer.

Template

Part A

Using properties of operations, explain why the expression [Term 1] × ([Term 2] + [Term 3] + [Term 4] + [Term 5]) can or cannot be used to find the value of [Term 6] × [Term 1].

Provide your answer and your explanation.

Part B

Write a new expression that can be used to find the value of [Term 6] × [Term 1].

Provide your expression in the space provided.

Part C

What is the value of [Term 6] × [Term 1]?

Fill in your answer in the box.

☐

Subtraction

Sample Item

Solve.

Fill in your answer in the box.

5,394 − 2,938 = ☐

Template Instructions

Select [Term 1] and [Term 2]. Insert them into the template.

Template Key

Term 1: A positive four-digit integer.

Term 2: A positive four-digit integer less than [Term 1].

Template

Solve.

Fill in your answer in the box.

[Term 1] − [Term 2] = ☐

Operation Not Specified

Sample Item

Represent the statement "17 times as many as 10 is 170" as an equation.

Fill in a number or symbol from the following list in each box to create the equation. Do not use any number or symbol more than once.

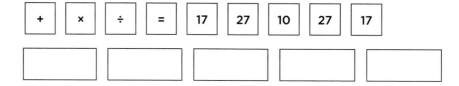

Template Instructions

1. Select [Quantity 1]. Insert it into the template.

2. Calculate [Quantity 2] and [Quantity 3]. Insert them into the template.

Template Key

Quantity 1: A positive two-digit integer, and a factor of [Quantity 3].

Quantity 2: The sum of [Quantity 1] and 10.

Quantity 3: The product of [Quantity 1] and 10.

Template

Represent the statement "[Quantity 1] times as many as 10 is [Quantity 3]" as an equation.

Fill in a number or symbol from the following list in each box to create the equation. Do not use any number or symbol more than once.

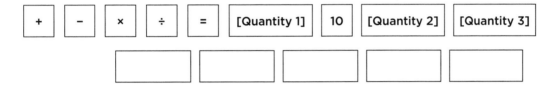

Quantity and Number

Comparison

Sample Item

Part A

Check the correct box in each row to show whether each fraction is less than or greater than $\frac{6}{10}$.

Fraction	Less than $\frac{6}{10}$	Greater than $\frac{6}{10}$
$\frac{1}{2}$	☐	☐
$\frac{9}{12}$	☐	☐
$\frac{5}{8}$	☐	☐
$\frac{30}{100}$	☐	☐

Part B

Circle the correct symbol to correctly complete each comparison.

$\frac{1}{2}$ < , > , = $\frac{9}{12}$

$\frac{9}{12}$ < , > , = $\frac{30}{100}$

$\frac{5}{8}$ < , > , = $\frac{30}{100}$

Template Instructions

1. Select [Fraction 1]. Insert it into the template.

2. Select [Fraction 2] through [Fraction 5]. Insert them into the template.

Template Key

Fraction 1: A proper fraction with an up-to-two-digit numerator and a denominator of either 2, 3, 4, 5, 6, 8, 10, 12, or 100.

Fractions 2–5: Unique proper fractions with denominators of either 2, 3, 4, 5, 6, 8, 10, 12, or 100. Denominators should be different from that of [Fraction 1], and the fractions should be not equal to [Fraction 1].

Template

Part A

Check the correct box in each row to show whether each fraction is less than or greater than [Fraction 1].

Fraction	Less than [Fraction 1]	Greater than [Fraction 1]
[Fraction 2]	☐	☐
[Fraction 3]	☐	☐
[Fraction 4]	☐	☐
[Fraction 5]	☐	☐

Part B

Circle the correct symbol to correctly complete each comparison.

[Fraction 2] < , > , = [Fraction 3]

[Fraction 3] < , > , = [Fraction 4]

[Fraction 4] < , > , = [Fraction 5]

Equivalence

Sample Item

Determine whether each expression is equivalent to $6 \times \frac{4}{5}$. Check the correct box in each row of the table.

	Equal to $6 \times \frac{4}{5}$	Not Equal to $6 \times \frac{4}{5}$
$4 \times \frac{6}{5}$	☐	☐
$5 \times \frac{4}{6}$	☐	☐
$24 \times \frac{1}{5}$	☐	☐

Template Instructions

1. Choose [Quantity 1] and [Quantity 2]. Insert them into the template.

2. Choose [Quantity 3]. Insert it into the template.

3. Calculate [Quantity 4]. Insert it into the template.

Template Key

Quantity 1: Either 2, 3, 4, 5, 6, 8, 10, 12, or 100.

Quantity 2: A positive single-digit integer.

Quantity 3: Either 2, 3, 4, 5, 6, 8, 10, 12, or 100. This value should be greater than [Quantity 2].

Quantity 4: The product of [Quantity 1] and [Quantity 2].

Template

Determine whether each expression is equivalent to $[Quantity 1] \times \frac{[Quantity 2]}{[Quantity 3]}$. Check the correct box in each row of the table.

	Equal to $[Quantity 1] \times \frac{[Quantity 2]}{[Quantity 3]}$	Not Equal to $[Quantity 1] \times \frac{[Quantity 2]}{[Quantity 3]}$
$[Quantity 2] \times \frac{[Quantity 1]}{[Quantity 3]}$	☐	☐
$[Quantity 3] \times \frac{[Quantity 2]}{[Quantity 3]}$	☐	☐
$[Quantity 4] \times \frac{1}{[Quantity 3]}$	☐	☐

Place Value

Sample Item

What is the expanded form of 7,419,083?

   A.   7,000,000 + 400,000 + 10,000 + 9,000 + 800 + 30

   B.   7,000,000 + 400,000 + 10,000 + 9,000 + 80 + 3

   C.   7,000,000 + 400,000 + 10,000 + 9,000 + 100 + 80 + 3

   D.   700,000 + 40,000 + 1,000 + 900 + 803

Template Instructions

   1.   Choose [Quantity]. Insert it into the template.

   2.   Create the correct expanded form of [Quantity].

   3.   Choose definitions for [Answer 1] through [Answer 4]. Insert them into
        the template.

Template Key

Quantity: A multi-digit positive integer with no more than seven digits (for example,
7,419,083).

Answers 1–4: Multi-digit positive integers written in expanded form, using the same
numerals as [Quantity] (for example, 7,000,000 + 400,000 + 10,000 + 9,000 + 80 + 3).
One of these is the correct answer.

Template

What is the expanded form of [Quantity]?

   A.   [Answer 1]

   B.   [Answer 2]

   C.   [Answer 3]

   D.   [Answer 4]

Grade 5

Expressions, Equations, Inequalities, and Functions (EEIF)

Expressions

Sample Item

Which expression correctly shows the quotient of the sum of 43 and 27 and the difference of 92 and 64?

A. $(43 \div 27) + (92 - 64)$

B. $43 \div 27 + 92 - 64$

C. $43 + (27 \div 92) - 64$

D. $(43 + 27) \div (92 - 64)$

Template Instructions

1. Select [Operation 1] through [Operation 3]. Insert them into the template.

2. Select [Quantity 1] through [Quantity 4]. Insert them into the template.

3. Create [Answer 1] through [Answer 4]. Insert them into the template.

Template Key

Operations 1–3: Three of the following four terms—*sum, difference, product,* and *quotient.* Each term should be used no more than once.

Quantities 1–4: Positive integers.

Answers 1–4: Expressions involving [Quantity 1] through [Quantity 4] using various combinations of the four operations and parentheses. One of these is the correct answer.

Template

Which expression correctly shows the [Operation 1] of the [Operation 2] of [Quantity 1] and [Quantity 2] and the [Operation 3] of [Quantity 3] and [Quantity 4]?

A. [Answer 1]

B. [Answer 2]

C. [Answer 3]

D. [Answer 4]

Geometry

Volume

Sample Item

A shipping container is in the shape of a right rectangular prism.

- The area of the base of the shipping container is 68 square feet.

- The height of the shipping container is 40 feet.

Fill in the volume, in cubic feet, of the shipping container.

Template Instructions

1. Choose definitions for [Object] and [Unit]. Insert them into the template.

2. Select [Quantity 1] and [Quantity 2]. Insert them into the template.

Template Key

Object: An object that is typically in the shape of a right rectangular prism (for example, shipping container, refrigerator, bookshelf)

Quantities 1–2: Whole numbers

Unit: A unit of length (for example, feet, meters, yards)

Template

An [Object] is in the shape of a right rectangular prism.

- The area of the base of the [Object] is [Quantity 1] square [Unit].

- The height of the [Object] is [Quantity 2] [Unit].

Fill in the volume, in cubic [Unit], of the [Object].

Area and Perimeter

Sample Item

The height of a road sign is $1\frac{5}{12}$ meters. The width of the sign is $2\frac{1}{3}$ meters.

What is the area, in square meters, of the road sign?

Fill in your answer in the box.

Template Instructions

1. Choose definitions for [Object] and [Unit]. Insert them into the template.

2. Select [Quantity 1] and [Quantity 2]. Insert them into the template.

Template Key

Object: A rectangular object (for example, road sign, cell phone, whiteboard)

Quantities 1–2: Mixed numbers

Unit: A unit of length (for example, meters, inches, feet)

Template

The height of [Object] is [Quantity 1] [Unit]. The width of [Object] is [Quantity 2] [Unit].

What is the area, in square [Unit], of [Object]?

Fill in your answer in the box.

[   ]

2-D and 3-D Shapes

Sample Item

Which of these figures are quadrilaterals but **not** trapezoids?

Select the **three** correct figures.

A.

D.

B.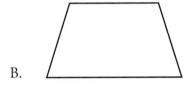

E.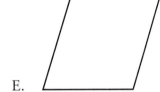

C.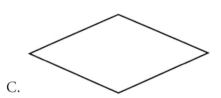

F.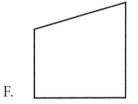

Template Instructions

1. Choose a definition for [Subcategory]. Insert it into the template.

2. Create [Shape 1] through [Shape 6]. Insert each shape into the template in place of one of the boxes.

Template Key

Subcategory: A subcategory of quadrilateral (for example, trapezoids, parallelograms, rhombi)

Shapes 1–6: Various polygons. Three should be non-[Subcategory] quadrilaterals

Template

Which of these figures are quadrilaterals but **not** [Subcategory]?

Select the **three** correct figures.

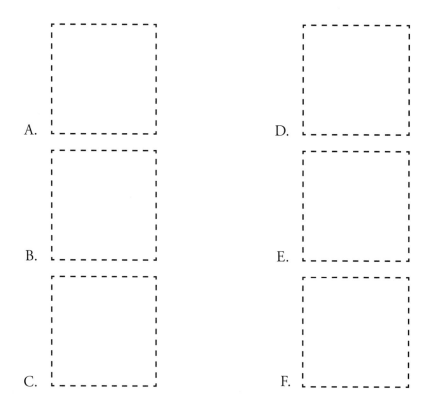

A.   D.

B.   E.

C.   F.

Operations

Operation Not Specified

Sample Item

A soda fountain dispenses 112 total cups of soda each day. There are three different sizes of cup.

- The small cup holds 12 ounces of soda, and $\frac{1}{8}$ of the cups are small.

- The medium cup holds 16 ounces of soda, and $\frac{3}{4}$ of the cups are medium.

- The large cup holds 24 ounces of soda, and the rest of the cups are large.

Determine how many of each size of cup are needed each day. Then determine how many ounces of soda are needed to fill the 112 cups. Show your work or explain your answers.

Template Instructions

1. Choose definitions for [Entity], [Produces], [Container], [Item], and [Time]. Insert them into the template.

2. Select [Quantity 1], [Fraction 1], and [Fraction 2]. Insert them into the template.

3. Select [Quantity 2] through [Quantity 4]. Insert them into the template.

Template Key

Entity: Something that produces or distributes containers of a particular item (for example, soda fountain, fast food restaurant, tile factory)

Produces: An act of production or distribution (for example, dispenses, makes, manufactures)

Container: A container that can hold multiple items (for example, cup, box, crate)

Item: An item that fits in [Container] (for example, ounces of soda, chicken nuggets, tiles)

Time: A unit of time (for example, day, week, month)

Quantity 1: A multi-digit whole number evenly divisible by the denominators of [Fractions 1–2]

Quantities 2–4: Single- or double-digit whole numbers, so [Quantity 2] is less than [Quantity 3], and [Quantity 3] is less than [Quantity 4]

Fractions 1–2: Positive fractions so the sum of [Fraction 1] and [Fraction 2] is less than 1

Template

[Entity] [Produces] [Quantity 1] total [Container] of [Item] each [Time]. There are three different sizes of [Container].

- The small [Container] holds [Quantity 2] [Item], and [Fraction 1] of the total [Container] are small.

- The medium [Container] holds [Quantity 3] [Item], and [Fraction 2] of the total [Container] are medium.

- The large [Container] holds [Quantity 4] [Item], and the rest of the total [Container] are large.

Determine how many of each size of [Container] are needed each [Time]. Then determine how many [Item] are needed to fill the [Quantity 1] [Container]. Show your work or explain your answers.

Multiplication

Sample Item

What is the product of $\frac{4}{9} \times \frac{16}{5}$?

- A. $\frac{64}{45}$

- B. $\frac{20}{14}$

- C. $\frac{20}{45}$

- D. $\frac{64}{14}$

Template Instructions

1. Select [Fraction 1] and [Fraction 2]. Insert them into the template.

2. Select [Answer 1] through [Answer 4]. Insert them into the template.

Template Key

Fractions 1–2: Positive fractions

Answers 1–4: Positive fractions, one of which is the product of [Fraction 1] and [Fraction 2]

Template

What is the product of [Fraction 1] × [Fraction 2]?

    A.   [Answer 1]

    B.   [Answer 2]

    C.   [Answer 3]

    D.   [Answer 4]

Addition

Sample Item

Fill in your answer in the box.

6.89 + 3.561 = ☐

Template Instructions

1. Select [Quantity 1] and [Quantity 2]. Insert them into the template.

Template Key

Quantities 1–2: Positive decimal values with up to three decimal places

Template

Fill in your answer in the box.

[Quantity 1] + [Quantity 2] = ☐

Division

Sample Item

Fill in your answer in the box.

4,941 ÷ 27 = ☐

Template Instructions

1. Select [Quantity 1] and [Quantity 2]. Insert them into the template.

Template Key

Quantity 1: A multi-digit whole number that is evenly divisible by [Quantity 2]

Quantity 2: A multi-digit whole number that is a factor of [Quantity 1]

Template

Fill in your answer in the box.

[Quantity 1] ÷ [Quantity 2] =

Quantity and Number

Coordinate Plane

Sample Item

Brian and Emmy are at the convenience store. They plan to go to the movie theater. The locations of the convenience store and the movie theater are plotted on the coordinate grid.

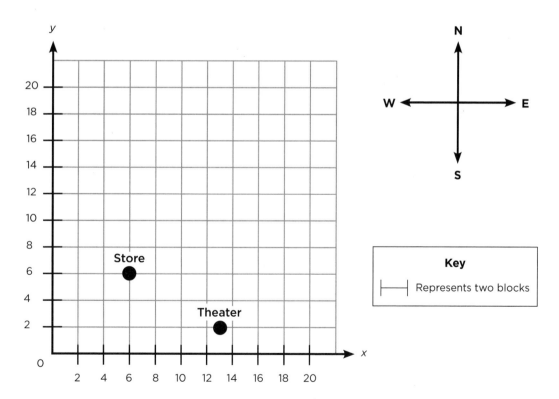

Brian suggests going 7 blocks east and 2 blocks south.

Emmy suggests going 4 blocks east, 4 blocks south, and 3 blocks east.

Which suggested route is the shortest way to get from the convenience store to the movie theater?

   A.   Brian's

   B.   Emmy's

   C.   Both Brian and Emmy's because each route is the same distance

   D.   Neither Brian nor Emmy's because neither route ends at the movie theater

Template Instructions

1.   Create a coordinate plane displaying only Quadrant I. The grid lines of the plane should represent intervals of more than one whole-number unit, and the plane should be accompanied by a key showing its scale and a compass rose showing the cardinal directions.

2.   Choose definitions for [Person 1], [Person 2], [Place 1], and [Place 2]. Insert them into the template.

3.   Create two points on the coordinate plane. One point should lie at an intersection of the horizontal and vertical grid lines while the other point should lie on either a horizontal grid line or a vertical grid line, but not both. The two points should not share x- or y-coordinates (that is, should not lie on the same horizontal or vertical grid line). Label one point as [Place 1] and the other point as [Place 2].

4.   Choose definitions for [Route 1] and [Route 2]. Insert them into the template.

Template Key

Person 1: An individual (for example, Brian, Jordan, Emmy)

Person 2: A second individual (for example, Rebecca, Jim, Andre)

Place 1: A location (for example, a convenience store, a home, a coffee shop)

Place 2: A different location than [Place 1] (for example, a movie theater, a school, a park)

Routes 1–2: Routes on the coordinate plane that begin at [Place 1] and end either at [Place 2] or elsewhere on the coordinate plane

Template

[Person 1] and [Person 2] are at [Place 1]. They plan to go to [Place 2]. The locations of [Place 1] and [Place 2] are plotted on the coordinate grid.

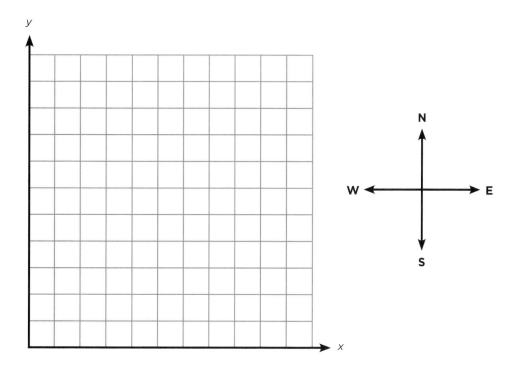

[Person 1] suggests going [Route 1].

[Person 2] suggests going [Route 2].

Which suggested route is the shortest way to get from [Place 1] to [Place 2]?

1. [Person 1]'s

2. [Person 2]'s

3. Both [Person 1] and [Person 2]'s, because each route is the same distance

4. Neither [Person 1] nor [Person 2]'s, because neither route ends at [Place 2]

Equivalence

Sample Item

Select the expression with a value equivalent to 10^5.

A. $5 \times 5 \times 5 \times 5 \times 5 \times 5 \times 5 \times 5 \times 5 \times 5$

B. 10×5

C. $10 \times 10 \times 10 \times 10 \times 10$

D. $10 + 5$

Template Instructions

1. Select [Exponent]. Insert it into the template.

2. Create [Answer 1] through [Answer 4]. Insert them into the template.

Template Key

Exponent: A whole number

Answers 1–4: Four expressions, each taking one of the following forms.

1.   10 + [Exponent]

2.   10 × [Exponent]

3.   10 × 10 × . . . (repeated for a total of [Exponent] terms)

4.   [Exponent] × [Exponent] × . . . (repeated for a total of 10 terms)

Template

Select the expression with a value equivalent to $10^{[Exponent]}$.

A.   [Answer 1]

B.   [Answer 2]

C.   [Answer 3]

D.   [Answer 4]

Place Value

Sample Item

In which number does the digit 6 have a value 10,000 times less than the digit 6 in the number 16,303,598.21?

A.   2,487,605.091

B.   68,455

C.   74,098,156.038

D.   924,161.4

Template Instructions

1.   Select [Digit], [Power of Ten], and [Greater or Less]. Insert them into the template.

2.   Select [Quantity]. Insert it into the template.

3.   Select [Answer 1] through [Answer 4]. Insert them into the template.

Template Key

Digit: A single-digit whole number

Power of Ten: A power of ten

Greater or Less: Either greater or less

Quantity: A multi-digit whole number or decimal value that includes [Digit] as one of the digits

Answers 1–4: Multi-digit whole numbers or decimal values that include [Digit] as one of the digits, with one of the values being the correct answer

Template

In which number does the digit [Digit] have a value [Power of Ten] times [Greater or Less] than the digit [Digit] in the number [Quantity]?

A. [Answer 1]

B. [Answer 2]

C. [Answer 3]

D. [Answer 4]

Comparison

Sample Item

The table shows the beam diameter of four lasers.

Laser	Beam Diameter (meters)
Beam 1	0.0016
Beam 2	0.0008
Beam 3	0.0045
Beam 4	0.0020

Fill in the empty boxes with the following symbols and numbers to create correct comparisons. Use each number and symbol no more than once.

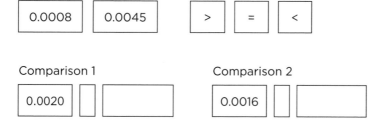

Template Instructions

1. Choose definitions for [Item], [Item Type 1] through [Item Type 4], [Measurement], and [Unit]. Insert them into the template.

2. Select [Quantity 1] through [Quantity 4]. Insert them into the template.

Template Key

Item: An object, person, or other entity with a dimension or characteristic you can express in decimal values (for example, laser, 100-meter runner, centipede)

Item Types 1–4: Unique variations of [Item] (for example, Beam 1, Usain, Centipede 1)

Measurement: A dimension or characteristic you can measure in decimal values (for example, beam diameter, race times, length)

Unit: A unit of measurement corresponding to [Measurement] (for example, meters, seconds, inches)

Quantities 1–4: Decimal values with equivalent values on the left side of the decimal point and the same number of decimal places

Template

The table shows the [Measurement] of four [Item].

[Item]	[Measurement] ([Unit])
[Item Type 1]	[Quantity 1]
[Item Type 2]	[Quantity 2]
[Item Type 3]	[Quantity 3]
[Item Type 4]	[Quantity 4]

Fill in the empty boxes with the following symbols and numbers to create correct comparisons. Use each number and symbol no more than once.

| [Quantity 2] | [Quantity 3] | | > | = | < |

Comparison 1

| [Quantity 4] | | |

Comparison 2

| [Quantity 1] | | |

Grade 6

Expressions, Equations, Inequalities, and Functions (EEIF)

Equations

Sample Item

The variable n represents a value in the set {2,8,10,14}. Which value of n makes $2(n - 4) + 7 = 19$ a true statement?

A.   2

B.   8

C.   10

D.   14

Template Instructions

1.   Choose a definition for [Variable]. Insert it into the template.

2.   Select a whole-number value for [Variable].

3.   Create [Equation]. Insert it into the template.

4.   Create three alternative solutions for the equation that are incorrect.

5.   Select [Quantity 1] through [Quantity 4]. Insert them into the template.

Template Key

Variable: Any variable (for example, x, n, r).

Quantity 1–4: Whole numbers; one of these is the correct value of [Variable].

Equation: An equation of the form $a(x + b) + c = d$ in which a and d are whole number constants; c is a positive or negative integer constant; b is a positive or negative integer constant such that $x + b > 0$; and x is [Variable].

Template

The variable [Variable] represents a value in the set {[Quantity 1], [Quantity 2], [Quantity 3], [Quantity 4]}. Which value of [Variable] makes [Equation] a true statement?

A.   [Quantity 1]

B.   [Quantity 2]

C.   [Quantity 3]

D.   [Quantity 4]

Expressions

Sample Item

The cost of hiring a junk removal company is $80. An additional $0.30 is charged for each pound of junk, p, the company removes. Which expression can you use to determine the total cost, in dollars, of hiring the junk removal company?

A. $80p - 0.30$

B. $80 + 0.30p$

C. $0.30 - 80p$

D. $0.30 + 80p$

Template Instructions

1. Choose a definition for [Purchase] and [Use of Purchase]. Insert them into the template.

2. Choose a definition for [Unit]. Insert it into the template.

3. Choose a definition for [Variable]. Insert it into the template.

4. Select [Quantity 1]. Insert it into the template.

5. Select [Quantity 2]. Insert it into the template.

6. Create [Expression 1] through [Expression 4]. Insert them into the template.

Template Key

Purchase: Any purchase that involves an initial cost plus an additional cost per use of the purchase (for example, renting a vehicle, junk removal, purchasing a pizza)

Use of Purchase: A use or modification of [Purchase] that adds additional costs per unit on top of the initial cost of [Purchase] (for example, miles driven, pounds of junk removed, additional toppings added)

Unit: Any unit relative to which [Use of Purchase] involves additional cost (for example, miles, pounds, additional toppings)

Variable: Any variable (for example, m, p, t) used to represent [Unit]

Quantity 1: A whole number that is the initial cost of [Purchase]

Quantity 2: A positive decimal value in hundredths that is the additional cost per [Unit] of [Use of Purchase]

Expressions 1–4: Possible expressions modeling the total cost of [Purchase], including additional costs incurred by [Use of Purchase], that take the form in which a and b are either [Quantity 1] or [Quantity 2] and x is [Variable]; one of these is the correct expression.

Template

The cost of [Purchase] is $[Quantity 1]. An additional $[Quantity 2] is charged for each [Unit], [Variable], [Use of Purchase]. Which expression can you use to determine the total cost, in dollars, of [Purchase]?

A. [Expression 1]

B. [Expression 2]

C. [Expression 3]

D. [Expression 4]

Geometry

Area and Perimeter

Sample Item

Part A

A figure shows the given dimensions.

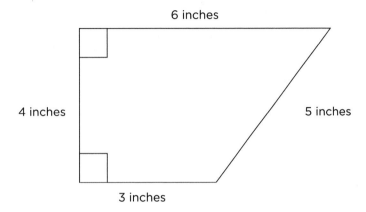

Which expressions can you use to determine the area, in square inches, of this figure?

Select **each** correct expression.

A. $(3 \times 4) + (6 \times 5)$

B. $(6 \times 4) - \frac{5 \times 4}{2}$

C. $(3 \times 4) + \frac{3 \times 4}{2}$

D. $(3 \times 4) + \frac{1}{2}(5 \times 3)$

E. $(6 \times 4) - \frac{1}{2}(3 \times 4)$

F. $(3 \times 4) + (6 + 5)$

Part B

What is the area, in square inches, of the figure?

Fill in your answer in the box.

_____ square inches

Template Instructions

1. Create a quadrilateral with two right angles and two non-right angles.

2. Select a length unit for the measurement of the side lengths of the quadrilateral from step 1 and insert it into the template as [Unit].

3. Select value [a] through value [d] for the side lengths of the quadrilateral from step 1.

4. Insert the created quadrilateral into the template in place of the box and label the sides with value [a] through value [d] and [Unit].

5. Create [Expression 1] through [Expression 6]. Insert them into the template.

Template Key

Expressions 1–6: Different possible expressions that may model the area of the quadrilateral created in step 1 of the instructions; two of these should correctly model the area.

Unit: Any unit of length measurement (for example, inches, feet, meters)

a–d: Any whole numbers that represent possible side lengths of the quadrilateral created in step 1 of the instructions

Template

Part A

A figure shows the given dimensions.

Which expressions can you use to determine the area, in square [Unit], of this figure?

Select **each** correct expression.

A. [Expression 1]

B. [Expression 2]

C. [Expression 3]

D. [Expression 4]

E. [Expression 5]

F. [Expression 6]

Part B

What is the area, in square [Unit], of the figure?

Fill in your answer in the box.

[   ] square [Unit]

Volume

Sample Item

This solid was created by joining 3 right rectangular prisms.

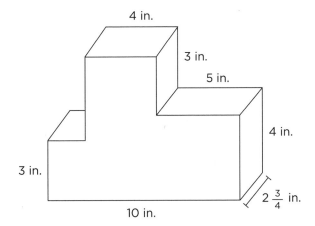

In the following box, fill in the volume of the solid in cubic inches.

| | cubic inches
|---|

Template Instructions

1. Create a 3-D rectilinear figure that is a composition of two or more rectangular prisms. Insert it into the template in place of the box.

2. Identify [Quantity]. Insert it into the template.

3. Choose a definition for [Unit]. Insert it into the template.

4. Select various distinct whole- or mixed-number values for the side lengths of the created figure. Include at least one mixed number. Label most, but not all, of the side lengths of the figure in [Unit]. Some side lengths should be left unlabeled, and care should be taken so it is possible to determine the lengths of the unlabeled sides by performing calculations on the labeled side lengths.

Template Key

Unit: Any unit of length measurement (for example, centimeters, inches, feet)

Quantity: A whole number corresponding to the number of rectangular prisms combined to create the rectilinear figure from step 1

Template

This solid was created by joining [Quantity] right rectangular prisms.

In the following box, fill in the volume of the solid in cubic [Unit].

[   ] cubic [Unit]

Operations

Division

Sample Item

What is the value of 12,105 ÷ 36?

Fill in your answer in the box.

[   ]

Template Instructions

1. Select [Quantity 1]. Insert it into the template.
2. Select [Quantity 2]. Insert it into the template.

Template Key

Quantity 1: Any multi-digit whole number

Quantity 2: Any multi-digit whole number greater than [Quantity 1]; care should be taken that, if [Quantity 2] ÷ [Quantity 1] results in a decimal value, the decimal should not be overly long.

Template

What is the value of [Quantity 2] ÷ [Quantity 1]?

Fill in your answer in the box.

[   ]

Operation Not Specified

Sample Item

Megan has a recipe for a bowl of fruit salad.

> **Fruit Salad**
>
> $3\frac{1}{2}$ cups grapes
>
> $1\frac{3}{4}$ cups diced pineapple
>
> $1\frac{1}{4}$ cups sliced kiwi
>
> $2\frac{1}{2}$ cups sliced strawberries

Part A

Megan estimates that each serving is $\frac{3}{4}$ cup of fruit salad.

How many bowls will Megan need to make 12 servings? Show or explain all the steps you use to answer the question.

Fill in your answer in the following space.

Part B

How much of each fruit will Megan need to make 12 servings? Show or explain all the steps you use to answer the question.

Fill in your answer in the space provided.

Template Instructions

1. Choose definitions for [Person], [Mix], [Mix Unit], [Portion], [Ingredient], [Ingredient 1] through [Ingredient 4], and [Unit]. Insert them into the template.

2. Select values for [Quantity 1] through [Quantity 5]. Insert them into the template.

3. Select a value for [Quantity 6]. Insert it into the template.

Template Key

Person: Any person or entity creating a product that is a mix of different parts or ingredients in different proportions (for example, Megan, caterer, paint company)

Mix: Any product that is a mix of different parts or ingredients in different proportions (for example, fruit salad, seasoning mix, blended paint color)

Mix Unit: The unit or package in which [Mix] is produced (for example, bowl, batch, quart)

Portion: The unit or package in which [Mix] is used or consumed (for example, serving, container, bucket)

Ingredient: The type of parts being mixed together to form [Mix] (for example, fruit, seasoning, paint color)

Ingredients 1–4: Unique variations of [Ingredient] (for example, pineapple, cayenne pepper, red paint)

Unit: Any standard measurement unit by which [Ingredient] is measured (for example, cup, tablespoon, quart)

Quantities 1–5: Any fraction or mixed number; care should be taken that these quantities do not all have the same denominator.

Quantity 6: Any whole number

Template

[Person] has a recipe for a [Mix Unit] of [Mix].

[Mix]

[Quantity 1] [Unit] [Ingredient 1]

[Quantity 2] [Unit] [Ingredient 2]

[Quantity 3] [Unit] [Ingredient 3]

[Quantity 4] [Unit] [Ingredient 4]

Part A

[Person] estimates that each [Portion] is [Quantity 5] [Unit] of [Mix].

How many [Mix Unit] will [Person] need to make [Quantity 6] [Portion]? Show or explain all the steps you use to answer the question.

Fill in your answer in the following space.

Part B

How much of each [Ingredient] will [Person] need to make [Quantity 6] [Portion]? Show or explain all the steps you use to answer the question.

Fill in your answer in the space provided.

Quantity and Number

Coordinate Plane

Sample Item

The graph shows the location of point J. The x-coordinate of point K is equal to the x-coordinate of point J. The y-coordinate of point K is the opposite of the y-coordinate of point J.

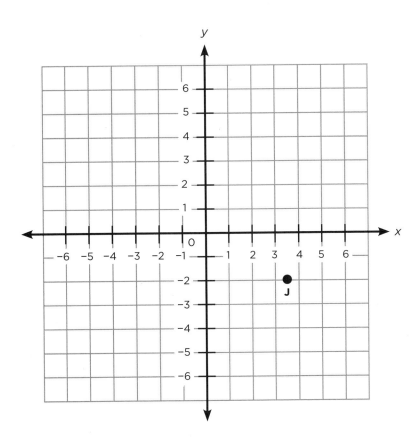

What are the coordinates of point *K*?

A. (–3.5, –2)

B. (3.5, –2)

C. (3.5, 2)

D. (–3.5, 2)

Template Instructions

1. Choose definitions for [A] and [B]. Insert them into the template.

2. Create a coordinate plane containing a single point in any quadrant. The location of the point should include at least one decimal coordinate ending in .5. Label the point as [A].

3. Choose definitions for [Relationship 1] and [Relationship 2]. Insert them into the template.

4. Create [Ordered Pair 1] through [Ordered Pair 4]. Insert them into the template.

Template Key

A: Any variable representing a point on the coordinate plane

B: Any variable representing a point on the coordinate plane

Relationship 1: An equal or opposite relationship between similar coordinates from two separate coordinate pairs (for example, equal to, the opposite of)

Relationship 2: An equal or opposite relationship between similar coordinates from two separate coordinate pairs (for example, equal to, the opposite of). If [Relationship 1] is *equal to*, then this should be *the opposite of*. If [Relationship 1] is *the opposite of*, then this may be either *equal to* or *the opposite of*.

Ordered Pair 1–4: Ordered pairs that represent possible locations on the coordinate plane, consisting of positive or negative coordinates with at least one coordinate of each pair being a decimal value ending in *.5*; one of these is the correct answer.

Template

The graph shows the location of point *[A]*. The *x*-coordinate of point *[B]* is [Relationship 1] the *x*-coordinate of point *[A]*. The *y*-coordinate of point *[B]* is [Relationship 2] the *y*-coordinate of point *[A]*.

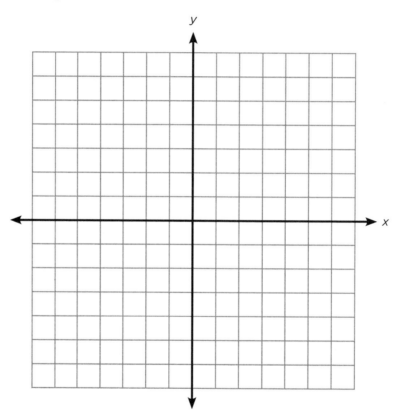

What are the coordinates of point *[B]*?

    A.   [Ordered Pair 1]

    B.   [Ordered Pair 2]

    C.   [Ordered Pair 3]

    D.   [Ordered Pair 4]

Equivalence

Sample Item

Select all the expressions equivalent to $3(7x + 5y)$.

    A. $21x + 5y$

    B. $3(7x) + 3(5y)$

    C. $21x + 15y$

    D. $3(12xy)$

    E. $10x + 8y$

Template Instructions

1. Create [Expression 1]. Insert it into the template.

2. Create [Expression 2] through [Expression 6]. Insert them into the template.

Template Key

Expression 1: An expression of the form $a(bx + cy)$ in which a, b, and c are whole number constants and x and y are variables

Expressions 2–6: Possible equivalent expressions to [Expression 1]; one or more of these, but not all, should be correct answers.

Template

Select all the expressions equivalent to [Expression 1].

    A.   [Expression 2]

    B.   [Expression 3]

    C.   [Expression 4]

    D.   [Expression 5]

    E.   [Expression 6]

Percentages

Sample Item

Angela used 75 percent of the paper plates she purchased for a birthday party. She used 84 paper plates.

Fill in the total number of paper plates she purchased for the party.

Template Instructions

1. Choose definitions for [Person], [Select], [Total Items], and [Item]. Insert them into the template.

2. Select [Quantity 1]. Insert it into the template.

3. Select [Quantity 2]. Insert it into the template.

Template Key

Person: Any person or entity (for example, a hotdog stand, a basketball team, Angela)

Select: Any act of selection or acquisition in which a percentage is selected from the available total (for example, selling hotdogs, scoring points in a game, using paper plates at a party)

Total Items: Any total group of items from which a percentage is selected (for example, total hotdogs prepared, total points scored in a game, paper plates purchased for a birthday party)

Item: The items selected or acquired (for example, hotdogs, points, paper plates)

Quantity 1: Any single- or double-digit whole number representing the percentage of [Item] selected by [Person]

Quantity 2: Any whole number representing the number of [Item] selected or acquired, so $\frac{[Quantity\ 2]}{[Quantity\ 1]} \times 100$ is equal to a whole number

Template

[Person] [Select] [Quantity 1] percent of [Total Items]. [Person] [Select] [Quantity 2] [Item].

Fill in the number of [Total Items].

```
┌─────────────┐
│             │
└─────────────┘
```

Ratios and Proportional Relationships

Rate and Ratio

Sample Item

A car factory produces cars at a constant rate. The factory produces 3,324 cars in 6 days. How many cars did the factory produce in 1 day?

Fill in your answer in the box.

```
┌──────────┐
│          │ cars
└──────────┘
```

Template Instructions

1. Choose definitions for [Person] and [Activity]. Insert them into the template.

2. Choose a definition for [Unit 1]. Insert it into the template.

3. Choose a definition for [Much or Many]. Insert it into the template.

4. Choose a definition for [Unit 2]. Insert it into the template.

5. Select [Quantity 2]. Insert it into the template.

6. Select a unit rate of [Unit 1] per [Unit 2]. Multiply the unit rate with [Quantity 2] and insert the product into the template as [Quantity 1].

Template Key

Person: Any person or entity (for example, Varun, a car factory, a freight train)

Activity: Any activity you can measure by two different units in a rate relationship (for example, walking, producing cars, traveling)

Much or Many: An adjective describing quantity or amount appropriate for use with [Unit 1] (for example, *much, many, far*)

Unit 1: Any measurement unit in which the first entity of the rate relationship is measured (for example, miles, cars, kilometers)

Unit 2: Any measurement unit in which the second entity of the rate relationship is measured (for example, weeks, days, hours)

Quantity 1: Any whole number greater than 1 and evenly divisible by [Quantity 2]

Quantity 2: Any whole number greater than 1 representing the number of [Unit 2] in the scenario

Template

[Person] [Activity] at a constant rate. [Person] [Activity] [Quantity 1] [Unit 1] in [Quantity 2] [Unit 2]. How [Much or Many] [Unit 1] did [Person] [Activity] in 1 [Unit 2]?

Fill in your answer in the box.

 [Unit 1]

Number Patterns

Sample Item

The median amount of rainfall in inches on 11 different days in a particular city is 6. The range of the number of inches of rainfall is 12.

Which statement is true based on the given information?

A. There must be 3 days that had 6 inches of rainfall.

B. The mean number of inches of rainfall in a day is greater than 6.

C. All days must have had less than 12 inches of rainfall.

D. If the greatest amount of rainfall on a day was 13 inches, then the least amount of rainfall on a day was 1 inch.

Template Instructions

1.   Choose a definition for [Data Set]. Insert it into the template.

2.   Select whole-number values for the points in the data set.

3.   Calculate [Quantity 1]. Insert it into the template.

4.   Calculate [Quantity 2]. Insert it into the template.

5.   Create one correct statement describing the data set. Take care that the veracity of the statement can be determined based *only* on the information presented in the problem.

6.   Create [Statement 1] through [Statement 4]. Insert them into the problem.

Template Key

Data Set: A statement describing a set of whole numbers (data points) having random values; this statement should not include the values of the data points, but should include the number of data points in the set (for example, number of yards run by 7 different players in a football game, inches of rainfall on 11 different days in a particular city, amount of money earned in tips for waiting tables on 12 different nights)

Data Point: The type of data points within [Data Set] (for example, yards run by one player, inches of rainfall in one day, amount of money earned waiting tables on one night)

Quantity 1: Any whole number representing the median of the data set

Quantity 2: Any whole number representing the range of the data set

Statements 1–4: Statements of inference about the data points in the set based on the information provided in the problem; one of these should be a true statement while the others should be false. Take care that the veracity of the statements can be determined based *only* on the information presented in the problem. Examples of statements, in which # represents whole numbers, may include:

- At least one [Data Point] is [Quantity 1].

- The greatest [Data Point] is greater than #.

- The mean [Data Point] is greater than [Quantity 1].

- If the greatest [Data Point] is #, then the least [Data Point] is #.

- The least [Data Point] could have been #.

- If the least [Data Point] was #, then the greatest [Data Point] was #.

- There must be # [Data Point] that are [Quantity 1].

- A [Data Point] could be less than [Quantity 1].

- A [Data Point] could be greater than #.

- All [Data Point] must be less than [Quantity 2].

- At least one [Data Point] is not [Quantity 1].

Template

The median [Data Set] is [Quantity 1]. The range of [Data Set] is [Quantity 2].

Which statement is true based on the given information?

A. [Statement 1]

B. [Statement 2]

C. [Statement 3]

D. [Statement 4]

Statistics

Measures of Center and Variance

Sample Item

The manager of a car dealership tracked the number of cars sold at the dealership in 16 different weeks. The list shows the number of cars sold in each week.

66, 68, 68, 68, 70, 80, 85, 87, 92, 93, 101, 105, 106, 109, 114, 118

Part A

What is the interquartile range of the number of cars sold in the 16 different weeks?

Fill in your answer in the box.

Part B

Suppose the week in which 80 cars were sold is changed to 103 cars sold. Which statement about the median and interquartile range after this change is true?

A. The median and interquartile range do not change.

B. The median increases, and the interquartile range does not change.

C. The median does not change, and the interquartile range increases.

D. The median and interquartile range both increase.

Template Instructions

1. Choose a definition for [Setting]. Insert it into the template.

2. Choose a definition for [Data Set]. Insert it into the template.

3. Select [Data Point List]. Insert it into the template.

4. Select [Data Point 1]. Insert it into the template.

5. Select [Data Point 2]. Insert it into the template.

6. Create one correct statement about changes in the median and interquartile range of the data set resulting from the substitution of [Data Point 1] with [Data Point 2].

7. Create [Statement 1] through [Statement 4]. Insert them into the template.

Template Key

Setting: A statement describing a scenario in which a set of whole numbers (data points) having random values is counted or tracked; this statement should identify the number of data points in the set (for example, a coach charting the number of points scored by a basketball team at 18 different games, management at a car dealership keeping track of the number of cars sold at the dealership in 16 different weeks, a jogger tracking the number of miles she jogged in 23 different months).

Data Point List: A list of whole numbers that make up the data points in [Data Set], ordered from least to greatest

Data Set: A word or phrase describing the data set in the problem (for example, the points scored, the number of cars sold, the number of miles jogged in each month)

Data Point 1: A specific data point from the data set (for example, the score of 89, the week in which 80 cars were sold, the person who jogged 68 miles)

Data Point 2: A new, alternative data point to which [Data Point 1] is being changed (for example, the score of 76, the week in which 103 cars were sold, the person who jogged 44 miles)

Statements 1–4: Statements indicating a change (or not) in both the median and interquartile range of the data set resulting from the substitution of [Data Point 1] with [Data Point 2]; one of these should be a correct statement while the others should be false. Examples of statements include:

- The median and interquartile range do not change

- The median and interquartile range both decrease

- The median and interquartile range both increase

- The median decreases, and the interquartile range does not change

- The median does not change, and the interquartile range decreases

- The median increases, and the interquartile range does not change

- The median does not change, and the interquartile range increases

Template

[Setting]. The list shows the [Data Set].

[Data Point List]

Part A

What is the interquartile range of [Data Set]?

Fill in your answer in the box.

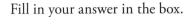

Part B

Suppose [Data Point 1] is changed to [Data Point 2]. Which statement about the median and interquartile range is true after this change?

A.   [Statement 1]

B.   [Statement 2]

C.   [Statement 3]

D.   [Statement 4]

Grade 7

Expressions, Equations, Inequalities, and Functions (EEIF)

Equations

Sample Item

Here are two equations.

$3x - 26 = -11$

$-5(r + 17) = -70$

Solve each equation. Give **only** your solutions.

$x =$

$r =$

Template Instructions

1. Choose separate variables for [Variable 1] and [Variable 2]. Insert them into the template.

2. Select positive or negative integer values for [Variable 1] and [Variable 2].

3. Create two separate equations of the form specified in the key that satisfy the values selected for [Variable 1] and [Variable 2] in step 2. Insert the equations into the template as [Equation 1] and [Equation 2].

Template Key

Equation 1: An equation of the form $ax \pm b = c$ where a, b, and c are positive or negative integer constants and x is [Variable 1]

Equation 2: An equation of the form $a(x + b) = c$ where a, b, and c are positive or negative integer constants and x is [Variable 2]

Variable 1: Any variable (for example, *x*, *n*, *r*)

Variable 2: Any variable (for example, *x*, *n*, *r*)

Template

Here are two equations.

[Equation 1]

[Equation 2]

Solve each equation. Give **only** your solutions.

[Variable 1] =

[Variable 2] =

Expressions

Sample Item

The length of Mario's hockey stick is *h* inches. The length of Connor's hockey stick is 5 percent shorter than Mario's. Which expressions represent the length, in inches, of Connor's hockey stick?

Select **each** correct answer.

    A. $0.05h$

    B. $0.95h$

    C. $h - 0.05$

    D. $h - 0.95$

    E. $h - 0.05h$

Template Instructions

1. Choose definitions for [Characteristic], [Item 1], [Item 2], [Unit], [Variable], and [More or Less]. Insert them into the template.

2. Select [Percentage]. Insert it into the template.

3. Convert [Percentage] into decimal form and insert it into the answer choices in the template as [Percentage in decimal form].

4. Based on the chosen adjective for [More or Less], select either + or −. Insert the correct symbol into the template in place of the ± symbol.

5. Perform the calculations for [1 ± [Percentage in decimal form]] in the answer choices involving this expression, and insert the result into these answers in the template.

6. Randomize the order of answer choices A–E.

Template Key

Characteristic: A measurable characteristic (for example, length, cost, weight)

Item 1: An item with a measurable characteristic (for example, Mario's hockey stick, an armchair, Janelle's first child)

Item 2: A different item of the same type as [Item 1] (for example, Connor's hockey stick, a dining chair, Janelle's second child)

Unit: A unit of measure (for example, inches, dollars, pounds)

Variable: A variable (for example, h, x, w)

More or Less: A comparative adjective related to [Characteristic] (for example, shorter, more expensive, heavier)

Percentage: A whole-number percentage expressed with the % sign (for example, 5%)

Percentage in decimal form: [Percentage] converted to decimal form (for example, 0.05)

Template

The [Characteristic] of [Item 1] is [Variable] [Unit]. The [Characteristic] of [Item 2] is [Percentage] [More or Less] than [Item 1]. Which expressions represent the [Characteristic], in [Unit], of [Item 2]?

Select **each** correct answer.

A. [Percentage in decimal form][Variable]

B. [1 ± [Percentage in decimal form]][Variable]

C. [Variable] ± [Percentage in decimal form]

D. [Variable] ± [1 ± [Percentage in decimal form]]

E. [Variable] ± [Percentage in decimal form][Variable]

Inequalities

Sample Item

Mark had 16 gallons of paint. He used 10 gallons. Each room of his house uses 2 gallons of paint.

Graph the solution set of the inequality you could use to determine r, the number of rooms that Mark can paint with the remaining gallons of paint.

Select the correct solution-set indicator, then draw the indicator across the appropriate location on the number line to display the solution set.

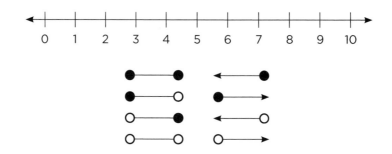

Template Instructions

1. Choose definitions for [Individual], [Item], [Object], [Make], and [Variable]. Insert them into the template.

2. Select [Quantity 1] through [Quantity 3]. Insert them into the template.

3. Create a number line with a range and scale appropriate for the quantities selected.

4. Create a set of eight line segments whose endpoints display different ways in which an inequality may be graphed on a number line (for example, a set of line segments that represent different combinations of closed, open, and infinite inequalities in interval notation); one of these line segments should correctly represent the solution set of the inequality in the problem.

Template Key

Individual: A person or other entity (for example, Mark, Anya, cell phone battery)

Item: Something you can use up or consume (for example, gallons of paint, dollars, hours of energy)

Object: Something on or for which [Item] can be used (for example, rooms of a house, stuffed animals, phone calls)

Variable: A variable (for example, *r*, *s*, *p*)

Make: The act of using [Item] for [Object] (for example, paint, purchase, power)

Quantity 1: A positive rational number

Quantity 2: A positive rational number less than [Quantity 1]

Quantity 3: A positive rational number less than [Quantity 1]

Template

[Individual] had [Quantity 1] [Item]. [Individual] used [Quantity 2] [Item]. Each [Object] uses [Quantity 3] [Item].

Graph the solution set of the inequality you could use to determine [Variable], the number of [Object] that [Individual] can [Make] with the remaining [Item].

Select the correct solution-set indicator, then draw the indicator across the appropriate location on the number line to display the solution set.

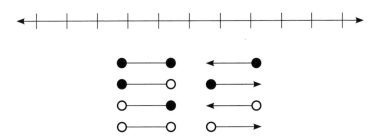

Geometry

2-D and 3-D Shapes

Sample Item

A right equilateral triangular prism is sliced into two pieces that are congruent. Which 2-D-plane sections **could result** from the slice?

Select **each** correct answer.

    A.   isosceles triangle

    B.   equilateral triangle

    C.   circle

    D.   rectangle

    E.   pentagon

Template Instructions

1. Choose definitions for [3-D Figure] and [Condition]. Insert them into the template.

2. Select [Answer 1] through [Answer 5]. Insert them into the template.

Template Key

3-D Figure: A 3-D figure (for example, right equilateral triangular prism, right circular cone, right square pyramid)

Condition: A condition on the slice made through the figure (for example, which are congruent; with the slice perpendicular to the base; with the slice parallel to the base)

Answers 1–5: 2-D-plane sections; at least one of these is a correct answer.

Template

A [3-D Figure] is sliced into two pieces [Condition]. Which 2-D-plane sections **could result** from the slice?

Select **each** correct answer.

A.   [Answer 1]

B.   [Answer 2]

C.   [Answer 3]

D.   [Answer 4]

E.   [Answer 5]

Area and Perimeter

Sample Item

The following figure is created by joining two rectangles.

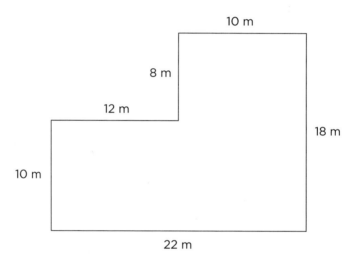

Fill in the area of the figure in square meters.

Template Instructions

1.   Select [Quantity]. Insert it into the template.

2.   Choose a definition for [Unit]. Insert it into the template.

3.   Create an irregular, rectilinear, 2-D figure composed of [Quantity] rectangles. Label each side with whole-number side lengths in [Unit]. Insert it into the template in place of the box.

Template Key

Quantity: A single-digit whole number of low value

Unit: A unit of length (for example, meters, inches, centimeters)

Template

The following figure is created by joining [Quantity] rectangles.

Fill in the area of the figure in square [Unit].

```
┌─────────────┐
│             │
└─────────────┘
```

Operations

Operation Not Specified

Sample Item

Joe bought one gallon of milk for $2.79 and some containers of yogurt that cost $0.39 each. He paid a total of $5.13 for these items.

How many containers of yogurt did Joe buy?

Fill in the box with your answer.

```
┌─────────────┐
│             │
└─────────────┘
```

Template Instructions

1. Choose definitions for [Individual], [Item 1], and [Item 2]. Insert them into the template.

2. Select [Quantity 1] and [Quantity 2]. Insert them into the template.

3. Select [Quantity 3]. Insert it into the template.

Template Key

Individual: A person or other entity that can purchase items (for example, Joe, Cecilia, Roland)

Item 1: An item (for example, gallon of milk, bag of soil, pair of pants)

Item 2: An item related to [Item 1] (for example, containers of yogurt, flowerpots, pairs of socks)

Quantity 1: An amount of money, in dollars and cents

Quantity 2: A different amount of money than [Quantity 1]

Quantity 3: An amount of money so the value of [Quantity 3] – [Quantity 1] is evenly divisible by [Quantity 2]

Template

[Individual] bought one [Item 1] for [Quantity 1] and some [Item 2] that cost [Quantity 2] each. [Individual] paid a total of [Quantity 3] for these items.

How many [Item 2] did [Individual] buy?

Fill in the box with your answer.

[   ]

Quantity and Number

Coordinate Plane

Sample Item

The graph shows the number of dollars charged for gallons of fuel purchased.

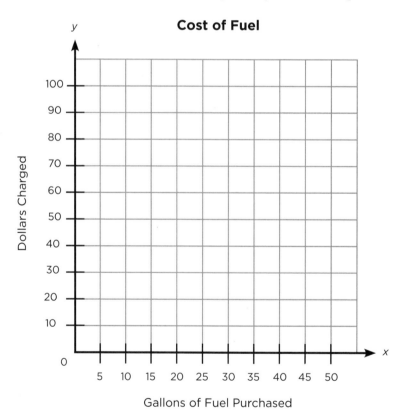

Which statement describes the meaning of the point (20, 50) on the graph?

    A.   There are 20 dollars charged per gallon of fuel purchased.

    B.   There are 50 dollars charged per gallon of fuel purchased.

C.   There are 20 dollars charged for 50 gallons of fuel purchased.

D.   There are 50 dollars charged for 20 gallons of fuel purchased.

Template Instructions

1.   Choose definitions for [Item 1] and [Item 2]. Insert them into the template.

2.   Create a coordinate plane graph displaying a proportional relationship between [Item 1] and [Item 2]. The graph should pass through the point ([Coordinate 1], [Coordinate 2]).

Template Key

Item 1: An item that exists in quantities proportional to [Item 2] (for example, dollars charged, ounces of bleach, dollars earned)

Item 2: An item that exists in quantities proportional to [Item 1] (for example, gallons of fuel purchased, liters of cleaning solution, hours worked)

Coordinate 1: A whole number corresponding to the *x*-coordinate of a point on the graph

Coordinate 2: A whole number corresponding to the *y*-coordinate of a point on the graph

Template

The graph shows the amount of [Item 1] for or in [Item 2].

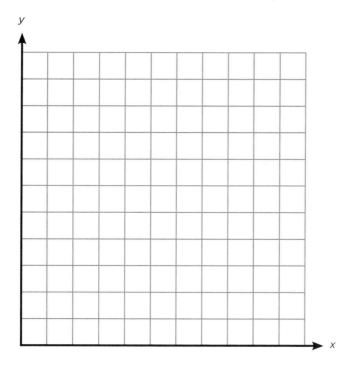

Which statement describes the meaning of the point ([Coordinate 1], [Coordinate 2]) on the graph?

A. There are [Coordinate 1] [Item 1] per [Item 2].

B. There are [Coordinate 2] [Item 1] per [Item 2].

C. There are [Coordinate 1] [Item 1] for or in [Coordinate 2] [Item 2].

D. There are [Coordinate 2] [Item 1] for or in [Coordinate 1] [Item 2].

Equivalence

Sample Item

Select **all** expressions equivalent to $-1.65x - 3.3(3x - 2) + 6.6$.

A. $-11.55x + 13.2$

B. $-11.55x$

C. $-1.65x - 9.9x - 6.6 - 6.6$

D. $-1.65 [x + 2(3x - 2) - 4]$

Template Instructions

1. Create [Expression 1]. Insert it into the template.

2. Create [Answer 1] through [Answer 4]. Insert them into the template.

Template Key

Expression 1: A linear expression in one variable with decimal and whole-number coefficients and constants

Answers 1–4: Linear expressions that meet the same parameters and use the same variable as [Expression 1], with at least one of these expressions being equivalent to [Expression 1]

Template

Select **all** expressions equivalent to [Expression 1].

A. [Answer 1]

B. [Answer 2]

C. [Answer 3]

D. [Answer 4]

Percentages

Sample Item

Jerome bought a phone. He paid 11% in tax. The tax added $38.50 to the price of the phone.

What was the price of the phone, not including the tax?

Template Instructions

1. Choose definitions for [Individual] and [Item]. Insert them into the template.

2. Select [Base Price].

3. Select [Percentage]. Insert it into the template.

4. Calculate [Quantity] using the selected [Base Price] and [Percentage]. Insert it into the template.

Template Key

Individual: A person or other entity that can purchase something (for example, Jerome, Tiffany, an office manager)

Base Price: The pretax price of [Item]

Item: An item you can purchase (for example, a phone, a car, a computer)

Percentage: A percentage so the value of [Percentage] × [Base Price] can be expressed in whole cents without rounding

Quantity: The dollar value of the tax on [Item], equal to [Percentage] × [Base Price]

Template

[Individual] bought [Item]. [Individual] paid [Percentage] in tax. The tax added [Quantity] to the price of [Item].

What was the price of [Item], not including the tax?

Ratios and Proportional Relationships

Proportional Relationships

Sample Item

Which table shows a proportional relationship between x and y?

A.

x	y
1	0
2	4
3	8

C.

x	y
1	2
2	3
3	4

B.

x	y
1	0
2	24
3	48

D.

x	y
1	4
2	8
3	12

Template Instructions

1. Select values for [Value 1] through [Value 12]. Insert them into the template.

Template Key

Values 1–12: Whole numbers so the sequence of numbers within each table displays a pattern (for example, a common difference); select these so one of the tables represents a proportional relationship while the others do not.

Template

Which table shows a proportional relationship between *x* and *y*?

A.

x	*y*
1	[Value 1]
2	[Value 2]
3	[Value 3]

C.

x	*y*
1	[Value 7]
2	[Value 8]
3	[Value 9]

B.

x	*y*
1	[Value 4]
2	[Value 5]
3	[Value 6]

D.

x	*y*
1	[Value 10]
2	[Value 11]
3	[Value 12]

Rate and Ratio

Sample Item

Jamie goes for a run. She runs at a constant rate of $\frac{2}{3}$ mile every $\frac{1}{11}$ hour. At this rate, what fraction represents the miles Jamie runs per hour? Give your answer as a fraction.

Fill in the boxes with your answer.

Template Instructions

1. Choose definitions for [Individual], [Activity], [Unit], and [Time]. Insert them into the template.

2. Select [Fraction 1] and [Fraction 2]. Insert them into the template.

Template Key

Individual: A person or other entity that can perform an activity at a certain rate (for example, Jamie, a farmer using a combine, a painter)

Activity: An activity you can perform at a constant rate (for example, running, harvesting wheat, painting a house)

Unit: A unit of measure (for example, mile, a field, a house)

Time: A unit of time (for example, hour, day, week)

Fraction 1: A positive fractional value

Fraction 2: A positive fractional value

Template

[Individual] [Activity]. [Individual] [Activity] at a constant rate of [Fraction 1] [Unit] every [Fraction 2] [Time]. At this rate, what fraction represents the [Unit] [Individual] [Activity] per [Time]? Give your answer as a fraction.

Fill in the boxes with your answer.

$$\frac{\boxed{}}{\boxed{}}$$

Scaling

Sample Item

The scale on a map shows that .25 inches = 10 miles.

Part A

What number of inches on the map represents an actual distance of .25 mile?

Fill in the box with your answer.

	inches

Part B

What is the actual number of miles represented by 10 inches on the map?

Fill in the box with your answer.

	miles

Template Instructions

1. Choose definitions for [Unit 1] and [Unit 2]. Insert them into the template.

2. Select [Quantity 1] and [Quantity 2]. Insert them into the template.

Template Key

Quantity 1: A positive rational number

Quantity 2: A positive rational number, different from [Quantity 1]

Unit 1: A unit of length feasible for use on a map (for example, centimeters, millimeters, inches)

Unit 2: A larger unit of length feasible for real-world distances (for example, kilometers, meters, miles)

Template

The scale on a map shows [Quantity 1] [Unit 1] = [Quantity 2] [Unit 2].

Part A

What number of [Unit 1] on the map represents an actual distance of [Quantity 1] [Unit 2]?

Fill in the box with your answer.

| |
|---------------------| [Unit 1]

Part B

What is the actual number of [Unit 2] represented by [Quantity 2] [Unit 1] on the map?

Fill in the box with your answer.

| |
|---------------------| [Unit 2]

Statistics

Measures of Center and Variance

Sample Item

A tire's air pressure changed –22.8 psi over 4 seconds. What was the mean change of air pressure in psi per second?

Fill in the box with your answer.

| |
|---------------------| psi per second

Template Instructions

1. Choose definitions for [Item], [Characteristic], [Unit 1], and [Unit 2]. Insert them into the template.

2. Select [Quantity 1] and [Quantity 2]. Insert them into the template.

Template Key

Item: An item with a measurable characteristic that can change (for example, a tire, a lake, a plant)

Characteristic: A changeable measurable characteristic of [Item] (for example, air pressure, water level, height)

Unit 1: A unit in which [Characteristic] can be measured (for example, psi, feet, centimeters)

Unit 2: A unit of time (for example, seconds, weeks, days)

Quantity 1: A positive or negative value

Quantity 2: A positive value

Template

[Item] [Characteristic] changed [Quantity 1] [Unit 1] over [Quantity 2] [Unit 2]. What was the mean change of [Characteristic] in [Unit 1] per [Unit 2]?

Fill in the box with your answer.

☐ [Unit 1] per [Unit 2]

Probability

Sample Item

A random number generator will run 56,000 times. Each result will be a digit from 2 to 9. Which statement best predicts how many times the digit 7 will appear among the 56,000 results?

A. It will appear exactly 7,000 times.

B. It will appear close to 7,000 times but probably not exactly 7,000 times.

C. It will appear exactly 8,000 times.

D. It will appear close to 8,000 times but probably not exactly 8,000 times.

Template Instructions

1. Select [Quantity 1] through [Quantity 4]. Insert them into the template.

2. Calculate the expected value of [Quantity 4] appearing among the [Quantity 1] results. Use this value as [Quantity 5] or [Quantity 6], and insert it into the template.

3. Select a different value for the remaining quantity ([Quantity 5] or [Quantity 6]). Insert it into the template.

Template Key

Quantity 1: A whole number

Quantities 2–3: A range of whole-number values, so the number of values encompassed by the range is a factor of [Quantity 1]

Quantity 4: A whole number within the range of [Quantity 2] to [Quantity 3]

Answers 1–4: Four statements in random order, each taking one of the following forms:

- It will appear exactly [Quantity 5] times.

- It will appear close to [Quantity 5] times but probably not exactly [Quantity 5] times.

- It will appear exactly [Quantity 6] times.

- It will appear close to [Quantity 6] times but probably not exactly [Quantity 6] times.

Quantities 5–6: Whole numbers, one of which is the expected value of [Quantity 4] appearing among the [Quantity 1] results

Template

A random number generator will run [Quantity 1] times. Each result will be a digit from [Quantity 2] to [Quantity 3]. Which statement best predicts how many times the digit [Quantity 4] will appear among the [Quantity 1] results?

A. [Answer 1]

B. [Answer 2]

C. [Answer 3]

D. [Answer 4]

Statistical Investigation

Sample Item

A restaurant owner wants to know if her customers like brussels sprouts. She is unable to ask the opinion of every customer, so she needs to select an appropriate sample of customers to represent her customer base.

Select which sample of customers the restaurant owner should choose.

  A.   One customer at each table in the restaurant during dinner one night

  B.   The largest group of customers at one table during dinner one night

  C.   Every customer who orders a vegetarian dish over one month

  D.   Every fifth customer who comes into the restaurant over one month

Template Instructions

  1.   Choose definitions for [Individual], [Population], [Member], and [Opinion].
       Insert them into the template.

  2.   Create [Answer 1] through [Answer 4]. Insert them into the template.

Template Key

Individual: A person or other entity that might survey a population (for example, a restaurant owner, an automobile manufacturer, a politician)

Population: The population [Individual] wants to survey (for example, the restaurant's customer base, all car buyers in the United States, her constituency)

Member: A member of [Population] (for example, customer, car buyer in the United States, constituent)

Opinion: An opinion on a topic that [Individual] wants to survey [Population] about (for example, like brussels sprouts, prefer SUVs or trucks, are in favor of a particular bill)

Answers 1–4: Descriptions of samples of the [Population] that could be selected; one of the answers should describe a representative sample of the [Population] and the remaining three answers should describe nonrepresentative or otherwise incorrect samples.

Template

[Individual] wants to know if [Population] [Opinion]. [Individual] is unable to ask the opinion of every [Member], so [Individual] needs to select an appropriate sample of [Member] to represent [Population].

Select which sample of [Member] [Individual] should choose.

  A.   [Answer 1]

  B.   [Answer 2]

  C.   [Answer 3]

  D.   [Answer 4]

Grade 8

Data Displays

Scatterplot

Sample Item

The scatterplot shows the height and weight of 9 patients at a clinic.

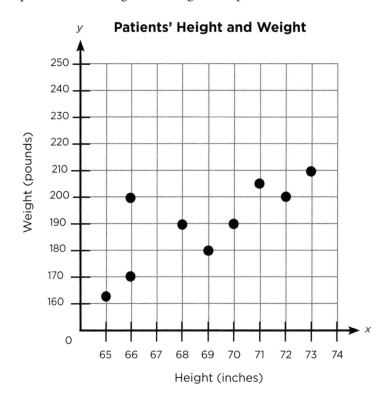

Which of these **most** closely approximates a line of best fit for the data in the scatterplot?

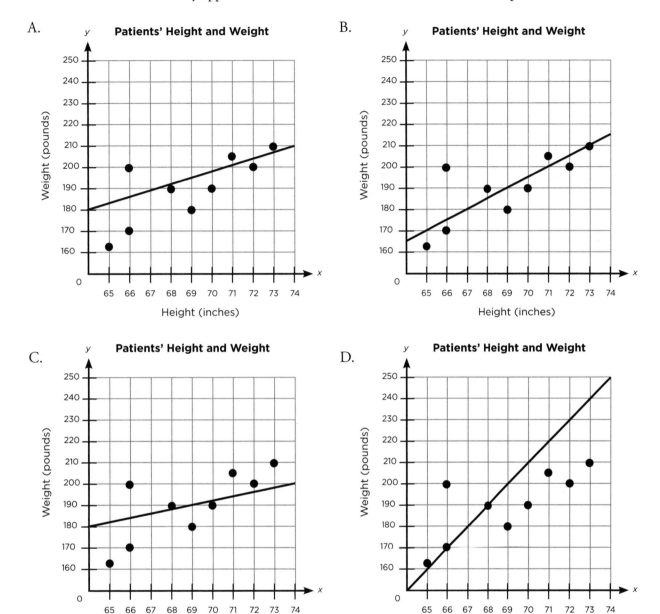

Template Instructions

1. Choose definitions for [Object], [Independent Variable], and [Dependent Variable]. Insert them into the template.

2. Select [Quantity]. Insert it into the template.

3. Create a scatterplot with points representing the relationships between the [Independent Variable] and [Dependent Variable] of each [Object]. The points on the plot should display a linear association.

4.   Create four copies of the scatterplot. On each copy, create a different line of best fit to model the points on the graph. One line should more closely fit the data than the others.

Template Key

Object: An object, person, or entity having two properties that are related in an independent and dependent variable relationship (for example, patients at a clinic, students in a class, cars)

Independent Variable: The independent variable property of [Object] (for example, height, hours of study, miles driven)

Dependent Variable: The dependent variable property of [Object] (for example, weight, percentage of questions answered correctly on a test, annual repair costs)

Quantity: Any whole number standing for the number of [Object] measured

Template

The scatterplot shows the [Independent Variable] and [Dependent Variable] of [Quantity] [Object].

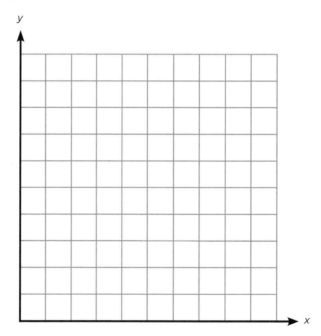

Which of these **most** closely approximates a line of best fit for the data in the scatterplot?

A.

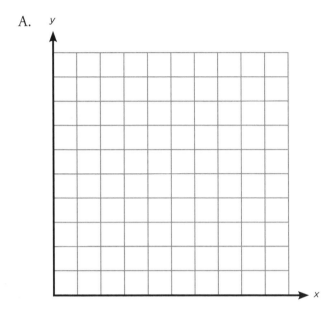

B.

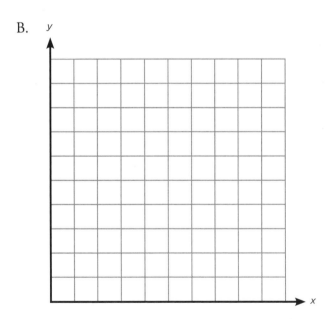

C. *y*

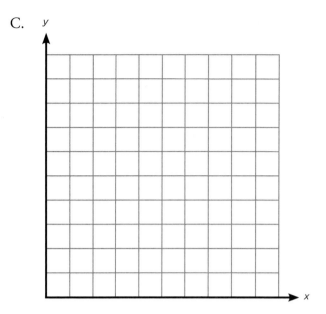

D. *y*

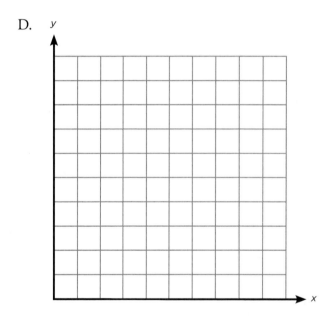

Expressions, Equations, Inequalities, and Functions (EEIF)

Equations

Sample Item

A line is graphed on the coordinate plane.

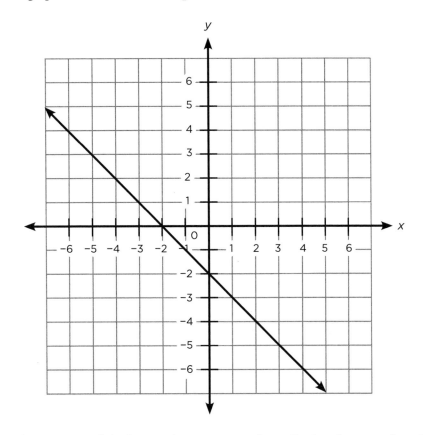

Write the equation of the line in slope-intercept form. Explain how you found the slope and the *y*-intercept.

Template Instructions

1. Create a coordinate plane with four quadrants. Draw a line on the plane that intercepts the *y*-axis at an integer value and that passes through at least two intersections of horizontal and vertical grid lines on the coordinate plane.

Template Key

(Not applicable)

Template

A line is graphed on the coordinate plane.

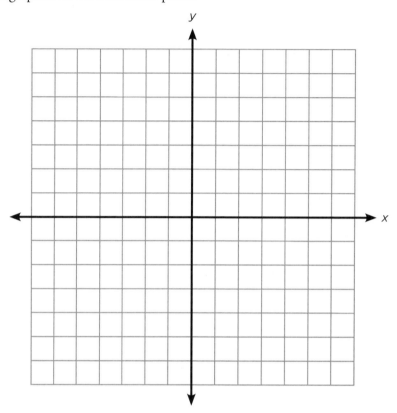

Write the equation of the line in slope-intercept form. Explain how you found the slope and the *y*-intercept.

Functions

Sample Item

The table shows a relation that is a function, where *x* is the input and *y* is the output.

x	y
5	0
−4	−2
6	3
−2	5

Which ordered pairs could you include in the table so the relation remains a function?

Select **each** correct answer.

A.   (5, 3)

B.   (–4, 4)

C.   (–1, 0)

D.   (–2, 3)

E.   (3, 2)

F.   (7, 8)

G.   (0, –1)

Template Instructions

1.   Create four ordered pairs. Insert them into the table in the template in place of #.

2.   Create [Answer 1] through [Answer 7]. Insert them into the template.

Template Key

#: Positive or negative integers that make up the values of four ordered pairs. The set of ordered pairs should represent a function relationship.

Answers 1–7: Seven ordered pairs consisting of positive or negative integers; one to six of the ordered pairs, when taken together with the ordered pairs in the table, should result in the relation remaining a function.

Template

The table shows a relation that is a function, where x is the input and y is the output.

x	y
#	#
#	#
#	#
#	#

Which ordered pairs could you include in the table so that the relation remains a function?

Select **each** correct answer.

A.   [Answer 1]   E.   [Answer 5]

B.   [Answer 2]   F.   [Answer 6]

C.   [Answer 3]   G.   [Answer 7]

D.   [Answer 4]

Expressions

Sample Item

Four rational numbers are represented by a, b, c, and d.

Part A

State all possible conditions that must be true for a and b so the product of this expression is negative.

$$5ab$$

Justify your response.

Fill in your response and your justification in the space provided.

Part B

What must be true for $(c - d)$ so the value of this expression is negative?

$$5 + (c - d)$$

Justify your response.

Fill in your response and your justification in the space provided.

Template Instructions

1. Choose definitions for [Sign] and [Variable 1] through [Variable 4]. Insert them into the template.

2. Choose definitions for [Quantity], [Operator 1], and [Operator 2]. Insert them into the template.

Template Key

Variables 1–4: Any four distinct variables (for example, x, y, j, n)

Sign: Either *positive* or *negative*

Quantity: Any positive or negative integer

Operator 1: Either + or –

Operator 2: Either + or –

Template

Four rational numbers are represented by [Variable 1], [Variable 2], [Variable 3], and [Variable 4].

Part A

State all possible conditions that must be true for [Variable 1] and [Variable 2] so the product of this expression is [Sign].

[Quantity][Variable 1][Variable 2]

Justify your response.

Fill in your response and your justification in the space provided.

Part B

What must be true for ([Variable 3] [Operator 1] [Variable 4]) so the value of this expression is [Sign]?

[Quantity] [Operator 2] ([Variable 3] [Operator 1] [Variable 4])

Justify your response.

Fill in your response and your justification in the space provided.

Geometry

Transformations

Sample Item

$\triangle XYZ$ is transformed to the image $\triangle X'Y'Z'$.

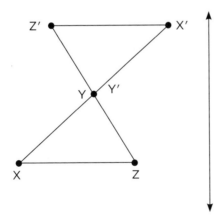

Part A

Describe the single transformation that maps $\triangle XYZ$ onto its image $\triangle X'Y'Z'$. Determine whether $\triangle XYZ$ maintains its shape as a result of the transformation.

Circle the word or phrase from each group that correctly completes the following statements.

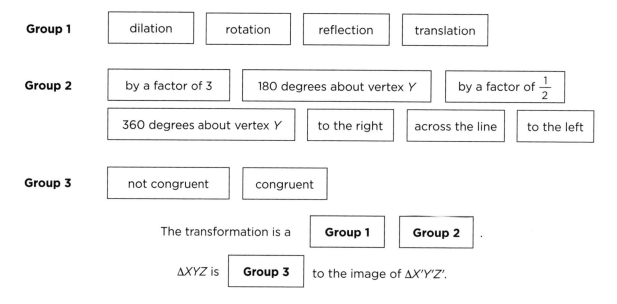

Group 1 | dilation | rotation | reflection | translation

Group 2 | by a factor of 3 | 180 degrees about vertex Y | by a factor of $\frac{1}{2}$
| 360 degrees about vertex Y | to the right | across the line | to the left

Group 3 | not congruent | congruent

The transformation is a **Group 1** **Group 2** .

$\triangle XYZ$ is **Group 3** to the image of $\triangle X'Y'Z'$.

Part B

A reflection is performed on $\triangle X'Y'Z'$ to create image $\triangle X''Y''Z''$. How does line segment $X''Y''$ compare to line segment $X'Y'$?

A. Line segment $X''Y''$ is longer than line segment $X'Y'$.

B. Line segment $X''Y''$ is shorter than line segment $X'Y'$.

C. Line segment $X''Y''$ is congruent to line segment $X'Y'$.

D. There is not enough information to compare the two line segments.

Template Instructions

1. Choose definitions for [V1], [V2], [V3], and [V]. Insert them into the template.

2. Create a triangle with vertices [V1], [V2], and [V3]. Insert it into the template in place of the box.

3. Create an image of the triangle after a single transformation, with vertices [V1]', [V2]', and [V3]'. If performing a rotation, it should be performed about vertex [V] in multiples of 90°. Insert it into the template in an appropriate location relative to the first triangle.

4. Select definitions for [Q1], [Q2], [Q3], and [Q4]. Insert them into the template.

5. Choose a definition for [Transformation]. Insert it into the template.

Template Key

V1–V3: Any variables (for example, *A*, *B*, *C*)

V: Either [V1], [V2], or [V3]

Q1–Q2: Rational numbers; if a dilation was performed, one of these values is the correct scale factor of the dilation.

Q3–Q4: A multiple of 90; if a rotation was performed, one of these values should be the angle measure of the rotation.

Transformation: Either *translation*, *reflection*, *rotation*, or *dilation*

Template

Δ*[V1][V2][V3]* is transformed to the image Δ*[V1]'[V2]'[V3]'*.

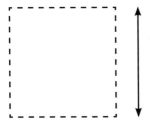

Part A

Describe the single transformation that maps Δ*[V1][V2][V3]* onto its image Δ*[V1]'[V2]'[V3]'*. Determine whether Δ*[V1][V2][V3]* maintains its shape as a result of the transformation.

Circle the word or phrase from each group that correctly completes the following statements.

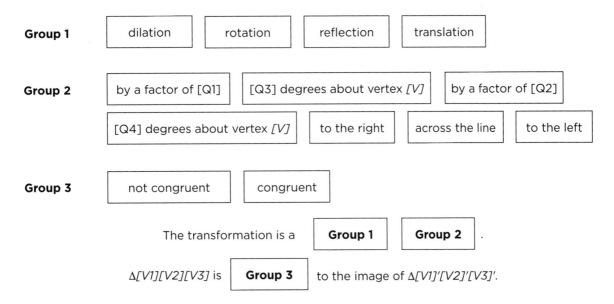

Part B

A [Transformation] is performed on Δ*[V1]'[V2]'[V3]'* to create image Δ*[V1]"[V2]"[V3]"*. How does line segment *[V1]"[V2]"* compare to line segment *[V1]'[V2]'*?

   A.   Line segment *[V1]"[V2]"* is longer than line segment *[V1]'[V2]'*.

   B.   Line segment *[V1]"[V2]"* is shorter than line segment *[V1]'[V2]'*.

   C.   Line segment *[V1]"[V2]"* is congruent to line segment *[V1]'[V2]'*.

   D.   There is not enough information to compare the two line segments.

Volume

Sample Item

The figure shows a right-circular cylinder and a right-circular cone. The cylinder and the cone have the same base and the same height.

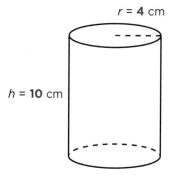 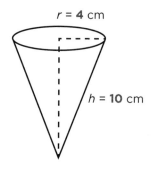

Part A

What is the volume of the cylinder in cubic centimeters?

   A. 40π

   B. 80π

   C. 160π

   D. 640π

Part B

What is the ratio of the cylinder's volume to the cone's volume?

   A. $\frac{2}{1}$

   B. $\frac{3}{1}$

   C. $\frac{4}{1}$

   D. $\frac{5}{1}$

Template Instructions

   1.   Choose a definition for [Unit]. Insert it into the template.

2. Create a right-circular cylinder and a right-circular cone with the same base and height. Each figure should be labeled with its height, *h*, and the radius of its base, *r*, in whole numbers of [Unit]. Insert the figures side-by-side into the template in place of the box.

3. Choose a definition for [Cone and Cylinder 1]. Insert it into the template.

4. Choose a definition for [Cone and Cylinder 2]. Insert it into the template.

5. Select [Answer 1] through [Answer 4]. Insert them into the template.

6. Select [Answer 5] through [Answer 8]. Insert them into the template.

Template Key

Unit: A unit of length (for example, centimeters, inches, feet)

Cone and Cylinder 1: Either *cone* or *cylinder*

Cone and Cylinder 2: Either *cone* or *cylinder*; whichever shape was not selected for [Cone and Cylinder 1].

Answers 1–4: Possible volumes of the selected shape, expressed in terms of π; one of the volumes is the correct answer.

Answers 5–8: Possible ratios of the volume of [Cone and Cylinder 1] to the volume of [Cone and Cylinder 2], expressed as fractions; one of the ratios is the correct answer.

Template

The figure shows a right-circular cylinder and a right-circular cone. The cylinder and the cone have the same base and the same height.

Part A

What is the volume of [Cone and Cylinder 1] in cubic [Unit]?

A. [Answer 1]

B. [Answer 2]

C. [Answer 3]

D. [Answer 4]

Part B

What is the ratio of the [Cone and Cylinder 1]'s volume to the [Cone and Cylinder 2]'s volume?

A.   [Answer 5]

B.   [Answer 6]

C.   [Answer 7]

D.   [Answer 8]

Lines and Angles

Sample Item

The figure shows lines *j* and *k* are parallel.

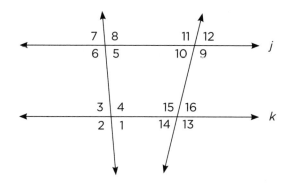

Jennifer claims that $m\angle15 + m\angle10 = m\angle3 + m\angle2$.

Is Jennifer correct? Use appropriate mathematical language to justify your response.

Fill in your answer and your justification in the space provided.

Template Instructions

1.   Choose definitions for [Person], [V1], and [V2]. Insert them into the template.

2.   Create a figure consisting of one pair of vertical lines intersecting one pair of horizontal lines. Either the vertical pair or the horizontal pair should be parallel while the other pair is not. The parallel lines should be labeled as [V1] and [V2], and each angle created by the intersection of two lines should be labeled with a number. Insert the figure into the template in place of the box.

3.   Choose definitions for [Q1] through [Q4]. Insert them into the template.

Template Key

Person: A person (for example, David, Lynn, Jennifer)

V1: Any variable (for example, *j*, *k*, *m*)

V2: Any variable (for example, *j*, *k*, *m*)

Q1–Q2: Numbers corresponding to angles in the figure; these should be adjacent interior angles that lie along the same transversal

Q3–Q4: Numbers corresponding to angles in the figure; these should be supplementary angles

Template

The figure shows lines [V1] and [V2] are parallel.

[Person] claims that $m\angle$[Q1] + $m\angle$[Q2] = $m\angle$[Q3] + $m\angle$[Q4].

Is [Person] correct? Use appropriate mathematical language to justify your response.

Fill in your answer and your justification in the space provided.

Triangles

Sample Item

The coordinate plane shows $\overline{AB}$.

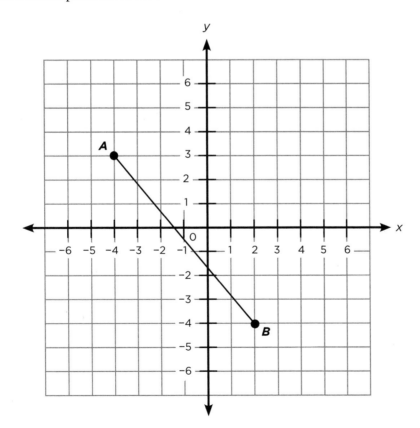

The coordinates of points *A* and *B* are integers. What is the length, to the nearest unit, of $\overline{AB}$? Fill in the box with your answer.

Template Instructions

1. Create a coordinate plane with four quadrants containing line segment $\overline{AB}$. The line segment should not be vertical or horizontal, and points *A* and *B* should have integer coordinates.

Template Key

(Not applicable)

Template

The coordinate plane shows $\overline{AB}$.

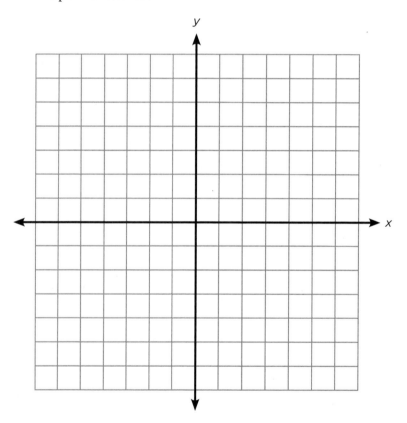

The coordinates of points *A* and *B* are integers. What is the length, to the nearest unit, of $\overline{AB}$?

Fill in the box with your answer.

Operations

Operation Not Specified

Sample Item

Joan is buying lattes.

- Each plain latte costs $5.

- Each flavored latte costs $6.

- Joan spends $69 on lattes.

- Joan buys 12 total lattes.

Fill in the total number of plain lattes and total number of flavored lattes Joan buys.

Plain lattes: [   ]

Flavored lattes: [   ]

Template Instructions

1. Choose definitions for [Person], [Item Type], [Item Subtype a], and [Item Subtype b]. Insert them into the template.

2. Select [Quantity 1], [Quantity 2], and [Quantity 4]. Insert them into the template.

3. Select [Quantity 3]. Insert it into the template.

Template Key

Person: A person or other entity (for example, Joan, a car rental company, a science teacher)

Quantity 1: A whole-number amount of money

Quantity 2: A whole-number amount of money, different from [Quantity 1]

Quantity 3: A whole-number amount of money, so a number of items of [Item Subtype a] multiplied by [Quantity 1], plus a number of items of [Item Subtype b] multiplied by [Quantity 2], equals [Quantity 3]

Quantity 4: A whole number comprising the sum of the number of items of [Item Subtype a] and the number of items of [Item Subtype b]

Item Type: Any type of object that costs money (for example, lattes, vehicles, measurement tools)

Item Subtype a: A unique variation of [Item Type] (for example, plain latte, sedan, scale)

Item Subtype b: A unique variation of [Item Type] (for example, flavored latte, van, graduated cylinder)

Template

[Person] is buying [Item Type].

- Each [Item Subtype a] costs [Quantity 1].

- Each [Item Subtype b] costs [Quantity 2].

- [Person] spends [Quantity 3] on [Item Type].

- [Person] buys [Quantity 4] total [Item Type].

Fill in the total number of [Item Subtype a] and total number of [Item Subtype b] [Person] buys.

[Item Subtype a]: _____

[Item Subtype b]: _____

Quantity and Number

Exponents, Radicals, and Scientific Notation

Sample Item

Which expression is equivalent to $(4^5)^2 \times 4^8$?

Select **each** correct answer.

- A. $4^{5 \times 2 \times 8}$

- B. $4^{5 \times 2 \cdot + 8}$

- C. $4^{5 + 2 + 8}$

- D. $4^{5(2 \cdot + 8)}$

- E. $4^{5 \times 2} \times 7^8$

- F. $4^{5 + 2} \times 4^8$

Template Instructions

1. Select [Quantity 1] through [Quantity 4]. Insert them into the template.

2. Create [Answer 1] through [Answer 6]. Insert them into the template.

Template Key

Quantities 1–4: Whole numbers

Answers 1–6: Expressions involving [Quantity 1] with exponential values expressed using various combinations of multiplication, addition, and parentheses; at least one of the expressions should be a correct answer.

Template

Which expression is equivalent to

([Quantity 1]$^{[Quantity\ 2]}$)$^{[Quantity\ 3]}$ × [Quantity 1]$^{[Quantity\ 4]}$?

Select **each** correct answer.

    A.   [Answer 1]

    B.   [Answer 2]

    C.   [Answer 3]

    D.   [Answer 4]

    E.   [Answer 5]

    F.   [Answer 6]

Equivalence

Sample Item

Which decimal is the equivalent of $\frac{7}{12}$?

    A. $0.58\overline{3}$

    B. $0.58\bar{3}$

    C. $1.71\overline{42857}$

    D. $1.7\overline{142857}$

Template Instructions

1.   Select [Fraction]. Insert this fraction into the template.

2.   Create [Answer 1] through [Answer 4]. Insert them into the template.

Template Key

Fraction: A fraction equivalent to a repeating decimal (for example, $\frac{7}{12}$, $\frac{1}{15}$; fractions in their most reduced forms having a prime denominator other than 2 or 5)

Answers 1–4: Repeating-decimal values; one of these is the correct answer.

Template

Which decimal is the equivalent of [Fraction]?

    A.   [Answer 1]

    B.   [Answer 2]

    C.   [Answer 3]

    D.   [Answer 4]

Ratios and Proportional Relationships

Rate and Ratio

Sample Item

Two cyclists track how long they ride in hours. The table shows the distance traveled for Cyclist 1. The distance traveled for Cyclist 2 can be found using the following equation, where y represents distance traveled in miles over x hours.

Cyclist 1		Cyclist 2
Riding Time (hours)	Distance Traveled (miles)	
4	92	$y = 22x$
6	138	

- Use the information provided to find the unit rate, in miles per hour, for each cyclist. Show your work or explain your answers.

- Find the distance traveled, in miles, over 5 hours of riding from the faster cyclist.

Enter your answers and your work or explanation in the space provided.

Template Instructions

1. Choose definitions for [Individual], [Individual 1], [Individual 2], [Item 1], [Item 2], [Unit 1], [Unit 2], and [Comparison]. Insert them into the template.

2. Select [Quantity 1] through [Quantity 4]. Insert them into the template.

3. Select [Quantity 5] and [Constant]. Insert them into the template.

Template Key

Individual: A type of person or other entity that can perform an activity at a constant rate (for example, cyclist, water company, heart)

Individual 1: A unique version of [Individual] (for example, Cyclist 1, Water Company 1, Jim's heart)

Individual 2: A unique version of [Individual] (for example, Cyclist 2, Water Company 2, Todd's heart)

Item 1: A measurable characteristic of [Individual]'s activity in a proportional relationship with another characteristic (for example, riding time, water used, time beating)

Item 2: A measurable characteristic of [Individual]'s activity in a proportional relationship with [Item 1] (for example, distance traveled, cost, heart activity)

Unit 1: A unit in which [Item 1] can be measured (for example, hours, gallons, minutes)

Unit 2: A unit in which [Item 2] can be measured (for example, miles, dollars, beats)

Comparison: A word comparing the rate of activity between [Individual 1] and [Individual 2] (for example, *faster, cheaper, slower*)

Quantities 1–4: Positive rational numbers so [Quantity 1] and [Quantity 2] are in a proportional relationship with [Quantity 3] and [Quantity 4]

Quantity 5: A quantity of [Item 1] different from [Quantity 1] or [Quantity 2]

Constant: A constant that is reasonably close to the unit rate in the table

Template

Two [Individual] [Item 1] in [Unit 1]. The [Item 2] for [Individual 1] is in the table. The [Item 2] for [Individual 2] can be found using the equation, where y represents [Item 2] in [Unit 2] for x [Unit 1].

[Individual 1]		[Individual 2]
[Item 1] ([Unit 1])	[Item 2] ([Unit 2])	$y = $ [Constant]x
[Quantity 1]	[Quantity 3]	
[Quantity 2]	[Quantity 4]	

- Use the information provided to find the unit rate, in [Unit 2] per [Unit 1], for each [Individual]. Show your work or explain your answers.

- Find the [Item 2], in [Unit 2], of [Quantity 5] [Unit 1] of [Item 1] from the [Comparison] [Individual].

Enter your answers and your work or explanation in the space provided.

High School

Expressions, Equations, Inequalities, and Functions (EEIF)

Functions

Sample Item

In a certain region, a viral infection is spreading at the rate in the table.

Days	Number of People Infected (millions)
0	2
2	2.08
5	2.21

Write an exponential function, $V(d)$, you can use to model the spread of the infection after d days.

Enter your function in the space provided.

$V(d) =$

Template Instructions

1. Create a setting in which some object or entity is undergoing a measurable exponential change in magnitude. Insert the setting, the object or entity, and a verb describing the exponential change into the template as [Setting], [Object], and [Change].

2. Identify the independent variable [Unit A] and the dependent variable [Unit B] which measures the change in magnitude of the object. Insert them into the template.

3. Select nonsequential values for [Quantity 1] and [Quantity 2] according to the specifications in the key. Insert them into the template.

4. Select a value for [Quantity 3] as an initial magnitude of [Object]. Insert it into the template.

5. Choose variables for [Function Variable] and [Argument Variable]. Insert them into the template.

6. Create a function that defines an exponential change in magnitude for [Object].

7. Use the function to calculate values for [Quantity 4] and [Quantity 5]. Insert those values into the template.

Template Key

Setting: The setting for the scenario in which an object or other entity is exponentially changing in magnitude at a measurable rate

Object: An object or other entity that is exponentially changing in magnitude at a measurable rate (for example, viral infection, nuclear reaction, rodent population)

Change: An exponential change in magnitude of [Object] in either the positive or negative direction (for example, spread, increase, grow)

Function Variable: Any variable used to represent a function (for example, f, h, g)

Argument Variable: Any variable used to represent the argument of a function (for example, x, n, j)

Unit A: The independent variable in relation to which the exponential change in magnitude of [Object] is measured (for example, days, seconds, weeks)

Unit B: The dependent variable by which the exponential change in magnitude of [Object] is measured (for example, people, fission events, rodents)

Quantity 1: Any whole number

Quantity 2: Any whole number greater than [Quantity 1]

Quantity 3: Any whole number or decimal value indicating the initial magnitude of [Object]

Quantity 4: Any whole number or decimal value indicating an exponential change in magnitude from [Quantity 3]

Quantity 5: Any whole number or decimal value indicating an exponential change in magnitude from [Quantity 4] that displays the same rate of change as that between [Quantity 3] and [Quantity 4]

Template

In [Setting], [Object] [Change] at the rate the table shows.

[Unit A]	[Unit B]
0	[Quantity 3]
[Quantity 1]	[Quantity 4]
[Quantity 2]	[Quantity 5]

Write an exponential function, *[Function Variable]*(*[Argument Variable]*), you can use to model the [Change] of the [Object] after *[Argument Variable]* [Unit A].

Enter your function in the space provided.

[Function Variable](*[Argument Variable]*) =

Equations

Sample Item

Solve the quadratic equation $-12x^2 + 9x = -3(4 + 3x)$.

Circle a number from each group to complete the following sentence:

The solutions are <u>(Group 1)</u> and <u>(Group 2)</u>.

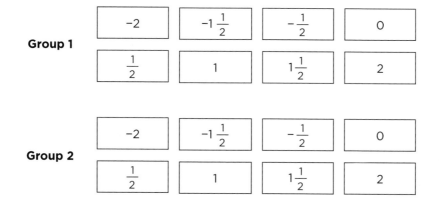

Template Instructions

1. Create [Equation]. Insert it into the template.

2. Select values for [#1] and [#2]. Insert them into the template.

Template Key

Equation: A quadratic equation with real roots not arranged in standard form (for example, should not be arranged in the form $ax^2 + bx + c = 0$)

#1: A set of eight real numbers that are possible values for the solutions of [Equation], arranged in order; two of these are correct answers.

#2: Identical to the values of [#1]

Template

Solve the quadratic equation [Equation].

Circle a number from each group to complete the following sentence:

The solutions are (Group 1) and (Group 2).

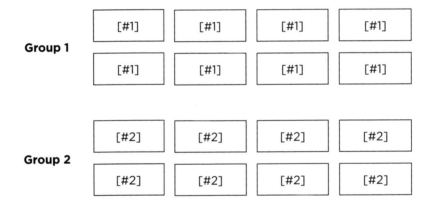

Inequalities

Sample Item

Which graph **best** represents the solution to this system of inequalities?

$$x - y \le 4$$

$$2x + 3y \ge 3$$

A.
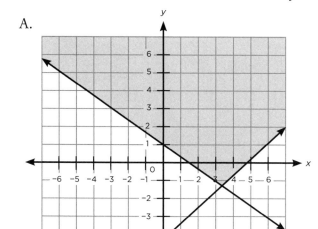

B.
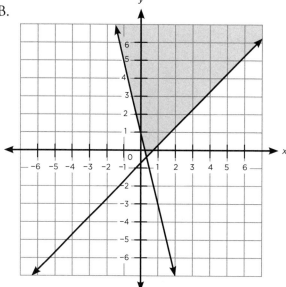

C.
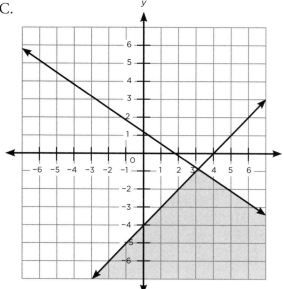

D.
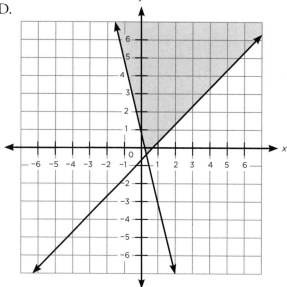

Template Instructions

1. Create [Inequality 1] and [Inequality 2]. Insert them into the template.

2. Create four coordinate plane graphs that each show a different system of two linear inequalities with the solution to the system shaded. One of the graphs should correctly represent the solution to the system in the problem.

Template Key

Inequality 1: A linear inequality in a system with [Inequality 2] so the system has a solution set (for example, does not include no solution)

Inequality 2: A linear inequality in a system with [Inequality 1] so the system has a solution set (for example, does not include no solution)

Template

Which graph **best** represents the solution to this system of inequalities?

[Inequality 1]   [Inequality 2]

A.

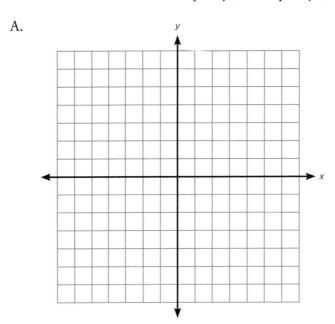

B.

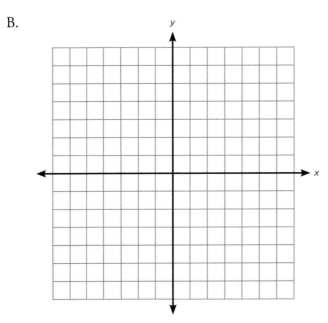

C.

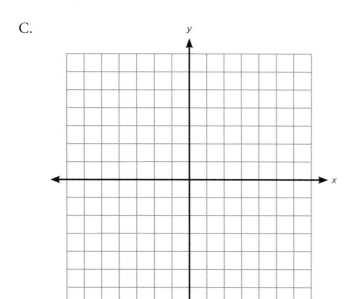

D.

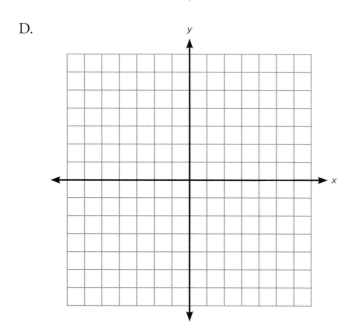

Expressions

Sample Item

The expression $8(1.22)^y$ represents the number of an invasive species of frog in an ecosystem at time y, in years. Which parts of the expression correspond to the number of frogs at their introduction to the ecosystem, the rate of growth per year, and the number of frogs when $y = 1$?

Draw a line connecting the parts and their corresponding box. Not all parts will be used.

| 1.22 | 0.22 | 8(1.22) | 8 | y |

| The number of frogs at their introduction to the ecosystem | The rate of growth per year | The number of frogs when $y = 1$ |

Template Instructions

1. Create a scenario in which some output is growing exponentially in relation to some input (for example, microorganisms growing in a culture, the incursion of an invasive species of frog, the spread of a disease). Choose definitions for [Input], [Input Unit], and [Output]. Insert them into the template.

2. Create [Expression]. Insert it into the template.

3. Choose a definition for [Input Variable]. Insert it into the template.

4. Choose definitions for [Change] and [Start]. Insert them into the template.

5. Choose definitions for [Answers 1–5]. Insert them into the template.

Template Key

Expression: An exponential expression of the form ab^x representing the exponential growth of [Output] in relation to [Input]

Change: A word or phrase indicating growth in [Output] (for example, *growth, infection*)

Start: A word or phrase indicating the point at which the exponential growth of [Output] begins (for example, the beginning, the introduction of the species to the ecosystem, the onset of the disease)

Output: A word or phrase representing the output that is growing exponentially in relation to [Input] (for example, the number of microorganisms in a culture, the number of an invasive species of frog in an ecosystem, the number of people infected with a disease)

Input: A word or phrase representing the input in relation to which [Output] is growing exponentially (for example, time)

Input Unit: The unit in which [Input] is measured (for example, day, year, week)

Input Variable: The variable in [Expression] that represents [Input] (for example, d, y, w)

Answers 1–5: A set of five different components of [Expression]; given that [Expression] takes the form ab^x, in which $b = 1 + r$, each term is one of the following: a, b, $a(b)$, r, x

Template

The expression [Expression] represents [Output] at [Input] [Input Variable], in [Input Unit]. Which parts of the expression correspond to [Output] at [Start], the rate of [Change] per [Input Unit], and [Output] when [Input Variable] = 1?

Appendix A
289

Draw a line connecting the parts and their corresponding box. Not all parts will be used.

[Answer 1]   [Answer 2]   [Answer 3]   [Answer 4]   [Answer 5]

[Output] at [Start]

The rate of [Change] per [Input Unit]

[Output] when [Input Variable] = 1

Geometry

Triangles

Sample Item

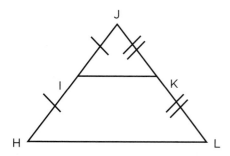

Given: I is the midpoint of $\overline{HJ}$ and K is the midpoint of $\overline{JL}$.

Prove: $\overline{IK} \parallel \overline{HL}$

Statement	Reason
1) I is the midpoint of $\overline{HJ}$; K is the midpoint of $\overline{JL}$.	1) Given
2)	2)
3)	3)
4) $\frac{IJ}{HJ} = \frac{JK}{JL}$	4) Transitive property of equality
5) $\angle J \cong \angle J$	5) Reflexive property of congruence
6) $\triangle HJL \sim \triangle IJK$	6) SAS similarity
7) $\angle JHL \cong \angle JIK$	7) Corresponding angles of similar triangles are congruent.
8) $\overline{IK} \parallel \overline{HL}$	8) If corresponding angles are congruent, then the lines are parallel.

Circle one option from each of the groups to complete the following statements:

In step 2 of the proof, the statement is (Group 1) and the reason is (Group 2).

In step 3 of the proof, the statement is (Group 3) and the reason is (Group 4).

GROUP 1	GROUP 2
$JK = \frac{1}{2}\,HJ$; $IJ = \frac{1}{2}\,JL$	Midpoint Theorem
$IJ = \frac{1}{3}\,HJ$; $JK = \frac{1}{3}\,JL$	Corresponding sides of similar triangles are proportional.
$IJ = \frac{1}{2}\,HJ$; $JK = \frac{1}{2}\,JL$	All sides of an equilateral triangle are congruent.

GROUP 3	GROUP 4
$\frac{IJ}{HJ} = \frac{1}{2}$; $\frac{1}{2} = \frac{JK}{JL}$	Corresponding sides of similar triangles are proportional.
$\frac{IJ}{JL} = \frac{1}{2}$; $\frac{1}{2} = \frac{JK}{HJ}$	Division property of equality
$\triangle HJL \sim \triangle IJK$	Reflexive property of equality
$\triangle HJL \cong \triangle IJK$	SAS similarity

Template Instructions

1. Select two steps from the proof in the template (these are the steps of the proof that the teacher requires students to supply). Delete those steps from the table, making sure to leave the empty cells and the numbers that label the deleted lines.

2. Choose definitions for [Step 1] and [Step 2]. Insert them into the template.

3. Choose definitions for [Group 1 Statement], [Group 2 Reason], [Group 3 Statement], and [Group 4 Reason]. Insert them into the template.

Template Key

Steps 1–2: Two numbers, each indicating one of the steps deleted from the proof in step 1 of the instructions

Group 1 Statement: A set of two or more different statements about the properties of the figure in the problem

- The statements may be correct or incorrect.

- One of these should be the statement deleted from [Step 1] of the proof in step 1 of the instructions.

- Examples may include: $\triangle HJL \sim \triangle IJK$, $\triangle HJL \cong \triangle IJK$, and so on.

Group 2 Reason: A set of two or more possible reasons for the [Group 1 Statements]

- These reasons may be correct or incorrect.

- One of these should be the reason associated with the statement deleted from [Step 1] of the proof in step 1 of the instructions.

- Examples may include: SSS congruence, SAS congruence, ASA congruence, AAS congruence, SSS similarity, AA similarity, HL similarity, SAS similarity, and so on.

Group 3 Statement: A set of two or more different statements about the properties of the figure in the problem

- The statements may be correct or incorrect.

- One of these should be the statement deleted from [Step 2] of the proof in step 1 of the instructions.

- Examples may include: $\angle JHL \cong \angle JIK$, $IK = \frac{1}{2} HL$, $\frac{IJ}{HJ} = \frac{JK}{JL} = \frac{IK}{HL}$, and so on.

Group 4 Reason: A set of two or more possible reasons for the [Group 3 Statements]

- These reasons may be correct or incorrect.

- One of these should be the reason associated with the statement deleted from [Step 2] of the proof in step 1 of the instructions.

- Examples may include: corresponding angles of similar triangles are congruent; corresponding angles of congruent triangles are congruent; corresponding sides of similar triangles are proportional; if the lines are parallel, then corresponding angles are congruent; if the lines are parallel, then alternate interior angles are congruent; in an isosceles triangle, base angles are congruent; vertical angles are congruent; Midpoint Theorem; and so on.

Template

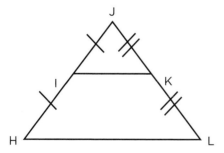

Given: I is the midpoint of $\overline{HJ}$ and K is the midpoint of $\overline{JL}$.

Prove: $\overline{IK} \parallel \overline{HL}$

Statement	Reason
1) I is the midpoint of $\overline{HJ}$; K is the midpoint of $\overline{JL}$.	1. Given
2) $IJ = \frac{1}{2}HJ$; $JK = \frac{1}{2}JL$	2. Midpoint theorem
3) $\frac{IJ}{HJ} = \frac{1}{2}$; $\frac{1}{2} = \frac{JK}{JL}$	3. Division property of equality
4) $\frac{IJ}{HJ} = \frac{JK}{JL}$	4. Transitive property of equality
5) $\angle J \cong \angle J$	5. Reflexive property of congruence
6) $\Delta HJL \sim \Delta IJK$	6. SAS similarity
7) $\angle JHL \cong \angle JIK$	7. Corresponding angles of similar triangles are congruent.
8) $\overline{IK} \parallel \overline{HL}$	8. If corresponding angles are congruent, then the lines are parallel.

Circle one option from each of the groups to complete the following statements:

In step [Step 1] of the proof, the statement is (Group 1) and the reason is (Group 2).

In step [Step 2] of the proof, the statement is (Group 3) and the reason is (Group 4).

GROUP 1	GROUP 2
[Group 1 Statement]	[Group 2 reason]
[Group 1 Statement]	[Group 2 reason]
[Group 1 Statement]	[Group 2 reason]
[Group 1 Statement]	[Group 2 reason]
GROUP 3	**GROUP 4**
[Group 3 Statement]	[Group 4 reason]
[Group 3 Statement]	[Group 4 reason]
[Group 3 Statement]	[Group 4 reason]
[Group 3 Statement]	[Group 4 reason]

Lines and Angles

Sample Item

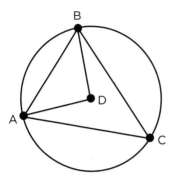

If *m∠ABD* = 43°, find *m∠BCA*, in degrees.

Fill in your answer in the box.

Template Instructions

1. Create a circle with an inscribed triangle, then create a central angle within the circle whose endpoints lie at two of the vertices of the triangle. Label the center of the circle and the vertices of the triangle. Insert the figure into the template in place of the box.

2. Choose a definition for [Angle 1]. Insert it into the template.

3. Select a value for [Quantity]. Insert it into the template.

4. Identify the definition of [Angle 2]. Insert it into the template.

Template Key

Quantity: A whole-number value representing the measure of [Angle 1] in degrees

Angle 1: Three letters that define an angle formed by one arm of the central angle and the side of the triangle that lies between the central angle's arms

Angle 2: Three letters that define the angle of the inscribed triangle that does not intersect with the central angle of the circle (that is, the vertex of [Angle 2] should be the vertex of the triangle that does *not* intersect with either arm of the central angle)

Template

If $m\angle$*[Angle 1]* = [Quantity]°, find $m\angle$*[Angle 2]*, in degrees.

Fill in your answer in the box.

Transformations

Sample Item

In the *xy*-coordinate plane, $\triangle ABC$ has vertices at $A(3, 2)$, $B(3, 4)$, and $C(5, 4)$. $\triangle DEF$ is shown in the plane.

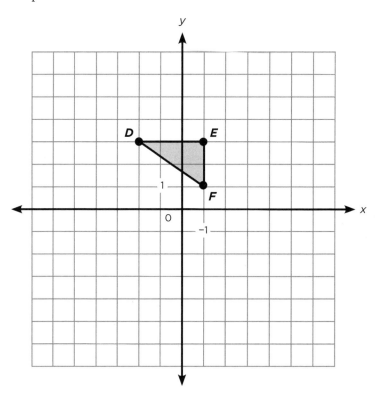

What is the scale factor and center of dilation that maps $\triangle ABC$ to $\triangle DEF$?

   A.   The scale factor is $1\frac{1}{2}$, and the center of dilation is the origin.

   B.   The scale factor is $1\frac{1}{2}$, and the center of dilation is point C.

   C.   The scale factor is $1\frac{2}{3}$, and the center of dilation is the origin.

   D.   The scale factor is $\frac{2}{3}$, and the center of dilation is point C.

Template Instructions

1.   Choose definitions for [A], [B], and [C]. Insert them into the template.

2.   Choose a center of dilation and a scale factor for mapping $\triangle ABC$ onto $\triangle DEF$. The center of dilation should be either the origin or one of the vertices of

$\triangle ABC$. Care should be taken that the center of dilation and scale factor are chosen so the vertices of $\triangle DEF$ are all integers.

3.   Create a coordinate plane containing $\triangle DEF$.

4.   Choose definitions for [Answer Scale Factor 1] through [Answer Scale Factor 4]. Insert them into the template.

5.   Choose definitions for [Answer Point 1] through [Answer Point 4]. Care should be taken that only one of the answer choices in the problem contains both the correct scale factor and correct center of dilation. Insert them into the template.

Template Key

A: An ordered pair consisting of integers and representing the coordinates of point A

B: An ordered pair consisting of integers and representing the coordinates of point B

C: An ordered pair consisting of integers and representing the coordinates of point C

Answer Scale Factors 1–4: Values representing possible scale factors for mapping $\triangle ABC$ onto $\triangle DEF$; one of these is the correct scale factor.

Answer Points 1–4: Each of these elements should be one of the following options: the origin, point A, point B, point C. They may be repeated and not all need be used. One of the elements should form part of the correct answer.

Template

In the xy-coordinate plane, $\triangle ABC$ has vertices at $A([A])$, $B([B])$, $C([C])$. $\triangle DEF$ is shown in the plane.

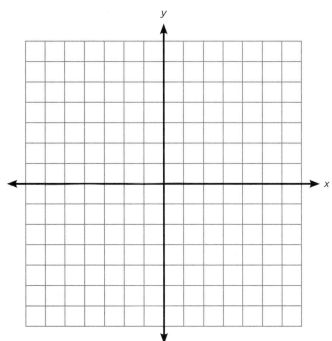

What is the scale factor and center of dilation that maps $\triangle ABC$ to $\triangle DEF$?

- A. The scale factor is [Answer Scale Factor 1], and the center of dilation is [Answer Point 1].

- B. The scale factor is [Answer Scale Factor 2], and the center of dilation is [Answer Point 2].

- C. The scale factor is [Answer Scale Factor 3], and the center of dilation is [Answer Point 3].

- D. The scale factor is [Answer Scale Factor 4], and the center of dilation is [Answer Point 4].

Circles

Sample Item

The equation $x^2 + 8x - 16 = -y^2 + 4y$ describes a circle in the coordinate plane.

Find the radius of the circle and the coordinates of its center.

Fill in your answers in the space provided. Fill in **only** your answers.

radius = [   ] units

center: ([   ] , [   ])

Template Instructions

1. Create [Equation]. Insert it into the template.

Template Key

Equation: An equation of a circle that should not be in standard form—that is, should not take the form $(x - h)^2 + (y - k)^2 = r^2$.

Template

The equation [Equation] describes a circle in the coordinate plane.

Find the radius of the circle and the coordinates of its center.

Fill in your answers in the space provided. Fill in **only** your answers.

radius = [   ] units

center: ([   ] , [   ])

Volume

Sample Item

A container is shaped like a right circular cylinder with diameter 3 inches and height 2.5 inches. The container is filled with cleaning solution to a height of 2 inches. One ring that is completely in the cleaning solution will displace about 0.15 fluid ounces of cleaning solution. (Note: 1 cubic inch is approximately 0.55 fluid ounces.)

A jeweler places tarnished rings in the cleaning solution to restore them. Create a model to determine the greatest number of tarnished rings that can be in the container before the cleaning solution overflows. Explain your reasoning.

Template Instructions

1. Choose definitions for [Container], [Substance], [Object], [Person], and [Placement]. Insert them into the template.

2. Choose definitions for [Length Unit] and [Volume Unit]. Insert them into the template.

3. Select values for [Container Diameter], [Container Height], [Substance Height], and [Volume]. Insert them into the template.

4. Select a value for [Ratio]. Insert it into the template.

Template Key

Container: A container in the shape of a right circular cylinder filled with some [Substance] in which [Objects] are placed (for example, a pool filled with water being entered by people, a container filled with a cleaning solution in which tarnished rings are being placed, a jar filled with vinegar in which cucumbers are being pickled)

Substance: The substance filling [Container] into which [Objects] are placed (for example, water, cleaning solution, vinegar)

Object: An item placed into a [Container] filled with [Substance] (for example, people, tarnished rings, cucumbers)

Person: A person or other entity placing or directing the placement of [Object] into a [Container] filled with [Substance] (for example, Angela, a jeweler, Seth)

Placement: A phrase describing the placement of [Object] into [Container] (for example, invites her friends over for a pool party, places tarnished rings in cleaning solution to restore them, makes pickles by submerging fresh cucumbers in the jar of vinegar)

Length Unit: The unit of length in which the diameter and height of [Container] are measured (for example, feet, inches, centimeters)

Volume Unit: The unit of volume in which the volume of [Substance] is measured (for example, gallons, fluid ounces, cups)

Container Diameter: A value representing the diameter of [Container], measured in [Length Unit]

Container Height: A value representing the height of [Container], measured in [Length Unit]

Substance Height: A value representing the height to which [Container] is filled with [Substance], measured in [Length Unit]

Volume: A value representing the amount of [Substance] displaced by one [Object], measured in [Volume Unit]

Ratio: A value indicating the number of [Volume Unit] equivalent to one cubic [Length Unit]; if necessary, round this value to an appropriate decimal place.

Template

A [Container] is shaped like a right circular cylinder with diameter [Container Diameter] [Length Unit] and height [Container Height] [Length Unit]. The [Container] is filled with [Substance] to a height of [Substance Height] [Length Unit]. One [Object] completely in the [Substance] will displace about [Volume] [Volume Unit] of [Substance]. (Note: 1 cubic [Length Unit] is approximately [Ratio] [Volume Unit].)

[Person] [Placement]. Create a model to determine the greatest number of [Object] that can be in the [Container] before the [Substance] overflows. Explain your reasoning.

2-D and 3-D Shapes

Sample Item

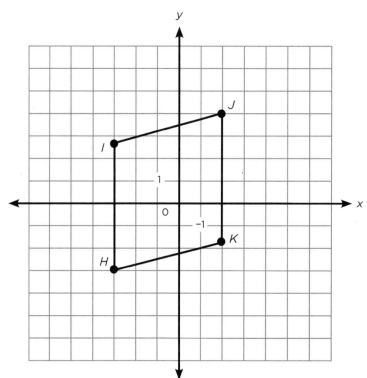

In the preceding figure, the vertices of *HIJK* are $H(-3, -3)$, $I(-3, 2\frac{3}{4})$, $J(2, 4)$, $K(2, -1\frac{3}{4})$. Give a mathematical justification that *HIJK* is a parallelogram.

Template Instructions

1. Create a coordinate plane containing a parallelogram and label its vertices.

2. Choose definitions for [V1], [V2], [V3], and [V4]. Insert them into the template.

3. Choose definitions for [C1], [C2], [C3], and [C4]. Insert them into the template.

Template Key

V1: A letter representing the first vertex of the parallelogram

V2: A letter representing the second vertex of the parallelogram

V3: A letter representing the third vertex of the parallelogram

V4: A letter representing the fourth vertex of the parallelogram

C1: The coordinates of [V1] in ordered-pair form

C2: The coordinates of [V2] in ordered-pair form

C3: The coordinates of [V3] in ordered-pair form

C4: The coordinates of [V4] in ordered-pair form

Template

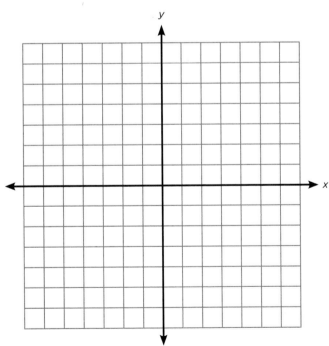

In the preceding figure, the vertices of *[V1][V2][V3][V4]* are *[V1]*[C1], *[V2]*[C2], *[V3]*[C3], and *[V4]*[C4]. Give a mathematical justification that *[V1][V2][V3][V4]* is a parallelogram.

Operations

Operation Not Specified

Sample Item

A furniture outlet sells two different sizes of table. A large table can seat more people than a small table. All large tables seat the same number of people and all small tables seat the same number of people.

A restaurant buys 6 large tables and 18 small tables to seat a total of 168 customers. A second restaurant buys 8 large tables and 12 small tables to seat a total of 152 customers. A third restaurant wants to be able to seat 172 people.

Enter the number of large tables the third restaurant buys after it buys 22 small tables.

```
┌─────────────────┐
│                 │
└─────────────────┘
```

Template Instructions

1. Choose a definition for [Scenario]. Insert it into the template.

2. Choose definitions for [Object], [Type 1], and [Type 2]. Insert them into the template.

3. Choose a definition for [Relative Magnitude]. Insert it into the template.

4. Choose a definition for [Same Magnitude]. Insert it into the template.

5. Select a different value of [Property] for each of the two types of [Object].

6. Choose definitions for [Person 1], [Person 2], and [Person 3]. Insert them into the template.

7. Choose the number of each type of [Object] that [Person 1] selects, acquires, or uses, and then calculate the combined magnitude of [Property] for the total [Object] of both types selected by [Person 1].

8. Using the number of each type of [Object] selected and the combined total [Property], choose a definition for [Person 1 Select]. Insert it into the template.

9. Choose the number of each type of [Object] that [Person 2] selects, acquires, or uses, and then calculate the combined magnitude of [Property] for the total [Object] of both types selected by [Person 2].

10. Using the number of each type of [Object] selected and the combined total [Property], choose a definition for [Person 2 Select]. Insert it into the template.

11. Choose the number of each type of [Object] that [Person 3] selects, acquires, or uses, and then calculate the combined magnitude of [Property] for the total [Object] of both types selected by [Person 3].

12. Using **only** the combined total [Property], choose a definition for [Person 3 Total]. Insert it into the template.

13. Choose a definition for [Person 3 Acquire]. Insert it into the template.

14. Select [Quantity]. Insert it into the template.

Template Key

Scenario: A statement describing a scenario in which two different types of objects or entities each have the same measurable [Property] and in which the magnitude of [Property] is different for each of the two types (for example, a pizza parlor sells both medium and large pizzas, bottles of water are sold in two different sizes, a furniture outlet sells two different sizes of table)

Relative Magnitude: A statement describing the relative magnitude (for example, *greater than* or *less than*) of [Property] for the two different types of [Object] (for example, a large pizza can feed more people than a medium pizza, a large bottle contains more water than a small bottle, a large table can seat more people than a small table)

Same Magnitude: A statement that all [Object] of the same type have the same magnitude of [Property] (for example, all large pizzas feed the same number of people and all medium pizzas feed the same number of people, all large bottles contain the same amount of water and all small bottles contain the same amount of water, all large tables seat the same number of people and all small tables seat the same number of people)

Object: An object or other entity that comes in two varieties, each having a different magnitude of [Property] (for example, different sizes of pizza that can feed different numbers of people, different sizes of bottled water that contain different amounts, different sizes of tables that can seat different numbers of people)

Property: A measurable property possessed by [Object] in which the two different types of [Object] each have a different value of [Property] (for example, medium pizzas feed 6 people while large pizzas feed 8, small bottles of water carry 8 fluid ounces while large bottles carry 16, small tables seat 6 people while large tables seat 10)

Type 1: The first of two different types of [Object] (for example, medium, small, large)

Type 2: The second of two different types of [Object] (for example, medium, small, large)

Person 1: A person or other entity selecting, acquiring, or using a number of each type of [Object] (for example, Robert, Julia, a restaurant)

Person 2: A person or other entity selecting, acquiring, or using a number of each type of [Object] (for example, Aiden, Sydney, a second restaurant)

Person 3: A person or other entity selecting, acquiring, or using an unknown number of each type of [Object] (for example, Cecilia, Varun, a third restaurant)

Person 1 Select: A statement in which [Person 1] selects, acquires, or uses a stated number of each type of object and in which the combined magnitude of [Property] across all [Object] is also stated (for example, Robert buys 6 medium pizzas and 4 large pizzas to feed 68 people, Julia packs 2 large bottles of water and 4 small bottles for a total of 64 fluid ounces of water, a restaurant buys 6 large tables and 18 small tables to seat a total of 168 customers)

Person 2 Select: A statement in which [Person 2] selects, acquires, or uses a stated number of each type of object and in which the combined magnitude of [Property] across all [Object] is also stated (for example, Aiden buys 5 medium pizzas and 3 large pizzas to feed 54 people, Sydney packs 1 large bottle of water and 6 small bottles for a total of 64 fluid ounces of water, a second restaurant buys 8 large tables and 12 small tables to seat a total of 152 customers)

Person 3 Total: A statement in which [Person 3] needs to acquire an unstated number of each type of [Object] to reach a stated total of [Property] (for example, Cecilia wants to feed 88 people, Varun wants to carry 72 fluid ounces of water on a hiking trip, a third restaurant wants to be able to seat 172 people)

Person 3 Acquire: A word or phrase describing the act of [Person 3] selecting, acquiring, or using [Object] (for example, Cecilia buys, Varun packs, the third restaurant buys)

Quantity: The number of [Type 2] [Object] that [Person 3] selects, acquires, or uses (that is, the number of [Type 2] [Object] chosen in step 11 of the instructions)

Template

[Scenario]. [Relative Magnitude]. [Same Magnitude].

[Person 1] [Person 1 Select]. [Person 2] [Person 2 Select]. [Person 3] [Person 3 Total].

Enter the number of [Type 1] [Object] [Person 3 Acquire] after [Person 3 Acquire] [Quantity] [Type 2] [Object].

Quantity and Number

Equivalence

Sample Item

Find the equation equivalent to the following quadratic equation.

$$x^2 - 5x + 27A = 0$$

A. $x(x - 5) = 27$

B. $(x - 5)^2 = 52$

C. $(x - 2\frac{1}{2})^2 = -20\frac{3}{4}$

D. $(x - 2\frac{1}{2})^2 = 33\frac{1}{4}$

Template Instructions

1. Create [Equation]. Insert it into the template.

2. Create [Answer 1] through [Answer 4]. Insert them into the template.

Template Key

Equation: A quadratic equation of the form $x^2 + ax + b = 0$.

Answers 1–4: Four quadratic equations, one of which is equivalent to [Equation] and three of which are not. These equations should possess the following properties:

- All variable terms should lie on one side of the equation.

- The side of the equation with no variable terms should be a non-zero number.

- The side of the equation with the variable terms should contain a binomial inside parentheses; this binomial may or may not be raised to the second power and may or may not be accompanied by other terms.

Template

Find the equation equivalent to the following quadratic equation.

[Equation]

A. [Answer 1]

B. [Answer 2]

C. [Answer 3]

D. [Answer 4]

Ratios and Proportional Relationships

Rate and Ratio

Sample Item

The graph models the height, h, in inches, at time t, in seconds, of a girl jumping rope. Each point indicated on the graph represents the girl's height at the end of each 0.25 second interval.

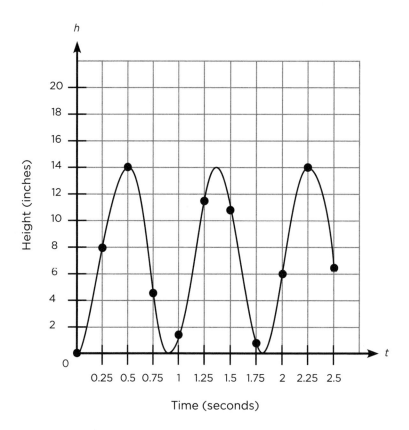

Time (seconds)

Select **1** time interval for which the average rate of change in height is approximately 5 inches per 0.25 seconds.

- A. from 0 seconds to 0.25 seconds
- B. from 0.25 seconds to 0.5 seconds
- C. from 0.5 seconds to 0.75 seconds
- D. from 0.75 seconds to 1 second
- E. from 1 second to 1.25 seconds
- F. from 1.25 seconds to 1.5 seconds
- G. from 1.5 seconds to 1.75 seconds
- H. from 1.75 seconds to 2 seconds
- I. from 2 seconds to 2.25 seconds
- J. from 2.25 seconds to 2.5 seconds

Template Instructions

1. Choose definitions for [Scenario], [Independent Variable], and [Dependent Variable]. Insert them into the template.

2. Choose definitions for [V1], [V2], [Unit 1], and [Unit 2]. Insert them into the template.

3. Create a wave graph on a coordinate plane to represent the relationship between [Dependent Variable] and [Independent Variable].

4. Identify [A] through [K]. Insert them into the template. Because the number of elements [A] through [K] will vary based upon the number of vertical grid lines in the graph, the number of answer choices in the problem may also vary. If adding additional answer choices, be sure to follow the pattern in the template.

5. Identify [Quantity 1]. Insert it into the template.

6. Choose a definition for [Quantity 2]. Insert it into the template.

7. Identify [Count]. Insert it into the template.

Template Key

Scenario: A phrase describing a relationship between an [Independent Variable] and a [Dependent Variable] that may be modeled by a wave graph (for example, the height over time of a girl jumping rope, the height over time of a tide, the height over time of a bouncing weight suspended from a spring); most of the maximum and minimum values of [Dependent Variable] (for example, the peaks and troughs of the wave that models the scenario) should **not** intersect with the vertical grid lines of the graph.

Independent Variable: The independent variable in [Scenario] (for example, time)

Dependent Variable: The dependent variable in [Scenario] (for example, height)

V1: A letter representing [Dependent Variable] (for example, h)

V2: A letter representing [Independent Variable] (for example, t)

Unit 1: The unit in which [Dependent Variable] is measured (for example, inches, feet, millimeters)

Unit 2: The unit in which [Independent Variable] is measured (for example, seconds, hours)

A–K: The values on the horizontal axis of the graph (for example, the x-values that correspond with the vertical grid lines on the graph) in sequential order, beginning with 0; the number of values will vary based upon the number of vertical grid lines in the created graph.

Quantity 1: A value representing the interval between adjacent vertical grid lines on the graph

Quantity 2: A value representing the approximate average rate of change in [Dependent Variable] across a chosen pair of adjacent vertical grid lines on the graph; these grid lines should be chosen so the interval between them includes either a peak or a trough of the graph.

Count: The number of different pairs of adjacent vertical grid lines on the graph across which [Dependent Variable] displays an approximate rate of change of [Quantity 2]

Template

The graph models the [Dependent Variable], *[V1]*, in [Unit 1], at [Independent Variable] *[V2]*, in [Unit 2], of [Scenario]. Each point indicated on the graph represents [Dependent Variable] at the end of each [Quantity 1] [Unit 2] interval.

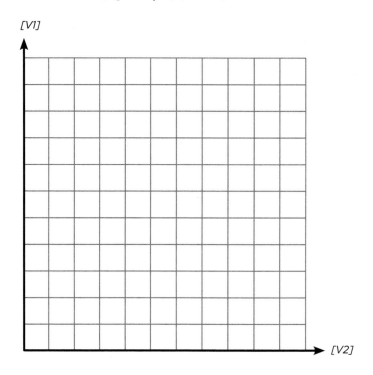

Select **[Count]** [Independent Variable] intervals for which the average rate of change in [Dependent Variable] is approximately [Quantity 2] [Unit 1] per [Quantity 1] [Unit 2].

A.   from [A] [Unit 2] to [B] [Unit 2]

B.   from [B] [Unit 2] to [C] [Unit 2]

C.   from [C] [Unit 2] to [D] [Unit 2]

D.   from [D] [Unit 2] to [E] [Unit 2]

E.   from [E] [Unit 2] to [F] [Unit 2]

F.   from [F] [Unit 2] to [G] [Unit 2]

G.   from [G] [Unit 2] to [H] [Unit 2]

H.   from [H] [Unit 2] to [I] [Unit 2]

I.   from [I] [Unit 2] to [J] [Unit 2]

J.   from [J] [Unit 2] to [K] [Unit 2]

Trigonometry

Sample Item

The figure shows triangle *JKL*.

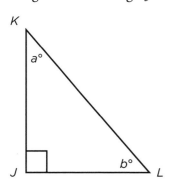

Select **all** expressions that **must be** equivalent to *sin K*.

A.   *cos b°*

B.   *sin (90 – a)°*

C.   *sin b°*

D.   *sin (90 – b)°*

E.   *cos (90 – a)°*

F.   *cos a°*

G.   *cos (90 – b)°*

Template Instructions

1.   Create a right triangle with vertices [V1], [V2], and [V3] and non-right angles [A1] and [A2]. Insert it into the template in place of the box.

2.   Insert [V1], [V2], [V3], [A1], and [A2] into the template.

3.   Identify [V]. Insert it into the template.

4.   Choose definitions for [Ratio 1] and [Ratio 2]. Insert them into the template.

5.   Choose definitions for [Answer 1] through [Answer 7]. Insert them into the template.

Template Key

V1–V3: Uppercase letters representing the vertices of the triangle

V: Either [V1], [V2], or [V3]; the label of the vertex that corresponds to [A1]

A1–A2: Lowercase letters representing the measures of the non-right angles of the triangle

Ratio 1: Either *sin* or *cos* and different from [Ratio 2]

Ratio 2: Either *sin* or *cos* and different from [Ratio 1]

Answers 1–7: Trigonometric expressions; at least one of these is a correct answer. Each expression should take one of the following forms:

- [*Ratio* 2] [*A1*]°

- [*Ratio* 2] [*A2*]°

- [*Ratio* 1] [*A2*]°

- [*Ratio* 1] (90 – [*A2*])°

- [*Ratio* 1] (90 – [*A1*])°

- [*Ratio* 2] (90 – [*A2*])°

- [*Ratio* 2] (90 – [*A1*])°

Template

The figure shows triangle *[V1][V2][V3]*.

Select **all** expressions that **must be** equivalent to [*Ratio* 1] *[V]*.

- A. [Answer 1]
- B. [Answer 2]
- C. [Answer 3]
- D. [Answer 4]
- E. [Answer 5]
- F. [Answer 6]
- G. [Answer 7]

SAT

Expressions, Equations, Inequalities, and Functions (EEIF)

Equations

Sample Item

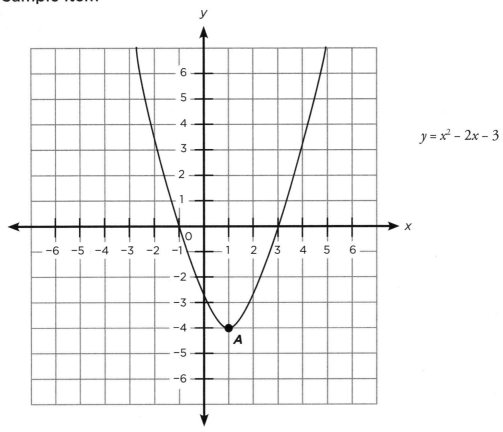

$$y = x^2 - 2x - 3$$

Which of the following is an equivalent form of the equation of the preceding graph in the *xy*-plane from which the coordinates of vertex *A* can be identified as constants in the equation?

A. $y = (x - 3)(x + 1)$

B. $y = (x + 3)(x - 1)$

C. $y = x(x - 2) - 3$

D. $y = (x - 1)^2 - 4$

Template Instructions

1. Create [Equation]. Insert it into the template.

2. Create a coordinate plane containing the graph of [Equation]. Label the vertex of the parabola *A*.

3. Create [Answer 1] through [Answer 4]. Insert them into the template.

Template Key

Equation: A quadratic equation in standard form with a leading coefficient of 1

Answers 1–4: Quadratic equations in nonstandard form that are possible solutions to the problem; one of these is the correct answer.

Template

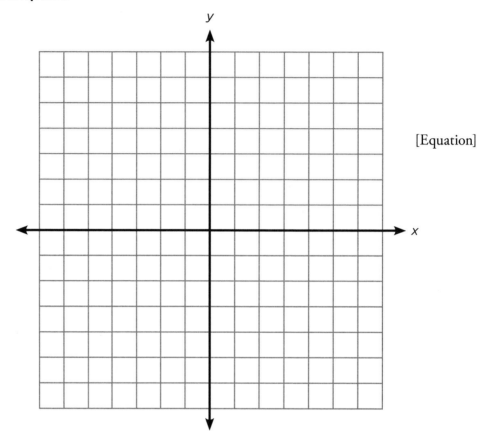

[Equation]

Which of the following is an equivalent form of the equation of the preceding graph in the *xy*-plane from which the coordinates of vertex *A* can be identified as constants in the equation?

    A.   [Answer 1]

    B.   [Answer 2]

    C.   [Answer 3]

    D.   [Answer 4]

Expressions

Sample Item

Prudence bought a book that had a 30 percent discount off its original price. The total amount she paid was d dollars, including an 11 percent sales tax on the discounted price. Which of the following represents the original price of the book in terms of d?

A. $0.81d$

B. $\dfrac{d}{0.81}$

C. $(0.7)(1.11)d$

D. $\dfrac{d}{(0.7)(1.11)}$

Template Instructions

1. Choose definitions for [Person], [Item], and [Variable]. Insert them into the template.

2. Select values for [Quantity 1] and [Quantity 2]. Insert them into the template.

3. Create [Answer 1] through [Answer 4]. Insert them into the template.

Template Key

Person: An individual who can purchase something (for example, Prudence, Javier, Lilly)

Item: An item that can be purchased (for example, a book, a table, a car)

Quantity 1: A single- or double-digit whole number that represents the discount rate on [Item]

Quantity 2: A single- or double-digit whole number that represents the sales tax rate on [Item]

Variable: A variable that represents the total price paid for [Item]

Answers 1–4: Expressions that represent possible solutions to the problem; one of these is the correct answer.

Template

[Person] bought [Item] that had a [Quantity 1] percent discount off its original price. The total amount [Person] paid was *[Variable]* dollars, including a [Quantity 2] percent sales tax on the discounted price. Which of the following represents the original price of the [Item] in terms of *[Variable]*?

A. [Answer 1]

B. [Answer 2]

C. [Answer 3]

D. [Answer 4]

Functions

Sample Item

$$f(x) = ax^2 + 238$$

For the function, f, a is a constant and $f(5) = 13$. What is the value of $f(-5)$?

- A. 13
- B. 0
- C. –9
- D. –13

Template Instructions

1. Select values for [Quantity 1] and [Quantity 2]. Insert them into the template.

2. Select an integer value for a and use the selected value to calculate [Quantity 3]. Insert it into the template.

3. Create [Answer 1] through [Answer 4]. Insert these values into the template.

Template Key

Quantity 1: An integer

Quantity 2: An integer

Quantity 3: An integer such that $f([Quantity 1]) = [Quantity 2]$ for the function $f(x) = ax^2 + [Quantity 3]$ when a is an integer constant

Answers 1–4: Integers that represent possible solutions to the problem; one of these is the correct answer.

Template

$$f(x) = ax^2 + [Quantity 3]$$

For the function f, a is a constant and $f([Quantity 1]) = [Quantity 2]$. What is the value of $f(-[Quantity 1])$?

- A. [Answer 1]
- B. [Answer 2]
- C. [Answer 3]
- D. [Answer 4]

Inequalities

Sample Item

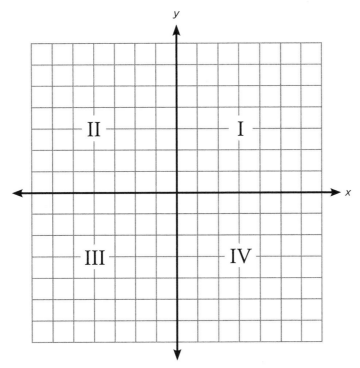

If the system of inequalities $y < -2x + 3$ and $y \geq \frac{1}{3}x - 1$ is graphed in the *xy*-plane, which quadrant contains no solutions to the system?

- A.   Quadrant I
- B.   Quadrant III
- C.   Quadrant IV
- D.   There are solutions in all four quadrants.

Template Instructions

1.   Construct the system of inequalities [Inequality 1] and [Inequality 2]. Insert them into the template.

2.   Select [Answer 1] through [Answer 4]. Insert these answer choices into the template.

Template Key

Inequality 1: A linear inequality in two variables with an integer or unit-fraction slope and a one-digit *y*-intercept

Inequality 2: A linear inequality in two variables with the same parameters as [Inequality 1] that intersects [Inequality 1]

Answers 1–4: Four out of the following five choices; at least one of these is a correct answer.

- Quadrant I
- Quadrant II
- Quadrant III
- Quadrant IV
- There are solutions in all four quadrants.

Template

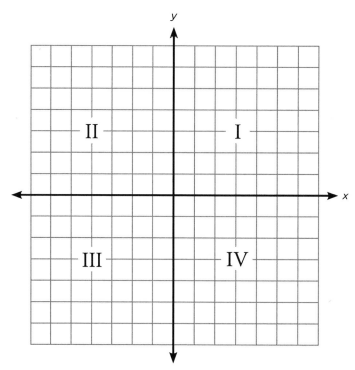

If the system of inequalities [Inequality 1] and [Inequality 2] is graphed in the *xy*-plane, which quadrant contains no solutions to the system?

A.   [Answer 1]

B.   [Answer 2]

C.   [Answer 3]

D.   [Answer 4]

Operations

Operation Not Specified

Sample Item

Two dog-food bowls hold different amounts of food. Rosco's bowl holds 4.5 cups, while Ollie's bowl holds 3 cups. The total amount of food eaten from 103 bowls was 385.5 cups. How many of the bowls of food were Rosco's?

- A.   51
- B.   52
- C.   86
- D.   129

Template Instructions

1. Choose definitions for [Category], [Item 1], [Item 2], [Action 1], [Action 2], [Object], and [Unit]. Insert them into the template.

2. Select values for x and y and use them to calculate [Quantity 3]. Insert it into the template.

3. Select values for [Quantity 1] and [Quantity 2] and use them, along with the selected values for x and y, to calculate [Quantity 4]. Insert [Quantity 1], [Quantity 2], and [Quantity 4] into the template.

4. Using the selected value for x as the correct answer, create [Answer 1] through [Answer 4]. Insert them into the template.

Template Key

Category: A category of items with some measurable characteristic (for example, dog-food bowls, frozen treats, building blocks)

Item 1: A specific type of [Category] (for example, Rosco's bowl, ice pops, red blocks)

Item 2: A specific type of [Category], different from [Item 1] (for example, Ollie's bowl, ice cream cones, blue blocks)

Action 1: The action that expresses the characteristic of [Category] (for example, hold, cost, are)

Action 2: An action done to [Object] (for example, eaten, spent, built)

Object: The measurable characteristic of [Category] (for example, amount of food, amount of money, height)

x: A positive value

y: A positive value different from x

Quantity 1: A positive value

Quantity 2: A positive value different from [Quantity 1]

Quantity 3: A value so $x + y$ = [Quantity 3]

Quantity 4: A value so [*Quantity* 1]x + [*Quantity* 2]y = [*Quantity* 4]

Unit: The unit of measurement for [Object] (for example, cups, dollars, inches)

Answers 1–4: Possible values for answer choices; one of these is the correct answer.

Template

Two [Category] [Action 1] different [Object]. [Item 1] [Action 1] [Quantity 1] [Unit], while [Item 2] [Action 1] [Quantity 2] [Unit]. The total [Object] [Action 2] from [Quantity 3] [Category] was [Quantity 4] [Unit]. How many of the [Category] were [Item 1]?

    A.   [Answer 1]

    B.   [Answer 2]

    C.   [Answer 3]

    D.   [Answer 4]

Quantity and Number

Equivalence

Sample Item

$$(x^2 - 2y - 6x^2y^2) + (4y - 2x^2 + 2x^2y^2)$$

Which of the following is equivalent to the preceding expression?

    A. $-4x^2y^2 + 5x^2 - 4y$

    B. $-4x^2y^2 - x^2 + 2y$

    C. $-5x^2y^2 + 2y$

    D. $-8x^2y^2 - 3x^2 + 6y$

Template Instructions

1. Construct [Expression]. Insert it into the template.

2. Create [Answer 1] through [Answer 4]. Insert them into the template.

Template Key

Expression: An expression in which a trinomial is added to or subtracted from another trinomial; each term of the trinomials should take one of the following forms, in which x and y are variables and a is a one-digit integer coefficient:

   • ax^2y^2

   • ax^2y

- axy^2

- axy

- ax^2

- ay^2

- ax

- ay

For example: $(x^2 - 2y - 6x^2y^2) + (4y - 2x^2 + 2x^2y^2)$

Answers 1–4: Polynomial expressions with like terms combined, representing possible solutions; one of these is the correct answer.

Template

[Expression]

Which of the following is equivalent to the preceding expression?

A. [Answer 1]

B. [Answer 2]

C. [Answer 3]

D. [Answer 4]

Ratios and Proportional Relationships

Rate and Ratio

Sample Item

Courtney can run at least 4 miles per hour and at most 8 miles per hour. Based on this information, what is a possible amount of time, in hours, that it could take Courtney to run 24 miles?

Template Instructions

1. Choose definitions for [Producer], [Produce], [Product], and [Time]. Insert them into the template.

2. Select values for [Quantity 1], [Quantity 2], and [Quantity 3]. Insert them into the template.

Template Key

Producer: A person or other entity capable of producing something or performing an action (for example, Courtney, a coal miner, an apple tree)

Produce: The action done by [Producer] (for example, run, mine, produce)

Product: The output generated by [Producer] (for example, miles, tons of coal, pounds of apples)

Time: A unit of time in which [Product] is produced (for example, hour, day, year)

Quantity 1: A one- or two-digit whole number that is a factor of [Quantity 3]

Quantity 2: A one- or two-digit whole number that is greater than [Quantity 1] and is a factor of [Quantity 3]

Quantity 3: A two- or three-digit whole number that is divisible by [Quantity 1] and [Quantity 2]

Template

[Producer] can [Produce] at least [Quantity 1] [Product] per [Time] and at most [Quantity 2] [Product] per [Time]. Based on this information, what is a possible amount of time, in [Time], it could take [Producer] to [Produce] [Quantity 3] [Product]?

ACT

Expressions, Equations, Inequalities, and Functions (EEIF)

Equations

Sample Item

The magnitude of an earthquake on the Richter scale, R, can be modeled by the equation $R = log(\frac{A}{A_0})$, where A is the measure of the amplitude of the earthquake wave and A_0 is a constant (the amplitude of the smallest detectable wave). What is the magnitude on the Richter scale of an earthquake with a wave amplitude 1,000 times the value of A_0?

A.   3

B.   5

C.   30

D.   100

E.   10,000

Template Instructions

1.   Select [Equation], [Variable 1], [Variable 2], and [Constant]. Insert them into the template.

2.   Select [Unit 1] and [Unit 2]. Insert them into the template.

3.   Select [Quantity]. Insert it into the template.

4.   Create [Answer 1] through [Answer 5]. Insert them into the template.

Template Key

Equation: An equation with a dependent variable, [Variable 1], on one side and the logarithm of a fraction on the other side; the fraction should consist of an independent variable, [Variable 2], over a constant, [Constant] (for example, decibel measure of sound, $d = 10log(\frac{I}{I_0})$; Richter scale magnitude of an earthquake, $R = log(\frac{A}{A_0})$).

Variable 1: The dependent variable in [Equation] (for example, d, R)

Variable 2: The independent variable in [Equation] (for example, I, A)

Constant: The constant in [Equation] (for example, I_0, A_0)

Unit 1: The unit in which the dependent variable in [Equation] is defined (for example, decibel, Richter scale magnitude)

Unit 2: The unit in which the independent variable in [Equation] is defined (for example, sound intensity, earthquake wave amplitude)

Quantity: Any multiple of 10

Answers 1–5: Values that are possible answers to the problem; one of these is the correct answer.

Template

[Unit 1], *[Variable 1]*, can be modeled by the equation [Equation], where *[Variable 2]* is [Unit 2] and *[Constant]* is a constant. What amount of [Unit 1] is produced by [Quantity] times the value of *[Constant]*?

  A. [Answer 1]

  B. [Answer 2]

  C. [Answer 3]

  D. [Answer 4]

  E. [Answer 5]

Functions

Sample Item

The graph of $f(x) = -x^2$ is in the standard (x, y) coordinate plane. Which of the following transformations, when applied to the graph of $f(x) = x^2$, results in the graph of $f(x) = -x^2$?

  A. Reflection across the x-axis

  B. Reflection across the y-axis

  C. Reflection across the line $y = -1$

  D. Translation down 1 coordinate unit

  E. Translation right 1 coordinate unit

Template Instructions

1. Create [Function 1] and [Function 2]. Insert them into the template.

2. Create [Answer 1] through [Answer 5]. Insert them into the template.

Template Key

Function 1: A function equation representing [Function 2] with a single transformation applied to it (for example, $f(x) = 3x$, $f(x) = -x^2$, $f(x) = |x + 12|$)

Function 2: A function equation (for example, $f(x) = x$, $f(x) = x^2$, $f(x) = |x|$)

Answers 1–5: Statements describing specific transformations on the coordinate plane; one of these statements correctly describes the transformation of [Function 2] to [Function 1] (for example, dilation by a scale factor of 3, reflection about the y-axis, translation to the left 12 coordinate units)

Template

The graph of [Function 1] is in the standard (x, y) coordinate plane. Which of the following transformations, when applied to the graph of [Function 2], results in the graph of [Function 1]?

  A.   [Answer 1]

  B.   [Answer 2]

  C.   [Answer 3]

  D.   [Answer 4]

  E.   [Answer 5]

Geometry

Area and Perimeter

Sample Item

The width of a rectangle is half as long as the length. The perimeter of the rectangle is 86 feet. What is the length of the rectangle, in feet?

  A. $28\frac{2}{3}$

  B. $57\frac{1}{3}$

  C. $13\sqrt{3}$

  D. $10\frac{3}{4}$

  E. $38\frac{2}{9}$

Template Instructions

1. Choose definitions for [Dimension 1], [Dimension 2], and [Unit]. Insert them into the template.

2. Choose a definition for [Relative size]. Insert it into the template.

3. Select a value for [Quantity]. Insert it into the template.

4. Create [Answer 1] through [Answer 5]. Insert them into the template.

Template Key

Dimension 1: Either *length* or *width* and different from [Dimension 2]

Dimension 2: Either *length* or *width* and different from [Dimension 1]

Relative size: A phrase describing a relative difference between the measure of [Dimension 1] and [Dimension 2] (for example, *5 inches shorter than, 3 feet longer than, half as long as*)

Unit: The unit of length in which [Dimension 1] and [Dimension 2] are measured (for example, inches, feet, meters)

Quantity: A value representing the measure of the rectangle's perimeter

Answers 1–5: Values that are possible answers to the problem; one of these is the correct answer.

Template

The [Dimension 1] of a rectangle is [Relative size] the [Dimension 2]. The perimeter of the rectangle is [Quantity] [Unit]. What is the [Dimension 2] of the rectangle, in [Unit]?

A. [Answer 1]

B. [Answer 2]

C. [Answer 3]

D. [Answer 4]

E. [Answer 5]

Lines and Angles

Sample Item

In the following *HIJK* parallelogram, $\overline{HJ}$ is a diagonal, the measure of $\angle HIJ$ is 46°, and the measure of $\angle HJK$ is 82°. What is the measure of $\angle JHK$?

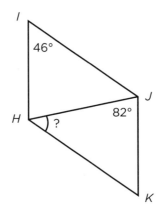

A. 49°

B. 36°

C. 46°

D. 82°

E. 52°

Template Instructions

1. Choose definitions for [V1], [V2], [V3], and [V4]. Insert them into the template.

2. Create a parallelogram.

    a. Label its vertices as [V1], [V2], [V3], and [V4].

    b. Create a diagonal of the parallelogram such that it divides ∠[V2][V3][V4], and ∠[V2][V1][V4].

    c. Label ∠[V3][V1][V4] with a question mark to indicate the unknown measure of ∠[V3][V1][V4].

    d. Insert the parallelogram into the template in place of the box.

3. Select values for [Q1] and [Q2] and insert them into the template.

4. Label ∠[V1][V2][V3] as [Q1]°.

5. Label ∠[V1][V3][V4] as [Q2]°.

6. Select [Answer 1] through [Answer 5]. Insert them into the template.

Template Key

V1–V4: Letters representing the vertices of the parallelogram

Q1: A value indicating the measure of ∠[V1][V2][V3]

Q2: A value indicating the measure of ∠[V1][V3][V4]

Answers 1–5: Values representing angle measures, in degrees, that are possible answers to the problem; one of these is the correct answer.

Template

In the following [V1][V2][V3][V4] parallelogram, $\overline{[V1][V3]}$ is a diagonal, the measure of ∠[V1][V2][V3] is [Q1]°, and the measure of ∠[V1][V3][V4] is [Q2]°. What is the measure of ∠[V3][V1][V4]?

A.   [Answer 1]

B.   [Answer 2]

C.   [Answer 3]

D.   [Answer 4]

E.   [Answer 5]

Volume

Sample Item

A mold in the shape of a cube has an interior side length of 24 centimeters and encloses a right circular cylinder with a radius of 6 centimeters and a height of 9 centimeters. The interior of the mold not occupied by the cylinder is filled with wax. Which of the following numerical expressions gives the number of cubic centimeters of the mold filled with wax?

A. $6(24)^2 - 2\pi(6)(12)$

B. $24^3 - \pi(9)^3$

C. $(24)^3 - \pi(6)^2(9)$

D. $6(24)^2 - 2\pi(6)(12) - 2\pi(6)^2$

E. $24^3 - \pi(6)(9)^2$

Template Instructions

1.   Choose definitions for [Object], [Contain], [Filling], and [Unit]. Insert them into the template.

2.   Select values for [Quantity 1], [Quantity 2], and [Quantity 3]. Insert them into the template.

3.   Create [Answer 1] through [Answer 5]. Insert them into the template.

Template Key

Object: A hollow object in the shape of a cube that is used to contain a right circular cylinder (for example, a box, an aquarium, a mold)

Contain: A word or phrase indicating that [Object] is used to enclose a right circular cylinder (for example, is used to store, holds, encloses)

Filling: A substance used to fill the remaining space in [Object] that is not filled by the right circular cylinder (for example, packing material, water, wax)

Unit: A unit of length measurement (for example, feet, inches, centimeters)

Quantity 1: A value representing the measure of the interior side lengths of [Object]

Quantity 2: A value representing the radius of the right circular cylinder; this value should be less than half the value of [Quantity 1].

Quantity 3: A value representing the height of the right circular cylinder; this value should be less than [Quantity 1].

Answers 1–5: Numerical expressions representing possible answers to the problem, in which pi is represented by the symbol π and [Quantity 1], [Quantity 2], and [Quantity 3] are represented as distinct values instead of being evaluated together or with other values (for example, the term $\pi r^2 h$, in which $r = 6$ and $h = 9$, would be represented as $\pi(6)^2(9)$ instead of being represented as 324π); one of these is the correct answer.

Template

An [Object] in the shape of a cube has an interior side length of [Quantity 1] [Unit] and [Contain] a right circular cylinder with a radius of [Quantity 2] [Unit] and a height of [Quantity 3] [Unit]. The interior of the [Object] not occupied by the cylinder is filled with [Filling]. Which of the following numerical expressions gives the number of cubic [Unit] of the [Object] filled with [Filling]?

  A. [Answer 1]

  B. [Answer 2]

  C. [Answer 3]

  D. [Answer 4]

  E. [Answer 5]

Operations

Multiples and Factors

Sample Item

Which of the following expressions is a factor of $a^3 - 216$?

A. $a - 36$

B. $a^2 - 12a + 36$

C. $a^2 - 36$

D. $a + 6$

E. $a - 6$

Template Instructions

1. Choose a definition for [V]. Insert it into the template.

2. Select a value for [Quantity]. Insert it into the template.

3. Create [Answer 1] through [Answer 5]. Insert them into the template.

Template Key

V: A variable (for example, x, y, k)

Quantity: A perfect cube (for example, 27, 64, 125)

Answers 1–5: Algebraic expressions that are possible answers to the problem; one of these is the correct answer.

Template

Which of the following expressions is a factor of $[V]^3 - [Quantity]$?

A. [Answer 1]

B. [Answer 2]

C. [Answer 3]

D. [Answer 4]

E. [Answer 5]

Operation Not Specified

Sample Item

The total score earned by a girl playing a racing video game is 12 points for each second below her opponent's completion time. The girl earned a total score of 84 points and her opponent's completion time was 193 seconds. What was the girl's race completion time, in seconds?

A. 12

B. 186

C. 7

D. 181

E. 200

Template Instructions

1. Choose definitions for [Person], [Possess], [Fixed Value], [Over or Under], [Dependent Variable], and [Independent Variable]. Insert them into the template.

2. Choose definitions for [Unit 1] and [Unit 2]. Insert them into the template.

3. Select values for [Quantity 1], [Quantity 2], and [Quantity 3]. Insert them into the template.

4. Select [Answer 1] through [Answer 5]. Insert them into the template.

Template Key

Dependent Variable: A word or phrase indicating the amount of a dependent variable possessed by [Person], measured in [Unit 1] (for example, the total score earned by a girl playing a racing video game, the total commission earned by a salesperson, the total cost for buying a set of books at a bookstore during a sale)

Independent Variable: A word or phrase indicating the amount of an independent variable possessed by [Person], measured in [Unit 2] (for example, the girl's race completion time, the total number of units sold by the salesperson, the number of books the boy bought)

Person: A person or other entity who has an amount of some [Dependent Variable] that is calculated based upon the amount of some [Independent Variable] they possess above or below some [Fixed Value] (for example, a girl, a salesperson, a boy)

Possess: A word or phrase indicating [Person]'s possession of the [Dependent Variable] (for example, earned, pays)

Over or Under: A word or phrase indicating either *greater than* or *less than* (for example, below, above, over)

Fixed Value: A word or phrase indicating a fixed amount of [Unit 2] (for example, her opponent's completion time, the salesperson's sales goal, the average number of books purchased by customers at the store during the previous month)

Unit 1: The units in which the [Dependent Variable] possessed by [Person] is measured (for example, points, dollars)

Unit 2: The units in which the [Independent Variable] possessed by [Person] is measured (for example, seconds, units sold, books)

Quantity 1: A value indicating the number of units of [Dependent Variable], measured in [Unit 1], for every [Unit 2] above or below a [Fixed Value]

Quantity 2: A value representing the amount of [Dependent Variable] [Person] possesses, measured in [Unit 1]. Care should be taken that this value is a multiple of [Quantity 1].

Quantity 3: A value representing the amount of [Unit 2] in [Fixed Value]

Answers 1–5: Values that are possible answers to the problem; one of these is the correct answer.

Template

[Dependent Variable] is [Quantity 1] [Unit 1] for each [Unit 2] [Over or Under] [Fixed Value]. [Person] [Possess] [Dependent Variable] of [Quantity 2] [Unit 1] and [Fixed Value] was [Quantity 3] [Unit 2]. What was [Person]'s [Independent Variable], in [Unit 2]?

- A.   [Answer 1]
- B.   [Answer 2]
- C.   [Answer 3]
- D.   [Answer 4]
- E.   [Answer 5]

Quantity and Number

Exponents, Radicals, and Scientific Notation

Sample Item

$\frac{7.5 \times 10^4}{1.5 \times 10^{-5}} = ?$

- A. 5.0×10^{-9}
- B. 5.0×10^{-1}
- C. 5.0×10^{9}
- D. 6.0×10^{-1}
- E. 6.0×10^{9}

Template Instructions

1.   Select values for [Quantity 1] through [Quantity 4]. Insert them into the template.

2.   Create [Answer 1] through [Answer 5]. Insert them into the template.

Template Key

Quantities 1–2: Values between 0 and 10 with one decimal place; [Quantity 1] must be evenly divisible by [Quantity 2].

Quantities 3–4: One- or two-digit integers

Answers 1–5: Possible solutions in scientific notation; one of these is the correct answer.

Template

$$\frac{[\text{Quantity 1}] \times 10^{[\text{Quantity 3}]}}{[\text{Quantity 2}] \times 10^{[\text{Quantity 4}]}} = ?$$

   A.   [Answer 1]

   B.   [Answer 2]

   C.   [Answer 3]

   D.   [Answer 4]

   E.   [Answer 5]

Percentages

Sample Item

A grocery store stocks soda packages that contain three different numbers of cans. The following table shows the store's soda package sales numbers from last week. How many cans did the store sell last week?

Type of soda package	Number of packages stocked	Percent sold
6 cans	90	70
12 cans	60	40
24 cans	40	25

   A.   97

   B.   190

   C.   367

   D.   906

   E.   936

Template Instructions

1.   Choose definitions for [Individual], [Attempt], [Success], [Group], [Contain], [Item], and [Time]. Insert them into the template.

2.   Select values for [Quantity 1], [Quantity 2], and [Quantity 3]. Insert them into the template.

3.   Select values for [Quantity 4], [Quantity 5], and [Quantity 6]. Insert them into the template.

4.   Select values for [Quantity 7], [Quantity 8], and [Quantity 9]. Insert them into the template.

5.   Select [Answer 1] through [Answer 5]. Insert them into the template.

Template Key

Individual: A person or other entity capable of performing an activity (for example, a grocery store, Michael, an artist)

Attempt: An attempt at the chosen activity (for example, stocks, attempts, tries to sell)

Success: A successful performance of the chosen activity (for example, sells, makes, sells)

Group: A group or other collective entity with three variations, each containing a different number of [Item] (for example, soda package, shot, painting)

Contain: A word that describes how [Group] contains or encompasses [Item] (that is, contain, worth, for)

Item: The individual item contained within [Group] (for example, cans, points, dollars)

Time: The unit of time over which the chosen activity was performed (for example, last week, last season, yesterday)

Quantities 1–3: Three different one- or two-digit whole numbers representing the number of [Item] in each [Group]

Quantities 4–6: Positive two-digit multiples of ten representing the number of [Attempt] for each [Group]

Quantities 7–9: Positive two-digit multiples of five or ten representing the percent [Success] rate for each [Group]; ensure each of these percentages represents a whole-number quantity of [Quantity 4], [Quantity 5], and [Quantity 6], respectively (for example, [Quantity 7] percent of [Quantity 4] should be equal to a whole number).

Answers 1–5: Five possible solutions to the problem; one of these is the correct answer.

Template

[Individual] [Attempt] [Group] [Contain] three different numbers of [Item]. The table shows [Individual] [Group] [Success] numbers from [Time]. How many [Item] did [Individual] [Success] [Time]?

Type of [Group]	Number [Attempt]	Percent [Success]
[Quantity 1] [Item]	[Quantity 4]	[Quantity 7]
[Quantity 2] [Item]	[Quantity 5]	[Quantity 8]
[Quantity 3] [Item]	[Quantity 6]	[Quantity 9]

- A. [Answer 1]
- B. [Answer 2]
- C. [Answer 3]
- D. [Answer 4]
- E. [Answer 5]

Statistics

Measures of Center and Variance

Sample Item

The list of numbers 83, 54, 38, *A*, *B*, 11 has a median of 32. The mode of the list of numbers is 11. To the nearest whole number, what is the mean of the list?

A. 26

B. 31

C. 32

D. 37

E. 38

Template Instructions

1. Select values for [Quantity 1] through [Quantity 4]. Insert them into the template.

2. Choose definitions for [*X*] and [*Y*]. Insert them into the template.

3. Select values for [*X*] and [*Y*].

4. Select [Quantity 5]. Insert it into the template.

5. Create [Answer 1] through [Answer 5]. Insert them into the template.

Template Key

Quantities 1–4: Four different two-digit whole numbers in order from greatest to least

Quantity 5: A value equal to $\frac{[\text{Quantity 3}] + [X]}{2}$

Quantity 6: A value equal to any of [Quantity 1] through [Quantity 4]

X: A variable; the value of this variable is a two-digit whole number less than [Quantity 3] and greater than [Quantity 4], such that [Quantity 3] + [*X*] is divisible by two.

Y: A variable; the value of this variable is equal to [Quantity 4].

Answers 1–5: Two-digit whole numbers representing possible solutions to the problem; one of these is the correct answer.

Template

The list of numbers [Quantity 1], [Quantity 2], [Quantity 3], [*X*], [*Y*], [Quantity 4] has a median of [Quantity 5]. The mode of the list of numbers is [Quantity 6]. To the nearest whole number, what is the mean of the list?

A. [Answer 1]

B. [Answer 2]

C.   [Answer 3]

D.   [Answer 4]

E.   [Answer 5]

Probability

Sample Item

Lilliana will play a game in which she will draw one marble from each of three jars containing 4 equal-size marbles each, with one green marble in each jar. She will be awarded 5 points for each green marble she draws. Let the random variable x represent the total number of points awarded on any round of drawing. What is the expected value of x?

A. $\frac{3}{4}$

B. $\frac{15}{4}$

C.   12

D.   15

E.   20

Template Instructions

1.   Select a value for [Quantity 1].

2.   Choose a definition for [Game]. Insert it into the template.

3.   Choose definitions for [Individual], [Success], and [Round]. Insert them into the template.

4.   Select [Quantity 2]. Insert it into the template.

5.   Create [Answer 1] through [Answer 5]. Insert them into the template.

Template Key

Individual: A person or other entity capable of performing an action (for example, Lilliana, John, Kenzie)

Game: A description of a game involving three independent actions, each with a probability of $\frac{1}{[Quantity\ 1]}$. Care should be taken that this description includes the size of the sample space if it is not already implied by the context (for example, draw a marble out of each of three jars containing [Quantity 1] equal-size marbles with one green marble in each jar; flip three separate coins; spin three spinners with each having [Quantity 1] equal-size, differently colored sections).

Quantity 1: A single-digit whole number

Quantity 2: A single-digit whole number

Success: The conditions for success within each part of the game (for example, draw a green marble, have tails land face-up, have the spinner land on blue)

Round: A complete round of [Game] (for example, round of drawing from all three jars, flip of all the coins, round of spinning all three spinners)

Answers 1–5: Possible solutions to the problem; one of these is the correct answer.

Template

[Individual] will play a game in which [Individual] will [Game]. [Individual] will be awarded [Quantity 2] points for each [Success]. Let the random variable x represent the total number of points awarded on any [Round]. What is the expected value of x?

    A.   [Answer 1]

    B.   [Answer 2]

    C.   [Answer 3]

    D.   [Answer 4]

    E.   [Answer 5]

Trigonometry

Sample Item

A line through the origin and ([x], [y]) is in the following standard (x, y) coordinate plane. The acute angle between the line and the positive x-axis has measure θ. What is the value of $sin\ \theta$?

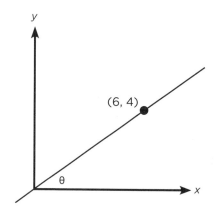

    A. $\dfrac{\sqrt{13}}{2}$

    B. $\dfrac{2}{\sqrt{13}}$

    C. $\dfrac{2}{3}$

    D. $\dfrac{3}{2}$

    E. $\dfrac{\sqrt{13}}{3}$

Template Instructions

1. Select values for [x] and [y]. Insert them into the template.

2. Create a coordinate plane containing a line that passes through the origin and point ([x], [y]) in Quadrant I. Label point ([x], [y]) with its coordinates and label the angle between the line and the positive x-axis as θ.

3. Select a function for [Trig Function]. Insert it into the template.

4. Create [Answer 1] through [Answer 5]. Insert them into the template.

Template Key

x: A single-digit whole number

y: A single-digit whole number

Trig Function: A basic trigonometric function (*sin*, *cos*, or *tan*)

Answers 1–5: Possible answer choices; one of these is the correct answer.

Template

A line through the origin and ([x], [y]) is in the following standard (x, y) coordinate plane. The acute angle between the line and the positive x-axis has measure θ. What is the value of [Trig Function] θ?

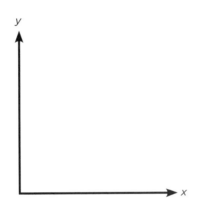

A. [Answer 1]

B. [Answer 2]

C. [Answer 3]

D. [Answer 4]

E. [Answer 5]

Appendix B: Science Topics

The following tables list the measurement topics and target-level (3.0) elements for each grade level of the Critical Concepts for science. The elements are organized by the five science topics identified in our analysis of science test items: earth and space science, physical science, life science, engineering and technology, and scientific investigation. For the engineering and technology and the scientific investigation categories, content is organized by grade bands. As described in chapter 4 (page 137), teachers can use the tables in this appendix to identify the specific content for which they wish to create practice science assessment items.

Grade 3

Science Category	Expectation for Student Knowledge	Critical Concepts Topic
Earth and Space Science	**CW1—Describe typical local weather conditions for each season** (for example, gather data about local weather conditions and how they change throughout the year to generalize about the typical weather conditions for each season).	Local Seasonal Weather Patterns
Earth and Space Science	**CW2—Describe different climates around the world** (for example, compare the characteristics and locations of climates around the world and the typical weather conditions they exhibit).	World Climates
Earth and Space Science	**NH1—Explain how to reduce the impacts of a weather-related natural hazard** (for example, describe the effects of weather-related natural hazards on humans, identify multiple methods that could lessen these effects, and compare their effectiveness).	Natural Hazards From Weather

continued →

Science Category	Expectation for Student Knowledge	Critical Concepts Topic
Physical Science	**F1—Explain the effects of balanced and unbalanced forces on an object's motion** (for example, identify and diagram forces acting on an object and explain how the direction and size of the resultant force determines the speed and direction of the object's motion).	Balanced and Unbalanced Forces
Physical Science	**M1—Use patterns to predict the future motion of objects** (for example, predict the motion of a pendulum with a certain length string after observing the motion of pendulums with strings of different lengths and determining how length of string affects swings per minute).	Predicting Object Motion
Physical Science	**E1—Explain how electrical charges can affect two objects not in contact with one another** (for example, create electrical charges in objects using friction and determine whether the charges of objects they interact with are similar, opposite, or neutral; experiment with changing the distance between objects, the friction used to build up the charge, or the materials of objects to determine patterns related to static electricity).	Effects of Electrical Charge
Physical Science	**MG1—Explain how magnetic forces can affect two objects not in contact with one another** (for example, determine how magnets interact with other objects [including different and similar poles of other magnets] and experiment with variables that affect these interactions, such as orientation of magnets and distance between or material of objects).	Effects of Magnetic Force
Life Science	**CO1—Explain how life cycles of organisms are similar and different** (for example, explain that all living organisms experience birth, growth, reproduction, and death, and compare different organisms' life cycles to determine similarities and differences among them).	Comparing Organism Life Cycles
Life Science	**OB1—Explain how group behavior helps organisms survive** (for example, use examples of animals living in groups to illustrate how group behavior can help organisms hunt, gather food, raise young, defend themselves, deal with changes to the environment, and mate).	Group Survival Behavior
Life Science	**OT1—Explain that plants and animals inherit traits from their parents** (for example, compare traits of offspring to that of their parents to explain that some traits are inherited and that inheritable traits tend to be physical and fairly permanent).	Inherited Traits
Life Science	**OT2—Explain that plants and animals' physical traits can be influenced by the environment** (for example, give examples of the environment physically changing the appearance of an organism's inherited trait [such as injuries] or influencing the way an inherited trait develops [such as weight]).	Environmental Impact on Physical Traits
Life Science	**OH1—Explain that different organisms are better suited to survive in different habitats** (for example, compare the characteristics and needs of animals that live in different habitats and explain how their unique characteristics would hurt their survival in a different habitat).	Organism Survival in Different Habitats

Science Category	Expectation for Student Knowledge	Critical Concepts Topic
Life Science	**OH2—Explain that variation of traits helps specific organisms survive or reproduce** (for example, identify traits that help organisms survive [such as size of thorns or coloration] and explain how variations of a specific trait would cause organisms with specific trait variations to survive better or worse in their habitat).	Organism Survival and Trait Variation
Life Science	**OH3—Explain how changes to an environment affect the organisms that can live there** (for example, describe the organisms in a habitat before and after a major change to show how changes to environment affect which organisms can survive there).	Effects of Environmental Change on Organisms

Source: Marzano Resources, n.d.

Grade 4

Science Category	Expectation for Student Knowledge	Critical Concepts Topic
Earth and Space Science	**GF1—Model patterns of Earth's features** (for example, chart the locations of a specific landform on a map, such as mountain ranges, coral reefs, volcanoes, or ocean ridges, to form conclusions about where this landform tends to develop).	Earth Features
Earth and Space Science	**EC1—Identify factors that contribute to weathering and erosion** (for example, explain how weathering and erosion are caused by water, ice, wind, and vegetation and identify factors that increase the effect and rate of weathering and erosion).	Factors Contributing to Weathering and Erosion
Earth and Space Science	**EC2—Use patterns in rock formations to explain how a landscape has changed over time** (for example, analyze specific rock formations and explain how weathering and erosion have contributed to their formation and changed the landscape over time).	Rock Formations and Earth Changes
Earth and Space Science	**EH1—Explain how fossils can be used to describe how a landscape has changed over time** (for example, determine the habitat an organism preserved in a fossil would likely live in, describe the location of where the fossil was found, and explain how disparities between the fossil and its location provide evidence that the landscape changed over time).	Investigating Landscape Changes Through Fossils
Earth and Space Science	**NH1—Explain how to reduce the impacts of a natural hazard caused by Earth processes** (for example, describe the effects of earthquakes on humans, identify multiple methods that could lessen these effects, and compare their effectiveness).	Natural Hazards From Earth Processes
Earth and Space Science	**NR1—Describe how different methods of energy production use natural resources** (for example, explain how different energy sources rely on renewable and nonrenewable resources for power).	Producing Energy From Natural Resources

continued →

Science Category	Expectation for Student Knowledge	Critical Concepts Topic
Earth and Space Science	**NR2—Describe the impacts of different methods of energy production on the environment** (for example, describe the impact renewable and nonrenewable energy sources can have on the environment by analyzing the effects of their production and consumption).	Environmental Impacts of Energy Production
Physical Science	**E1—Explain how energy converts between different forms** (for example, use the law of conservation of energy to explain how energy changes form and identify how energy changes in a real-world scenario).	Energy Conversion
Physical Science	**E2—Explain that energy can travel over a distance** (for example, observe instances of sound, light, heat, or electricity traveling across a distance to explain how energy can be transferred from place to place).	Energy Transfer
Physical Science	**M1—Explain the relationship between the speed and energy of an object** (for example, relate the concept of energy as ability to do work to comparisons of objects of the same mass moving at different speeds).	Energy and Speed of Objects
Physical Science	**M2—Explain how energy is transferred when objects collide** (for example, make predictions about the outcomes of various collisions as the speed, mass, and angle of the objects involved in the collision change and explain how energy is transferred between the objects as well as to their surroundings as heat or sound).	Collisions and Energy Transfer
Physical Science	**LV1—Explain how vision is a product of light reflecting off objects and entering the eye** (for example, diagram how light moves from a luminous object, reflects off an object, and enters the eye; explain how the reflected light travels through the eye to hit the retina; and describe how the information from both eyes is turned into an image by the brain).	Light, Vision, and the Eye
Physical Science	**W1—Identify patterns related to a wave's amplitude and wavelength** (for example, model waves to determine how changes to period, amplitude, frequency, wavelength, and speed affect movement and explain how the disturbances that cause waves determine amplitude and wavelength).	Wave Properties
Physical Science	**W2—Explain how waves can cause objects to move** (for example, compare the movement of particles within transverse, longitudinal, and ocean waves to explain how particles within a wave oscillate but do not travel over a distance).	Wave Motion
Physical Science	**IT1—Explain how patterns can be used to transfer information** (for example, analyze a method of communication that uses patterns to transfer information over a distance, such as Morse code and the mechanics of the technology that sends and receives Morse code).	Information Transfer

Science Category	Expectation for Student Knowledge	Critical Concepts Topic
Life Science	**PN1—Explain how specific plant structures contribute to a plant's survival, growth, or reproduction** (for example, describe the internal and external structures of a specific plant and explain how they are adapted to the organism's habitat, such as by explaining how a cactus's lack of leaves, waxy external coating, thick stem, and long roots help it to survive in the desert).	Plant Structures
Life Science	**AN1—Explain how specific animal structures contribute to an animal's survival, growth, or reproduction** (for example, explain how a camel's eyelashes, nostrils, humps, hooves, and coloration help it to survive in the desert).	Animal Structures
Life Science	**AN2—Explain how animals' response to stimuli support their survival, growth, or reproduction** (for example, explain how an animal responds to danger by running away, becoming very still, or preparing to fight).	Animal Behaviors

Source: Marzano Resources, n.d.

Grade 5

Science Category	Expectation for Student Knowledge	Critical Concepts Topic
Earth and Space Science	**G1—Explain that Earth's gravitational force pulls objects toward it** (for example, explain how gravity keeps objects on Earth by pulling them down toward its center and compare this phenomenon to the orbit of objects in Earth's gravitational field).	Earth's Gravitational Force
Earth and Space Science	**CM1—Describe how the Earth's movement in relation to the sun creates patterns of day and night** (for example, explain how the sun illuminates one face of the Earth using a model and incorporate Earth's rotation into the model to show how the Earth's movement creates day and night).	Daylight, Nighttime, and Earth's Motion
Earth and Space Science	**CM2—Describe how the Earth's movement in relation to the sun creates patterns that affect the appearance of shadows** (for example, gather data about the length and direction of shadows at different times of day and create and analyze graphs that represent this data to determine patterns in shadows' appearance).	Shadows and Earth's Motion
Earth and Space Science	**CM3—Describe how the Earth's movement in relation to the sun creates patterns that affect the appearance of constellations in the night sky** (for example, identify constellations in the night sky and relate constellations' movement across the night sky as well as the presence and disappearance of specific constellations depending on the season to the Earth's rotation and revolution).	Constellations and Earth's Motion

continued ➞

Science Category	Expectation for Student Knowledge	Critical Concepts Topic
Earth and Space Science	**CO1—Relate the apparent brightness of stars to their distance from the Earth** (for example, compare the true brightness and size of stars as well as their distance from Earth to explain why the sun is the most visible star from Earth and to determine factors that affect the apparent brightness of stars).	Apparent Brightness of Stars
Earth and Space Science	**ES1—Describe interactions between the atmosphere, biosphere, geosphere, and hydrosphere** (for example, given an interaction between multiple spheres [such as a volcanic eruption or a specific ecosystem], model how the four spheres interact and impact one another).	Interactions Among Earth Systems
Earth and Space Science	**ES2—Explain the distribution of water on Earth** (for example, describe the distribution of Earth's water in terms of total water [fresh water and salt water], fresh water [among icecaps, glaciers, groundwater, and surface water], and fresh surface water [among lakes, swamps, and rivers], and compare how access to fresh surface water and rate of precipitation varies around the world).	Distribution of Water on Earth
Physical Science	**M1—Explain that all matter is composed of small, invisible particles** (for example, explain that all solids, liquids, and gases are composed of atoms and demonstrate the existence of atoms by conducting experiments that show that gases have weight and volume).	Particle Composition of Matter
Physical Science	**M2—Explain that the weight of matter is conserved when substances change temperature** (for example, conduct experiments that involve measuring the weight of substances as they change between states and relate the measurements to the concept of conservation of mass).	Temperature and the Conservation of Matter
Physical Science	**M3—Explain that the weight of matter is conserved when substances are mixed** (for example, conduct experiments that involve measuring the weight of substances before and after they are mixed and relate the measurements to the concept of conservation of mass).	Conservation of Matter in Mixtures
Physical Science	**PM1—Identify materials based on their properties** (for example, given descriptions of the properties of different materials, test unknown substances for different properties to determine what materials they are made of).	Identifying Materials by Properties
Life Science	**EI1—Explain how the resources plants need for growth are obtained and used** (for example, explain how plants use water, carbon dioxide, light from the sun, and nutrients for growth, and identify the parts of the plants used to get these resources from the ecosystem they live within).	Plant Resource Usage
Life Science	**EI2—Explain how the energy used by animals started as energy from the sun** (for example, explain the transfer of energy from the sun to plants through photosynthesis and to animals as plants and animals within an ecosystem are eaten using food chains).	The Sun and Energy in Ecosystems

Science Category	Expectation for Student Knowledge	Critical Concepts Topic
Life Science	**EI3—Explain how matter moves between plants, animals, decomposers, and the environment** (for example, explain how plants take matter from their environment to create food, use food chains to show the movement of matter among plants and animals, and explain the role of decomposers in recycling waste back into useable matter).	Movement of Matter in Ecosystems

Source: Marzano Resources, n.d.

Grades 3–5

Science Category	Expectation for Student Knowledge	Critical Concepts Topic
Engineering and Technology	**DEDP1—Specify the criteria for an engineering design problem** (for example, when designing a plant growth chamber for the lunar surface, state that it must have systems that support plant life and produce plants that will nourish humans).	Criteria in Engineering Design
Engineering and Technology	**DEDP2—Specify the constraints for an engineering design problem** (for example, when designing a plant growth chamber for the lunar surface, state that it can only require materials that are already on the moon or can be reasonably transported in a space shuttle, can only require a specific amount of tending, and can only take up a specific amount of space).	Constraints in Engineering Design
Engineering and Technology	**SEDP1—Research an engineering design problem** (for example, collect facts about differences between the Earth and the moon when designing a plant growth chamber for the lunar surface).	Researching Engineering Design Problems
Engineering and Technology	**SEDP2—Generate possible solutions to an engineering design problem** (for example, suggest three different ways to create a plant growth chamber for the lunar surface).	Generating Engineering Design Solutions
Engineering and Technology	**SEDP3—Test possible solutions to an engineering design problem to identify failure points or difficulties** (for example, if a possible solution to creating a plant growth chamber for the lunar surface involves growing plants in a sealed environment, investigate whether plants will grow on Earth in a similar sealed environment).	Testing Engineering Design Solutions
Scientific Investigation	**SM1—Use the scientific method to conduct an experiment** (for example, after generating a simple hypothesis, develop an experiment to determine the accuracy of the hypothesis).	Scientific Method

Source: Marzano Resources, n.d.

Middle School

Science Category	Expectation for Student Knowledge	Critical Concepts Topic
Earth and Space Science	**G2—Explain how gravity affects objects in the solar system** (for example, explain gravity as the force that holds the solar system together by using examples of how it affects the motion of objects within the solar system).	Gravity and the Solar System
Earth and Space Science	**G3—Explain how the gravitational force between the Earth and the moon creates tides** (for example, model the effect of the gravitational force of the moon and sun on Earth's oceans, and explain how the position of the moon primarily determines tide patterns).	Gravity and Tides
Earth and Space Science	**CM1—Explain the cyclic nature of lunar phases using a model of the Earth, sun, and moon** (for example, explain how the location of the moon in its orbit around the Earth affects the lunar phases visible from Earth).	Lunar Phases
Earth and Space Science	**CM2—Explain the cyclic nature of eclipses using a model of the Earth, sun, and moon** (for example, explain how the position and movement of the Earth and moon in relation to the sun determine the appearance of lunar and solar eclipses from Earth).	Eclipses
Earth and Space Science	**CM3—Explain the cyclic nature of the seasons using a model of the Earth and sun** (for example, explain how the Earth's tilt creates seasons and why seasons are reversed between the northern and southern hemispheres).	Seasons
Earth and Space Science	**CO1—Describe characteristics of objects within the universe** (for example, describe general characteristics of asteroids, comets, meteors, moons, planets, and stars, and differentiate between the individual planets within the solar system).	Characteristics of Celestial Objects
Earth and Space Science	**CO2—Describe the scale of objects within the solar system** (for example, create a model that relates the size and position of objects within the solar system to familiar objects).	Scale of Objects in the Solar System
Earth and Space Science	**WC1—Explain the water cycle and the sources of energy that power it** (for example, create a diagram of the water cycle and explain how the movement of water between various stores is powered by the sun or the force of gravity).	Water Cycle
Earth and Space Science	**EC1—Explain how geological processes change the Earth's surface at varying scales** (for example, compare the time and spatial scales that various geologic processes operate on and draw conclusions about the relationship between the speed of an event and its spatial scale).	Geological Processes
Earth and Space Science	**EC2—Explain the past movement of tectonic plates** (for example, use the shapes of continents and an understanding of seafloor spreading as well as the distribution of similar fossils, landforms, and glacial evidence to create a model for how the continents could have previously fit together as one landmass).	Plate Tectonics

Science Category	Expectation for Student Knowledge	Critical Concepts Topic
Earth and Space Science	**EH1—Explain how the geologic time scale is used to organize Earth's history** (for example, create a timeline of Earth's history, and provide information about each eon, era, and period).	Geologic Time Scale
Earth and Space Science	**EH2—Explain how the fossil record can be used to show how organisms have developed and changed throughout Earth's history** (for example, create a timeline of the development of organisms from prokaryotic to eukaryotic; use fossil evidence to show the development of humans over time).	Fossil Record
Earth and Space Science	**CW1—Explain factors that change weather conditions** (for example, predict weather conditions from given information about current and incoming air masses and fronts).	Influences on Weather
Earth and Space Science	**CW2—Explain how regional climate is determined by patterns of oceanic and atmospheric movement** (for example, model convection currents in the Earth's atmosphere and ocean, explain how they are powered by the unequal heating of Earth by the sun as well as the Coriolis effect, and explain how they create regional climates).	Influences on Climate
Earth and Space Science	**CW3—Explain factors that have caused the rise in global temperatures over the past century** (for example, explain how changes in greenhouse gases in the atmosphere, Earth's orbit, and solar activity can cause global temperature to rise and explain the role that humans have played in rising global temperatures).	Influences on Global Temperatures
Earth and Space Science	**NH1—Explain how data on natural hazards can be used to develop technology that mitigates their effects** (for example, explain how data on earthquakes can be used to forecast future earthquakes, create improvements to warning technology, and inform responses to future events as they occur and as communities rebuild).	Natural Hazard Mitigation
Earth and Space Science	**HI1—Explain how humans impact the environment** (for example, explain how specific human activities, such as water usage, land usage, or pollution, have impacted the environment, including cascading effects that impact ecosystem services, biodiversity, and biogeochemical cycles).	Human Impact on the Environment
Earth and Space Science	**NR1—Explain how Earth processes create and unevenly distribute natural resources** (for example, describe the Earth processes that create fossil fuels, metal ore deposits, fresh water, and soil; explain why these processes only occur given specific conditions).	Distribution of Natural Resources
Earth and Space Science	**NR2—Explain how human consumption of natural resources impacts Earth's systems** (for example, describe the processes required to obtain and modify renewable and nonrenewable resources for human consumption; explain how these processes negatively impact the Earth).	Consumption of Natural Resources

continued ➔

Science Category	Expectation for Student Knowledge	Critical Concepts Topic
Earth and Space Science	**EP1—Explain patterns of interaction among organisms in an ecosystem** (for example, create food webs that explain the interactions of organisms within an ecosystem, and relate organism interactions to competition for resources).	Interactions Within Ecosystems
Earth and Space Science	**EP2—Explain the relationship between resource availability and populations of organisms in an ecosystem** (for example, compare models of how predator and prey populations change as a specific resource becomes scarce or abundant and relate the fluctuations in population to limiting factors and carrying capacity).	Resources and Population Levels
Earth and Space Science	**EP3—Explain how changes to an ecosystem can affect population** (for example, identify changes to abiotic and biotic parts of an ecosystem, determine their cause, and explain how these changes affect the populations of organisms within the ecosystem).	Ecosystem Changes
Earth and Space Science	**EP4—Relate human population and per-capita consumption of natural resources to concepts of competition and carrying capacity** (for example, explain how humans compete with other species for natural resources and compare human population and per-capita consumption with the ability of other organisms to survive).	Competition and Carrying Capacity
Earth and Space Science	**MEE1—Explain how matter cycles and energy flows through the living and nonliving parts of an ecosystem** (for example, model a biogeochemical cycle and explain how the cycle depends on the movement of matter between biotic and abiotic parts of an ecosystem).	Matter and Energy in Ecosystems
Earth and Space Science	**MEE2—Explain how interactions between living and nonliving parts of an ecosystem provide specific services that are of value to humans** (for example, relate specific ecosystem services that humans rely on to the interaction of biotic and abiotic aspects of an ecosystem, such as how trees provide fiber, filter air, and prevent runoff and erosion).	Ecosystem Services
Physical Science	**E1—Explain factors that change the average potential energy of an object** (for example, use the equation for potential energy to explain the relationship between the gravitational potential energy of an object, its height, and its mass; relate these factors to potential energy in other fields).	Potential Energy
Physical Science	**E2—Explain factors that change the average kinetic energy of an object** (for example, use the equation for kinetic energy to explain the relationship between the kinetic energy of an object, its speed, and its mass).	Kinetic Energy
Physical Science	**E3—Explain how energy converts between kinetic and potential energy** (for example, determine how the energy of a swinging pendulum converts between potential energy and kinetic energy and explain why the pendulum will not swing indefinitely).	Converting Energy

Science Category	Expectation for Student Knowledge	Critical Concepts Topic
Physical Science	**ET1—Explain changes in particle motion when thermal energy is changed** (for example, identify a situation in which conduction, convection, and radiation occur [such as water boiling in a pot heated by an open flame] and describe the movement and energy of the particles).	Changes in Particle Motion
Physical Science	**ET2—Explain how to minimize or maximize energy transfer** (for example, develop a method to minimize or maximize thermal energy transfer between substances and explain why the method is effective).	Minimizing and Maximizing Energy Transfer
Physical Science	**M1—Explain factors that change an object's motion** (for example, use Newton's first and second laws of motion to explain how the net force acting on an object determines whether its motion accelerates, decelerates, or remains constant).	Changes in Motion
Physical Science	**M2—Explain how Newton's laws of motion inform an understanding of collisions** (for example, compare collisions between a stationary object and a moving object and two moving objects in a head-on collision on Earth and in space, and use Newton's laws of motion to explain their outcomes).	Objects in Collisions
Physical Science	**G1—Relate the strength of the attractional force of gravity to the masses of and distance between interacting objects** (for example, compare the attractional force of gravity between objects of different sizes and objects at different distances; determine how changes in mass and distance affect the force of gravity).	Gravitational Force
Physical Science	**EM1—Explain factors that affect the size of an electric or magnetic force** (for example, conduct experiments to determine the effect charge and distance have on the strength of electric and magnetic forces).	Size of Electric and Magnetic Fields
Physical Science	**EM2—Explain how electric and magnetic fields can exert forces on objects, even when the objects are not in contact** (for example, explain how charged objects exert noncontact forces on other charged objects by creating diagrams of electric and magnetic fields and their effect on charged objects within their field of influence).	Force of Electric and Magnetic Fields
Physical Science	**C1—Explain how circuits produce electricity** (for example, use a circuit to complete a function [such as designing a simple flashlight] and explain why and how it works).	Circuits
Physical Science	**W1—Relate the parts of a simple wave to the energy it carries** (for example, calculate the amplitude, wavelength, and frequency of different waves and compare these calculations to the energy of the waves).	Wave Components and Energy
Physical Science	**W2—Explain the different ways waves interact as they encounter different media** (for example, give examples of waves being reflected, transmitted, or absorbed by different materials and explain why each interaction occurs).	Wave Interactions

continued →

Science Category	Expectation for Student Knowledge	Critical Concepts Topic
Physical Science	**W3—Explain why digital signals are more reliable than analog signals for encoding and transmitting information** (for example, compare the legibility of analog and digital signals before and after interference to explain why digital signals tend to be more reliable).	Digital Signals
Physical Science	**CR1—Explain how atoms organize to create larger structures** (for example, model different types of atoms, elements, molecules, and compounds to determine similarities and differences between their structures).	Chemical Structure
Physical Science	**CR2—Explain how chemical reactions change the properties of interacting substances** (for example, given descriptions of changes to substances, determine whether chemical reactions have or have not occurred).	Chemical Reactions
Physical Science	**CR3—Explain how mass is conserved on an atomic scale during a chemical reaction** (for example, apply the law of conservation of matter to chemical reactions to explain how atoms within reactants rearrange to create products; use subscripts and coefficients to balance chemical equations).	Conservation of Mass
Physical Science	**CR4—Explain how chemical reactions either absorb or release energy** (for example, explain what makes a chemical reaction endothermic or exothermic by examining energy within the chemical bonds of its reactants and products).	Endothermic and Exothermic Reactions
Life Science	**ON1—Explain how photosynthesis provides energy to organisms** (for example, model how autotrophs obtain energy from the sun, carbon dioxide, and water to create sugars and oxygen, identify where these processes occur within a plant, and explain how glucose is used).	Photosynthesis
Life Science	**ON2—Explain how the digestion of food provides energy to organisms** (for example, model how heterotrophs obtain sugar, oxygen, and water to create energy, carbon dioxide, and water, identify where these processes occur within a cell, and explain how adenosine triphosphate is used).	Digestion
Life Science	**OSF1—Explain how the parts of a cell contribute to its function** (for example, diagram the structure of prokaryotic and eukaryotic cells as well as plant and animal cells, and explain how differences in structure relate to these cells' different functions).	Cellular Structure
Life Science	**OSF2—Explain how the body is organized into specialized subsystems** (for example, create a model of the human body by diagramming organ systems and explaining how the organs within them contribute to their functioning).	Organ Systems
Life Science	**OB1—Explain how organisms respond to stimuli** (for example, model how signals are sent from sensory receptors to the brain and how the brain either sends signals for a reflex or learned action in response to a stimulus or stores the signal as memory).	Response to Stimuli

Science Category	Expectation for Student Knowledge	Critical Concepts Topic
Life Science	**OT1—Explain how genes determine which traits are expressed by organisms** (for example, explain how genes on DNA code for specific proteins which determine specific traits of an organism, and explain how mutations can affect the construction of specific proteins within an organism).	Genetic Influences on Traits
Life Science	**OT2—Explain how environmental factors can affect organism growth** (for example, identify how an organism's phenotypes are the product of its genotypes as well as environmental factors, and give examples of environment shaping an organism's traits).	Environmental Influences on Traits
Life Science	**OT3—Explain how human technologies can influence the inheritance of desired traits in organisms** (for example, compare selective breeding and gene splicing, their processes, their effects, and how they are used to modify organism growth).	Human Influences on Traits
Life Science	**GV1—Explain how asexual reproduction results in offspring with identical genes** (for example, compare the different methods for asexual reproduction, and explain why each result in offspring with identical genetic information to their parents).	Genetic Results of Asexual Reproduction
Life Science	**GV2—Explain how sexual reproduction results in offspring with genetic variation** (for example, explain the process for sexual reproduction in humans, and use Punnett squares to predict the probability of traits being passed down from parents to offspring).	Genetic Results of Sexual Reproduction
Life Science	**NS1—Explain how a trait can affect the probability of an organism's reproduction and survival in a specific environment** (for example, describe different physical and behavioral traits, describe environments in which traits would be advantageous or disadvantageous, and determine whether these traits are heritable or acquired).	Effects of Traits on Survival
Life Science	**NS2—Explain how natural selection leads to increases and decreases of specific traits within a population over time** (for example, give examples of desirable and undesirable traits in a population and describe how the frequency of these traits in the population changes over time).	Natural Selection
Life Science	**ER1—Use anatomical similarities between modern organisms and fossils to infer evolutionary relationships** (for example, compare homologous and vestigial structures among modern and ancient organisms to infer evolutionary relationships, and explain why these similar structures imply common ancestry while analogous structures do not).	Anatomical Evidence of Evolutionary Relationships
Life Science	**ER2—Use embryological similarities across multiple species to infer evolutionary relationships** (for example, compare images of different organisms' embryonic development to determine similarities and differences among the embryonic stages; relate these similarities and differences to the concept of common ancestry).	Embryological Evidence of Evolutionary Relationships

continued →

Science Category	Expectation for Student Knowledge	Critical Concepts Topic
Life Science	**ER3—Explain how taxonomic groups and the phylogenetic tree organize organisms by evolutionary relationship** (for example, explain why modern humans are classified as *Homo sapiens* in the phylogenetic tree of life based on their genetics and specific characteristics).	Phylogenetic Tree
Engineering and Technology	**DEDP1—Describe scientific principles that affect the criteria for an engineering design problem** (for example, for an engineering design problem that involves sending an object into higher levels of the atmosphere, solutions will need to be able to withstand fluctuations in atmospheric pressure).	Scientific Principles in Engineering Design Problems
Engineering and Technology	**DEDP2—Describe potential impacts on people and natural environments that represent constraints for an engineering design problem** (for example, for an engineering design problem that involves protecting an endangered species, solutions cannot endanger humans or another species).	Potential Impacts of Design Solutions
Engineering and Technology	**SEDP1—Test possible solutions to engineering design problems** (for example, create a model that can be used to collect data from tests of various solutions to an engineering design problem).	Testing Design Solutions
Engineering and Technology	**SEDP2—Evaluate possible solutions to engineering design problems** (for example, use a systematic process to describe how well various solutions meet the criteria and account for the constraints of an engineering design problem).	Evaluating Solutions to Design Problems
Engineering and Technology	**SEDP3—Revise possible solutions to engineering design problems** (for example, use data from testing to modify solutions, combine solutions, or create new solutions that incorporate the most promising characteristics of tested solutions to an engineering design problem).	Revising Solutions to Design Problems
Engineering and Technology	**ED1—Explain how to design a replicable experiment** (for example, for a given problem, generate a hypothesis, follow the steps of a given experiment procedure, determine a conclusion, and assess whether the experiment is replicable).	Experiment Design

Source: Marzano Resources, n.d.

High School

Science Category	Expectation for Student Knowledge	Critical Concepts Topic
Earth and Space Science	**G2—Predict the motion of orbiting objects in the solar system** (for example, use equations to find the velocity, period, frequency, and distance of objects in both circular and elliptical orbits).	Predicting Orbital Motion

Science Category	Expectation for Student Knowledge	Critical Concepts Topic
Earth and Space Science	**CO1—Explain the stages of a star's life cycle** (for example, model the potential life paths for a star, identify splits in the pathways [such as one pathway for main-sequence stars and one pathway for massive stars; within the pathway of massive stars, one pathway for neutron stars and one pathway for black holes], and compare differences between the pathways related to time, temperature, size, and color).	Life Cycle of Stars
Earth and Space Science	**CO2—Explain how nuclear fusion in a star's core releases radiation** (for example, explain why [at the molecular level] specific conditions [high pressure and high temperature] allow nuclear forces to overcome the Coulomb forces keeping atoms apart and relate nuclear fusion to a loss of mass and release of energy using the equation $E = mc^2$).	Fusion in Stars
Earth and Space Science	**CO3—Explain how stars produce elements throughout their life cycle** (for example, explain how nuclear fusion can produce elements lighter than iron and why supernovas can produce elements heavier than iron; relate the production of elements by nuclear fusion and supernovas to the distribution of elements throughout the universe).	Stellar Nucleosynthesis
Earth and Space Science	**BBT1—Explain the big bang theory using multiple strands of evidence** (for example, explain how cosmic background radiation, the observance of red shifting, and ratios of elements in the universe over time provide evidence to support the big bang theory).	Big Bang Theory
Earth and Space Science	**ES1—Explain how changes to one of Earth's spheres can affect its other spheres** (for example, explain how the atmosphere, biosphere, geosphere, and hydrosphere are interconnected by biogeochemical cycles and relate changes in one sphere to the creation of feedback loops that affect other spheres over various timespans).	Connections Among Earth's Spheres
Earth and Space Science	**ES2—Explain how human activity impacts Earth systems** (for example, explain how human activity negatively affects the atmosphere, biosphere, geosphere, and hydrosphere; relate the effects of human activity to population and consumption habits of developed versus developing nations; and describe ways in which humans try to mitigate their impact on Earth systems).	Human Impact on Earth Systems
Earth and Space Science	**ES3—Explain how water's unique properties play a critical role in Earth systems** (for example, relate water's unique properties to its effect on the atmosphere [through its facilitation of weather and the climate and its role as a greenhouse gas], biosphere [through its facilitation of the existence of life both biologically and ecologically], and geosphere [through its effect on Earth's surface and internal processes]).	Water in Earth Systems
Earth and Space Science	**ES4—Explain the cycling of carbon among the Earth's spheres** (for example, describe how carbon flows within and between the hydrosphere, atmosphere, geosphere, and biosphere).	Carbon Cycling

continued →

Science Category	Expectation for Student Knowledge	Critical Concepts Topic
Earth and Space Science	**EC1—Explain how matter is cycled by thermal convection within the Earth** (for example, diagram the process of thermal convection within the interior of the Earth, explain how heat from the Earth's core powers thermal convection in the mantle, and relate thermal convection currents to temperature and density).	Thermal Convection
Earth and Space Science	**EC2—Relate the ages of crustal rocks to the theory of plate tectonics** (for example, use the absolute ages of rocks [gathered from radioactive dating], the densities of continental and oceanic plates, records of reversals in the Earth's polarity, and a knowledge of seafloor spreading and subduction zones as evidence for the theory of plate tectonics).	Ages of Crustal Rocks
Earth and Space Science	**EC3—Explain how Earth's geologic processes form continental and ocean-floor features** (for example, explain how water, wind, and different types of plate boundaries create specific geologic features and compare the timespans over which these geologic features are created).	Formation of Earth Features
Earth and Space Science	**EH1—Explain theories regarding the formation of the Earth and Earth's early history** (for example, create a timeline of the Earth's history that begins at the creation of the solar system and ends at the present; use a comparison of planetary surfaces, the composition and age of Earth and other space objects, the theory of plate tectonics, and evidence for continental drift to support this timeline).	Formation of the Earth
Earth and Space Science	**CC1—Explain how the flow of energy within Earth's systems contributes to climate change** (for example, model how energy from the sun moves between the atmosphere, biosphere, geosphere, and hydrosphere; explain how changes to energy inputs or outputs in one part of the model affect other parts of the model [feedback loops]; and relate energy inputs and outputs to local and global climates).	Energy Flow and Climate Change
Earth and Space Science	**CC2—Predict the future impact of global and regional climate change at current rates** (for example, explain how human activity contributes to the rate of climate change and how human activities create feedback loops which further affect the rate of climate change).	Predicting Impact of Climate Change
Earth and Space Science	**CC3—Explain how climate change has affected human activity** (for example, explain how global and regional climate change affects the atmosphere, biosphere, geosphere, and hydrosphere as well as other Earth systems and relate these effects to human migration and settlement, the spread of disease, availability of food and water, and the occurrence of natural hazards).	Effects of Climate Change on Human Activity
Earth and Space Science	**NH1—Explain how natural hazards impact human activity** (for example, explain why specific natural hazards occur, how they affect humans on various scales [both temporal and spatial], and how the occurrence of these events has previously driven specific events in human history).	Natural Hazards

Science Category	Expectation for Student Knowledge	Critical Concepts Topic
Earth and Space Science	**NR1—Explain how the availability of natural resources affects human activity** (for example, explain how humans use renewable and nonrenewable resources and how the availability of these resources has impacted human activity both globally and locally as well as culturally, economically, and politically).	Availability of Natural Resources
Earth and Space Science	**NR2—Explain how cost-benefit ratios inform humans' use of natural resources** (for example, compare short-term and long-term cost-benefit ratios that consider the use of both renewable and nonrenewable resources as well as various stakeholders).	Use of Natural Resources
Earth and Space Science	**BE2—Explain the theory of simultaneous coevolution of Earth systems with life on Earth** (for example, critique a proposed example of the coevolution of life on Earth with Earth's systems [such as coral reefs altering coastlines, which eventually provided habitats for the evolution of new life] or of organisms in coevolutionary relationships [such as bumblebees and flowers]).	Coevolution of Earth's Life and Systems
Earth and Space Science	**B1—Explain the importance of biodiversity** (for example, explain why species biodiversity, genetic biodiversity, and ecosystem biodiversity are essential for ecosystems and humans at the local and global levels).	Importance of Biodiversity
Earth and Space Science	**B2—Explain the relationship between human activity and biodiversity** (for example, explain the loss of biodiversity in recent history in terms of the competition for resources between humans and other organisms and the consumption of natural resources by humans).	Human Activity and Biodiversity
Physical Science	**ECV1—Explain how to convert energy from one form to another** (for example, explain how a Rube Goldberg machine converts energy into multiple forms—such as a marble rolling down a ramp [potential energy into kinetic energy], which turns on speakers [kinetic energy into mechanical energy into sound energy], which produces vibrations that push a ball placed in the speakers to knock down a series of dominoes [sound energy into potential energy into kinetic energy]).	Converting Energy
Physical Science	**CE1—Calculate the change in energy of one component in a system when energy changes of the other components and energy flows in and out of the system are known** (for example, by substituting variables for constants and specific equations, solve the equation for change in a system's internal energy or enthalpy).	Changes in Energy
Physical Science	**EN1—Explain why thermal energy uniformly distributes among components of a closed system when two components of different temperatures are combined** (for example, confirm the statistical tendency toward high entropy and the relationship between higher temperatures and higher entropy and create a diagram showing the movement of components of different temperatures when combined).	Entropy

continued →

Science Category	Expectation for Student Knowledge	Critical Concepts Topic
Physical Science	**F1—Use Newton's second law of motion to describe the mathematical relationships between net force, acceleration, and mass** (for example, calculate an object's mass using Newton's second law of motion when given its force and acceleration).	Newton's Second Law of Motion
Physical Science	**F2—Explain why the total momentum of a system of objects is conserved when there is no net force on the system** (for example, create a proof for the law of conservation of momentum and explain the proof using real-world examples).	Conservation of Momentum
Physical Science	**F3—Explain how to minimize force on an object during a collision** (for example, explain why the force of a collision decreases as the length of the collision increases using equations for impulse and momentum change and provide real-world examples that support the explanation).	Minimizing Force
Physical Science	**G1—Use Newton's law of gravitation to describe the gravitational forces between objects** (for example, using known equations and Newton's law of gravitation, find the values for force, acceleration, velocity, mass, or the distance between two objects based upon given information).	Newton's Law of Universal Gravitation
Physical Science	**EM1—Identify similarities and differences between electrical and magnetic fields** (for example, compare the field lines that run directly between the north and south poles of a magnet and the asymptote that runs perpendicularly between the positive and negative poles of an electric dipole).	Comparing Electrical and Magnetic Fields
Physical Science	**EM2—Draw conclusions about the ability of electric currents to produce magnetic fields** (for example, relate the movement of the needle of a compass to an electric current as it is turned on and off).	Production of Magnetic Fields by Electric Currents
Physical Science	**EM3—Draw conclusions about the ability of magnetic fields to produce electric currents** (for example, relate the movement of the needle of a galvanometer to the movement of a bar magnet through a coil of copper wire).	Production of Electric Currents by Magnetic Fields
Physical Science	**FWF1—Explain how the forces acting upon a charged object in a field (electric or magnetic) affect the object** (for example, diagram the forces acting upon a charged object in an electric field and use Coulomb's law to quantitatively define the forces).	Forces on a Charged Object in a Field
Physical Science	**FWF2—Explain how the potential energy of a charged object changes at different points within a field** (electric or magnetic) (for example, relate an object's potential energy to the force exerted on it by the force of a field [electric or magnetic] and show how its potential energy changes as it moves within the field).	Potential Energy of a Charged Object in a Field

Science Category	Expectation for Student Knowledge	Critical Concepts Topic
Physical Science	**ER1—Explain differences between the particle model and the wave model for electromagnetic radiation** (for example, explain wave-particle duality by comparing the particle model with the wave model and explaining why each falls short when describing photon behavior).	Models of Electromagnetic Radiation
Physical Science	**ER2—Explain the effects of different frequencies of electromagnetic radiation on matter when absorbed** (for example, organize the electromagnetic spectrum from highest energy to lowest energy and explain uses for each type of radiation and why they can be used in that way).	Frequencies of Electromagnetic Radiation
Physical Science	**IT1—Explain how different technological devices transmit and capture energy and information using waves** (for example, compare how radio communication and sonar imaging rely on different types of waves [radio and sound respectively] to accomplish a goal and how the waves affect the performance of the technology).	Transmission Through Waves
Physical Science	**IT2—Explain the advantages of digital storage and transmission of information** (for example, compare how vinyl records or analog televisions store and transmit information to how MP3s or digital televisions store and transmit information to identify advantages of digital over analog technologies).	Digital Storage and Transmission of Information
Physical Science	**AS1—Explain the atomic structure and electron configurations of specific elements** (for example, given an element, write and diagram its electron configuration in multiple ways).	Atomic Structure
Physical Science	**AS2—Explain the organization of the periodic table** (for example, identify organizational structures in the periodic table [such as by atomic number, groups, or periods] and explain how these structures predict the properties of an element based upon its outermost electron valence).	Periodic Table
Physical Science	**MS1—Relate the strength of electrical forces among particles to the molecular-level structure of substances at the bulk scale** (for example, identify materials that rely on hydrogen bonding, dipole-dipole bonding, and dispersion forces and compare how the strength of their bonds affects the structure and properties of the material).	Molecular-Level Structure
Physical Science	**MS2—Explain how the molecular-level structure of substances affects their function** (for example, identify the molecular-level structure of simple materials, explain how the molecular-level structure informs their specific physical and chemical properties, and compare how these properties relate to the function of the material).	Molecular-Level Structure and Function
Physical Science	**CR1—Explain how atoms' valence electrons inform the outcome of a simple chemical reaction** (for example, given multiple reactants, identify the atoms' oxidation numbers; predict the type of bond they will form; correctly diagram and write the chemical reaction; and correctly name the chemical compound produced).	Valence Electrons in Chemical Reactions

continued →

Science Category	Expectation for Student Knowledge	Critical Concepts Topic
Physical Science	**CR2—Use the law of conservation of mass to explain why chemical reaction equations must be balanced** (for example, identify the reactants and products of a chemical reaction; using coefficients and subscripts, write a balanced chemical equation for the reaction; and relate the balanced chemical equation to the law of conservation of mass).	Balancing Chemical Equations
Physical Science	**CR3—Explain how the absorption or release of energy from a chemical reaction depends on changes in total bond energy** (for example, explain why energy is absorbed in order to break bonds during an endothermic reaction or why energy is released in order to form bonds during an exothermic reaction; relate the formation or breaking of chemical bonds to the potential energy between two atoms [Morse curve], bond energy, bond length, and bond strength).	Bond Energy in Chemical Reactions
Physical Science	**CRF1—Explain factors that affect chemical reaction rate** (for example, explain activation energy as the amount of energy reactants need to convert into products, relate activation energy to the rate of a chemical reaction, and explain why specific factors [such as pressure, temperature, concentration, phase, surface area, and presence of a catalyst] shift the activation energy to the left or right).	Chemical Reaction Rate
Physical Science	**CRF2—Explain factors that affect the equilibrium of a chemical system** (for example, explain a reversible reaction and equilibrium state in terms of ratios of reactants and products and use Le Chatelier's principle to identify how a chemical system at equilibrium will shift to accommodate given changes in concentration, volume, pressure, or temperature).	Equilibrium of Chemical Systems
Physical Science	**FFRD1—Explain how changes in the composition of an atom's nucleus during radioactive decay release energy** (for example, write and explain chemical equations for the alpha decay of iridium-168 isotope, the beta negative decay of calcium-46, the beta positive decay of potassium-40, and the gamma decay of argon-40).	Radioactive Decay
Physical Science	**FFRD2—Explain how changes in the composition of an atom's nucleus during fission release energy** (for example, create a diagram of uranium-235 undergoing nuclear fission and the chain reaction it sets off and write a series of chemical equations to accompany the image).	Nuclear Fission
Physical Science	**FFRD3—Explain how changes in the composition of an atom's nucleus during fusion release energy** (for example, explain a series of chemical equations that show how four hydrogen atoms can combine to create one heavier helium atom and relate the mass defect created to a release of energy using the mass-energy equivalence formula).	Nuclear Fusion

Science Category	Expectation for Student Knowledge	Critical Concepts Topic
Life Science	**OSF1—Explain the role of cellular division (mitosis) in maintaining and producing complex organisms** (for example, diagram each phase of mitosis, explain what occurs during each phase, and explain how the products of mitosis are used for growth or repair within a multicellular organism).	Mitosis
Life Science	**OSF2—Explain how cellular differentiation creates specialized cells from stem cells** (for example, explain how a zygote, through mitosis and cellular differentiation, develops into a multicellular organism, and relate this process to internal and external cues for differential gene expression and a cell's ability to transform [totipotent, pluripotent, multipotent, unipotent]).	Cellular Differentiation
Life Science	**OSF3—Explain how specialized cells work together to create interacting systems that provide specific functions within a multicellular organism** (for example, explain how cells create tissues, how tissues form organs, and how organs form organ systems, and describe various organ systems, their functions, and their components).	Formation of Systems from Cells
Life Science	**CM1—Explain how the structure of carbon-based molecules impacts their function** (for example, explain how the amino acids composing a protein molecule determine its function).	Carbon-Based Molecules
Life Science	**CRP1—Explain photosynthesis as a chemical process** (for example, diagram the process of light-dependent photosynthesis and the Calvin cycle, showing how various products from one step start another, and write proper chemical equations to represent the diagram).	Photosynthesis as a Chemical Process
Life Science	**CRP2—Explain cellular respiration as a chemical process** (for example, diagram the process of glycolysis, the Krebs cycle, and the electron transport chain, showing how various products from one step start another, and write proper chemical equations to represent the diagram).	Cellular Respiration as a Chemical Process
Life Science	**PS1—Explain how DNA controls the process of protein synthesis** (for example, explain the various stages of DNA transcription and translation and identify where and when each stage occurs).	Protein Synthesis
Life Science	**H1—Explain feedback loops that maintain homeostasis in an organism** (for example, describe the processes that activate negative feedback loops that govern thermoregulation).	Homeostasis
Life Science	**OT1—Explain the role of DNA in passing inheritable genetic traits from parents to offspring** (for example, explain how the structure of DNA contains genetic material and how chromosomes package DNA and are inherited from parents to offspring).	DNA

continued ➞

Science Category	Expectation for Student Knowledge	Critical Concepts Topic
Life Science	**OT2—Explain the role of meiosis in passing inheritable genetic traits from parents to offspring** (for example, diagram the phases of meiosis, explain what occurs during each phase, and explain how the products of meiosis are used in sexual reproduction).	Meiosis
Life Science	**OT3—Explain how inheritable genetic mutations are created** (for example, explain how specific inheritable genetic mutations are created during the DNA replication process and relate their mutation type to the probability of error during the DNA replication process).	Genetic Mutations
Life Science	**GV1—Explain the distribution and variation of expressed traits in a population** (for example, explain how natural selection affects allele frequency within a gene pool and use the Hardy-Weinberg equation to determine the distribution of specific traits throughout a nonevolving population).	Genetic Variation
Life Science	**NS1—Explain how advantageous traits increase an organism's chances of reproduction and survival** (for example, determine whether advantageous traits are physical or behavioral and heritable or acquired and explain how they increase an organism's chances of reproduction or survival).	Advantageous Traits
Life Science	**NS2—Explain how natural selection leads to the adaptation of populations** (for example, using finches in the Galapagos Islands or giraffes, explain how natural selection led to the adaptation of populations over time by allowing those organisms with advantageous physical or behavioral traits to survive).	Adaptation
Life Science	**BE1—Explain the theory that natural selection, over time, led to the evolution of organisms from a common ancestor** (for example, critique a proposed line of common ancestry [such as humans from apes, whales from land mammals, or birds from dinosaurs] using multiple lines of evidence).	Biological Evolution
Life Science	**EP1—Explain why ecosystems tend to maintain relatively consistent numbers and types of organisms in stable conditions** (for example, explain that ecosystems have carrying capacities and negative feedback loops that regulate their populations).	Ecosystem Population Regulation
Life Science	**EP2—Explain how feedback loops maintain homeostasis in an ecosystem** (for example, describe the feedback loops that occur when biotic and abiotic factors cause homeostatic disruptions and identify how these feedback loops permeate the ecosystem).	Feedback Loops in Ecosystems
Life Science	**EP3—Explain how changes to an environment can result in a new ecosystem** (for example, list potential short-term and long-term changes to an environment, describe how each affects the populations of specific organisms, and explain how those changes in population affect the ecosystem as a whole over time).	Formation of New Ecosystems

Science Category	Expectation for Student Knowledge	Critical Concepts Topic
Life Science	**MEE1—Explain the cycling of matter among organisms in an ecosystem** (for example, explain why key nutrients like nitrogen are critical to living organisms and the role living organisms play in specific biogeochemical cycles).	Cycling Matter in Ecosystems
Life Science	**MEE2—Explain the flow of energy among organisms in an ecosystem** (for example, use food webs and ecological pyramids [of energy, biomass, and numbers] to model how energy flows between organisms at different trophic levels of an ecosystem and compare energy flows of different ecosystems).	Flow of Energy in Ecosystems
Engineering and Technology	**DEDP1—Describe a major global challenge as an engineering design problem** (for example, articulate a problem such as the need for clean water and food or the need for energy sources that minimize pollution as an engineering design problem by identifying qualitative and quantitative criteria and constraints for solutions).	Global Challenges as Engineering Design Problems
Engineering and Technology	**DEDP2—Explain the requirements set by society that are criteria or constraints for a specific engineering design problem** (for example, quantify issues of risk mitigation to the greatest extent possible and state them so one can tell if a given design meets them).	Social Criteria and Constraints for Engineering Design Problems
Engineering and Technology	**DEDP3—Prioritize criteria related to an engineering design problem** (for example, break criteria into smaller, simpler parts and decide which ones are more important than others to inform decisions about trade-offs).	Prioritizing Criteria for Engineering Design Problems
Engineering and Technology	**SEDP1—Evaluate possible solutions to engineering design problems according to a range of constraints and impacts** (for example, evaluate a solution according to constraints such as cost, safety, reliability, and aesthetics, and social, cultural, and environmental impacts).	Evaluating Solutions to Engineering Design Problems According to Constraints and Impacts
Engineering and Technology	**SEDP2—Use technological simulations to evaluate possible solutions to engineering design problems** (for example, create computer simulations to test different ways of solving a problem, see which solutions are more efficient or economical, model the impacts of specific solutions, or consider interactions within and between systems relevant to the problem).	Evaluating Solutions to Engineering Design Problems with Simulations

Source: Marzano Resources, n.d.

References

ACT. (2006). *Reading between the lines: What the ACT reveals about college readiness in reading.* Accessed at https://act.org/content/dam/act/unsecured/documents/reading_report.pdf on April 22, 2020.

ACT. (2017, July 21). *What the research says about the effects of test prep* [Blog post]. Accessed at leadershipblog.act.org/2017/07/what-research-says-about-effects-of.html on April 20, 2020.

ACT. (2018). *The condition of college and career readiness: National 2018.* Accessed at https://act.org/content/dam/act/secured/documents/cccr2018/National-CCCR-2018.pdf on February 8, 2021.

ACT. (2020). *Preparing for the ACT test.* Accessed at http://act.org/content/dam/act/unsecured/documents/Preparing-for-the-ACT.pdf on January 23, 2021.

American Educational Research Association, American Psychological Association, & National Council on Measurement in Education. (2014). *Standards for educational and psychological testing.* Washington, DC: American Educational Research Association.

Associated Press. (2020a, December 14). Study suggests video games can help mental health. *Newsela.* Accessed at https://newsela.com/read/video-games-mental-health/id/2001016255/ on June 7, 2021.

Associated Press. (2020b, December 20). Listening to athletes, USOPC won't punish Olympic protests. *Newsela.* Accessed at https://newsela.com/read/us-olympians-allowed-protest/id/2001017183/?search_id=20e7a235-a021-49e7-a321-559858c9c049 on June 7, 2021.

Atkinson, R. C., & Geiser, S. (2009). Reflections on a century of college admissions tests. *Educational Researcher, 38*(9), 665–676.

Bangert-Drowns, R. L., Hurley, M. M., & Wilkinson, B. (2004). The effects of school-based writing-to-learn interventions on academic achievement: A meta-analysis. *Review of Educational Research, 71*(4), 29–58.

Barnett, R. (2013, May 22). Exit exams may be on their way out. *USA Today.* Accessed at https://usatoday.com/story/news/nation/2013/05/22/exit-exams-high-school-diploma/2351009 on February 8, 2021.

Barnum, M. (2016, June 12). The exit exam paradox: Did states raise standards so high they then had to lower the bar to graduate? *74.* Accessed at https://www.the74million.org/article/the-exit-exam-paradox-did-states-raise-standards-so-high-they-then-had-to-lower-the-bar-to-graduate on February 8, 2021.

Baum, L. F. (1900). *The wonderful wizard of Oz.* Chicago: George M. Hill Company.

Belasco, A. S., Rosinger, K. O., & Hearn, J. C. (2015). The test-optional movement at America's selective liberal arts colleges: A boon for equity or something else? *Educational Evaluation and Policy Analysis, 37*(2), 206–223.

Bransford, J. D., & Johnson, M. K. (1972). Contextual prerequisites for understanding: Some investigations of comprehension and recall. *Journal of Verbal Learning & Verbal Behavior, 11*(6), 717–726.

Britton, J. (1982). *Prospect and retrospect: Selected essays of James Britton* (G. M. Pradl, Ed.). Montclair, NJ: Boynton/Cook.

Card, D., & Giuliano, L. (2016, March). *Can tracking raise the test scores of high-ability minority students?* (Working Paper No. 22104). Cambridge, MA: National Bureau of Economic Research. Accessed at https://nber.org/papers/w22104.pdf on February 8, 2021.

Cheng, A. (2017a, October 10). *How to improve your SAT reading score: 8 strategies* [Blog post]. Accessed at https://blog.prepscholar.com/how-to-improve-your-low-sat-reading-score-6 -strategies on February 8, 2021.

Cheng, A. (2017b, October 13). *Khan Academy SAT will never be enough—here's why* [Blog post]. Accessed at https://blog.prepscholar.com/khan-academy-sat-will-never-be-enough-heres-why on February 8, 2021.

Clarke, M. M., Madaus, G. F., Horn, C. L., & Ramos, M. A. (2000). Retrospective on educational testing and assessment in the 20th century. *Journal of Curriculum Studies, 32*(2), 159–181.

College Board. (2015). *Test specifications for the redesigned SAT.* Accessed at https://collegereadiness .collegeboard.org/pdf/test-specifications-redesigned-sat-1.pdf on February 8, 2021.

College Board. (2016). *The SAT practice test #1.* Accessed at https://collegereadiness.collegeboard .org/pdf/sat-practice-test-1.pdf on January 23, 2021.

College Board. (2018a, May 7). *The College Board and Khan Academy team up for better SAT prep* [Blog post]. Accessed at https://blog.collegeboard.org/college-board-khan-academy-for-better -sat-prep on February 8, 2021.

College Board. (2018b). *SAT suite of assessments annual report.* Accessed at https://reports .collegeboard.org/pdf/2018-total-group-sat-suite-assessments-annual-report.pdf on February 8, 2021.

Colorado Department of Education. (2019). *Colorado academic standards: Mathematics.* Accessed at https://www.cde.state.co.us/comath/2020cas-ma-p12 on May 19, 2021.

Colorado Measures of Academic Success. (n.d.). *CMAS practice resources.* Accessed at http:// download.pearsonaccessnext.com/co/co-practicetest.html?links=1 on January 22, 2021.

Darling-Hammond, L., Rustique-Forrester, E., & Pecheone, R. (2005). *Multiple measures approaches to high school graduation.* Accessed at https://edpolicy.stanford.edu/library /publications/238 on February 8, 2021.

Ericsson, K. A., Krampe, R. T., & Tesch-Römer, C. (1993). The role of deliberate practice in the acquisition of expert performance. *Psychological Review, 100*(3), 363–406.

FairTest. (2021). *1,400+ Accredited, 4-Year Colleges & Universities with ACT/SAT-Optional Testing Policies for Fall, 2022 Admissions.* Accessed at https://www.fairtest.org/university /optional on May 14, 2021.

Fu, C., & Mehta, N. (2018). Ability tracking, school and parental effort, and student achievement: A structural model and estimation. *Journal of Labor Economics, 36*(4), 923–979.

Galla, B. M., Shulman, E. P., Plummer, B. D., Gardner, M., Hutt, S. J., Goyer, J. P., et al. (2019). Why high school grades are better predictors of on-time college graduation than are admissions test scores: The roles of self-regulation and cognitive ability. *American Educational Research Journal, 56*(6), 2077–2115.

Gallagher, C. J. (2003). Reconciling a tradition of testing with a new learning paradigm. *Educational Psychology Review, 15*(1), 83–99.

Gamoran, A. (1992). Is ability grouping equitable? *Educational Leadership, 50*(2), 11–17.

Geiser, S., & Santelices, M. V. (2007). *Validity of high-school grades in predicting student success beyond the freshman year: High-school record vs. standardized tests as indicators of four-year college outcomes.* Berkeley, CA: Center for Studies in Higher Education, University of California, Berkeley. Accessed at https://cshe.berkeley.edu/sites/default/files/publications /rops.geiser._sat_6.13.07.pdf on February 9, 2021.

Gershenson, S. (2018, September 19). *Grade inflation in high schools (2005–2016).* Accessed at https://fordhaminstitute.org/national/research/grade-inflation-high-schools-2005-2016 on February 15, 2021.

Gewertz, C. (2019, April 9). Which states require an exam to graduate? An interactive breakdown of states' 2016–17 testing plans. *Education Week.* Accessed at https://www .edweek.org/ew/section/multimedia/states-require-exam-to-graduate.html on February 9, 2021.

Goff, D. A., Pratt, C., & Ong, B. (2005). The relations between children's reading comprehension, working memory, language skills and components of reading decoding in a normal sample. *Reading and Writing: An Interdisciplinary Journal, 18*(7–9), 583–616.

Graham, S., Kiuhara, S. A., & MacKay, M. (2020). The effects of writing on learning in science, social studies, and mathematics: A meta-analysis. *Review of Educational Research, 90*(2), 179–226.

Graham, S., & Perin, D. (2007). *Writing next: Effective strategies to improve writing of adolescents in middle and high schools—A report to Carnegie Corporation of New York.* Alliance for Excellent Education. Accessed at https://production-carnegie.s3.amazonaws.com/filer _public/3c/f5/3cf58727-34f4-4140-a014-723a00ac56f7/ccny_report_2007_writing.pdf on May 19, 2021.

Greene, J. P., & Winters, M. A. (2004). *The positive effects of exit exams.* Accessed at https://www .manhattan-institute.org/html/positive-effects-exit-exams-1731.html on February 9, 2021.

Greene, J. P., & Winters, M. A. (2007). Revisiting grade retention: An evaluation of Florida's test-based promotion policy. *Education Finance and Policy, 2*(4), 319–340. Accessed at https:// www.mitpressjournals.org/doi/pdfplus/10.1162/edfp.2007.2.4.319 on February 9, 2021.

Haladyna, T. M. (2016). Item analysis for selected-response test items. In S. Lane, M. R. Raymond, & T. M. Haladyna (Eds.), *Handbook of test development* (2nd ed., pp. 392–409). New York: Routledge.

Haladyna, T. M., & Downing, S. M. (2004). Construct-irrelevant variance in high-stakes testing. *Educational Measurement: Issues and Practice, 23*(1), 17–27.

Harrington, T., & Freedberg, L. (2017, October 17). California joins trend among states to abandon high school exit exam. *EdSource.* Accessed at https://edsource.org/2017/california -joins-trend-among-states-to-abandon-high-school-exit-exam/588640 on February 9, 2021.

Heflebower, T., Hoegh, J. K., Warrick, P. B., & Flygare, J. (2019). *A teacher's guide to standards-based learning.* Bloomington, IN: Marzano Resources.

Hoegh, J. K. (with Heflebower, T., & Warrick, P. B.). (2020). *A handbook for developing & using proficiency scales in the classroom.* Bloomington, IN: Marzano Resources.

Holme, J. J., Richards, M. P., Jimerson, J. B., & Cohen, R. W. (2010). Assessing the effects of high school exit examinations. *Review of Educational Research, 80*(4), 476–526.

Hyslop, A. (2014, July 15). *The case against exit exams* [Policy paper]. Accessed at https:// newamerica.org/education-policy/policy-papers/the-case-against-exit-exams on February 16, 2021.

Jaschik, S. (2017, July 17). High school grades: Higher and higher. *Inside Higher Ed.* Accessed at https://insidehighered.com/admissions/article/2017/07/17/study-finds-notable-increase -grades-high-schools-nationally on February 9, 2021.

Jaschik, S. (2018, April 27). Large study finds colleges that go test optional become more diverse and maintain academic quality. *Inside Higher Ed.* Accessed at https://insidehighered.com /print/news/2018/04/27/large-study-finds-colleges-go-test-optional-become-more-diverse -and-maintain on February 9, 2021.

Jean, M. (2016). *Can you "Work your way up?"—Ability grouping and the development of academic engagement.* Doctoral dissertation, University of Chicago, Chicago, IL, United States of America. Accessed at https://knowledge.uchicago.edu/record/577 on February 9, 2021.

Jimerson, S. R. (2001). Meta-analysis of grade retention research: Implications for practice in the 21st century. *School Psychology Review, 30*(3), 420–437. Accessed at https://www.cde.state .co.us/sacpie/metaanalysisofgraderetentionresearch on February 9, 2021.

Kaestle, C. (2012). *Testing policy in the United States: A historical perspective.* Accessed at https:// ets.org/Media/Research/pdf/kaestle_testing_policy_us_historical_perspective.pdf on February 16, 2021.

Kaplan. (n.d.). *ACT math: Pacing and strategy overview.* Accessed at https://www.kaptest.com /study/act/act-math-test-pacing-strategy-overview on February 9, 2021.

Khan Academy. (n.d.). Maximize your score with official SAT practice. *Khan Academy.* Accessed at https://www.khanacademy.org/sat on February 9, 2021.

Koshmrl, M. (2018, July 4). Hunting, wolves, fewer elk cut cat numbers. *Jackson Hole News and Guide.* Accessed at https://www.jhnewsandguide.com/news/environmental/hunting-wolves -fewer-elk-cut-cat-numbers/article_7a01b894-3ae3-57cb-b9cc-66dd0c80b87f.html on May 11, 2021.

Ladner, M., & Burke, L. M. (2010). Closing the racial achievement gap: Learning from Florida's reforms. *Backgrounder.* Washington, DC: The Heritage Foundation.

Lemann, N. (1999). *The big test: The secret history of the American meritocracy.* New York: Farrar, Straus & Giroux.

Lleras, C., & Rangel, C. (2009). Ability grouping practices in elementary school and African American/Hispanic achievement. *American Journal of Education, 115*(2), 279–304.

Los Angeles Times. (2015, April 6). Man rescued after 66 days adrift at sea in his crippled boat. *Newsela.* Accessed at https://newsela.com/read/fisherman-found/id/8450/?search _id=5288f8e9-326a-4362-b883-c3ca3c05550f on June 11, 2021.

Loveless, T. (2013). *The 2013 Brown Center report on American education: How well are American students learning? With sections on the latest international tests, tracking and ability grouping, and advanced math in 8th grade.* Accessed at https://brookings.edu/wp-content/uploads /2016/06/2013-brown-center-report-web-3.pdf on February 9, 2021.

Loveless, T. (2016). *The 2016 Brown Center report on American education: How well are American students learning? With sections on reading and math in the Common Core era, tracking and Advanced Placement (AP), and principals as instructional leaders.* Accessed at https:// brookings.edu/wp-content/uploads/2016/03/Brown-Center-Report-2016.pdf on February 10, 2021.

Mann, H. (Ed.). (1845). *The common school journal.* Boston: Marsh, Capen, Lyon, and Webb.

Martin, E. (2015). Four ways to outsmart any multiple-choice test. *Business Insider.* Accessed at https://businessinsider.com/4-ways-to-outsmart-any-multiple-choice-test-2015-6 on February 10, 2021.

Marzano Resources. (n.d.). *The Critical Concepts.* Accessed at https://www.marzanoresources .com/educational-services/critical-concepts on February 22, 2021.

Marzano, R. J. (1992). *A different kind of classroom: Teaching with dimensions of learning.* Alexandria, VA: Association for Supervision and Curriculum Development.

Marzano, R. J. (2010). *Formative assessment and standards-based grading.* Bloomington, IN: Marzano Resources.

Marzano, R. J. (2017). *The new art and science of teaching.* Bloomington, IN: Solution Tree Press.

Marzano, R. J. (2018). *Making classroom assessments reliable and valid.* Bloomington, IN: Solution Tree Press.

Marzano, R. J., Norford, J. S., & Ruyle, M. (2019). *The new art and science of classroom assessment.* Bloomington, IN: Solution Tree Press.

Mathews, J. (2017, December 31). Sharp decline in high school graduation exams is testing the educational system. *Washington Post.* Accessed at https://washingtonpost.com/local/education /sharp-decline-in-high-school-graduation-exams-is-testing-the-education-system/2017/12 /31/662dc31c-eb5d-11e7-9f92-10a2203f6c8d_story.html on February 10, 2021.

McIntosh, S. (2012, September). *State high school exit exams: A policy in transition.* Accessed at https://cep-dc.org/displayDocument.cfm?DocumentID=408 on February 10, 2021.

Messick, S. (1982). Issues of effectiveness and equity in the coaching controversy: Implications for educational and testing practice. *Educational Psychologist, 17*(2), 67–91.

Missouri Department of Elementary and Secondary Education. (2018). *Released practice form grade 5 science.* Accessed at https://dese.mo.gov/sites/default/files/asmt-gl-practice-form -sci-gr5.pdf on January 23, 2021.

Nadvornick, D. (2019, May 10). WA high school graduation requirements changed. *Inland Journal* [Audio podcast]. Accessed at https://www.spokanepublicradio.org/post/inland -journal-may-10-2019-wa-high-school-graduation-requirements-changed#stream/0 on February 16, 2021.

National Center for Education Statistics. (n.d.). *NAEP questions tool.* Accessed at https://nces .ed.gov/nationsreportcard/nqt on January 23, 2021.

National Center for Education Statistics. (1993). *120 years of American education: A statistical portrait.* Accessed at https://nces.ed.gov/pubs93/93442.pdf on February 10, 2021.

National Center for Education Statistics. (2012). *The nation's report card: Vocabulary results from the 2009 and 2011 NAEP reading assessments.* Accessed at https://nces.ed.gov/nationsreport card/pdf/main2011/2013452.pdf on April 22, 2020.

National Center for Education Statistics. (2018a). *Table 203.20: Enrollment in public elementary and secondary schools, by region, state, and jurisdiction: Selected years, fall 1990 through fall 2028.* Accessed at https://nces.ed.gov/programs/digest/d18/tables/dt18_203.20.asp on February 10, 2021.

National Center for Education Statistics. (2018b). *Table 302.60: Percentage of 18- to 24-year-olds enrolled in college, by level of institution and sex and race/ethnicity of student: 1970 through 2017.* Accessed at https://nces.ed.gov/programs/digest/d18/tables/dt18_302.60.asp on February 10, 2021.

National Commission on Excellence in Education. (1983). *A nation at risk: The imperative for educational reform.* Washington, DC: Author.

National Governors Association Center for Best Practices & Council of Chief State School Officers. (2010). *Common Core State Standards for English language arts & literacy in history/ social studies, science, and technical subjects.* Washington, DC: Authors. Accessed at www .corestandards.org/assets/CCSSI_ELA%20Standards.pdf on February 16, 2021.

National Reading Panel. (2000). *Teaching children to read: An evidence-based assessment of the scientific research literature on reading and its implications for reading instruction—Reports of the subgroups.* Washington, DC: U.S. Government Printing Office. Accessed at https://nichd.nih .gov/sites/default/files/publications/pubs/nrp/Documents/report.pdf on April 22, 2020.

National Research Council. (1999). *High stakes: Testing for tracking, promotion, and graduation.* Washington, DC: National Academies Press. Accessed at https://doi.org/10.17226/6336 on February 10, 2021.

National Research Council. (2011). *Incentives and test-based accountability in education.* Washington, DC: National Academies Press.

Olszewski-Kubilius, P. (2013, May 20). Setting the record straight on ability grouping. *Education Week.* Accessed at https://edweek.org/tm/articles/2013/05/20/fp_olszewski.html on February 10, 2021.

Paige, D. D. (2011). Engaging struggling adolescent readers through situational interest: A model proposing the relationships among extrinsic motivation, oral reading proficiency, comprehension, and academic achievement. *Reading Psychology, 32*(5), 395–425.

Pearson, P. D. (2013). Research foundations of the Common Core State Standards in English language arts. In S. B. Neuman & L. B. Gambrell (Eds.), *Quality reading instruction in the age of Common Core State Standards* (pp. 237–262). Newark, DE: International Reading Association.

Pearson, P. D., & Hamm, D. N. (2005). The assessment of reading comprehension: A review of practices—past, present, and future. In S. G. Paris & S. A. Stahl (Eds.), *Children's reading comprehension and assessment* (pp. 13–69). Mahwah, NJ: Erlbaum. Accessed at https:// researchgate.net/publication/232594874 on February 10, 2021.

Pearson, P. D., & Liben, D. (2013). *The progression of reading comprehension.* Accessed at http:// achievethecore.org/page/1195/the-progression-of-reading-comprehension on April 22, 2020.

Penfield, R. D. (2010). Test-based grade retention: Does it stand up to professional standards for fair and appropriate test use? *Educational Researcher, 39*(2), 110–119.

Powers, D. E. (1985). Effects of test preparation on the validity of a graduate admissions test. *Applied Psychological Measurement, 9*(2), 179–190.

Powers, D. E. (2017). Understanding the impact of special preparation for admissions tests. In R. E. Bennett & M. von Davier (Eds.), *Advancing human assessment: The methodological, psychological and policy contributions of ETS* (pp. 553–564). New York: Springer.

Reese, W. J. (2013). *Testing wars in the public schools: A forgotten history.* Cambridge, MA: Harvard University Press.

Rodriguez, M. C. (2016). Selected-response item development. In S. Lane, M. R. Raymond, & T. M. Haladyna (Eds.), *Handbook of test development* (2nd ed., pp. 259–273). New York: Taylor & Francis.

Rothstein, J. M. (2004). College performance predictions and the SAT. *Journal of Econometrics, 121*(1–2), 297–317.

Sandburg, C. A. (1914). *Chicago.* Accessed at https://www.poetryfoundation.org/poetrymagazine /poems/12840/chicago on June 22, 2021.

Selingo, J. (2020, September 16). The SAT and the ACT will probably survive the pandemic— thanks to students. *Atlantic.* Accessed at https://theatlantic.com/ideas/archive/2020/09/even -coronavirus-cant-kill-sat-and-act/616360/ on February 10, 2021.

Shepard, L. A. (2008). A brief history of accountability testing, 1965–2007. In K. E. Ryan & L. A. Shepard (Eds.), *The future of test-based educational accountability* (pp. 25–46). New York: Routledge.

Simms, J. A. (2016). *The critical concepts (final version: English language arts, mathematics, and science).* Accessed at https://www.marzanoresources.com/the-critical-concepts.html on May 11, 2021.

Smithsonianmag.com. (2020, December 17). Your cherished family recipes could be featured in a museum exhibition. *Newsela.* Accessed at https://newsela.com/read/family-recipes-exhibit /id/2001017153/?search_id=c04b18da-84cc-40eb-9973-c49677bb3747 on June 11, 2021.

South Carolina Department of Education. (2018). *South Carolina end of course examination program biology 1.* Accessed at https://ed.sc.gov/tests/tests-files/eocep-files/2018-biology1 -sample-release-items on January 23, 2021.

Sparks, S. D. (2020, July 9). Standardized testing and COVID-19: Four questions answered. *Education Week.* Accessed at https://edweek.org/ew/articles/2020/07/09/standardized -testing-and-covid-19-4-questions-answered.html on February 10, 2021.

Strauss, V. (2014, September 14). Will Common Core double the high school dropout rate? *Washington Post.* Accessed at https://washingtonpost.com/news/answer-sheet/wp/2014 /09/04/will-common-core-double-the-high-school-dropout-rate/ on February 10, 2021.

Student Achievement Partners. (2015). Research supporting the ELA standards and shifts. *Achieve the Core.* Accessed at http://achievethecore.org/page/2669/research-supporting -the-ela-standards-and-shifts on April 22, 2020.

Syverson, S. T., Franks, V. W., & Hiss, W. C. (2018). *Defining access: How test-optional works.* Accessed at https://nacacnet.org/news--publications/Research/Defining-Access on February 10, 2021.

Ujifusa, A. (2020, November 20). *States push to ditch or downplay standardized tests during virus surge* [Blog post]. Accessed at https://blogs.edweek.org/edweek/campaign-k-12/2020/11 /state-standardized-tests-ditch-downplay-coronavirus.html?intc=main-mpsmvs on February 10, 2021.

University of Northern Colorado. (2011). Student retention vs. social promotion: A false dichotomy [Policy brief]. *Education Innovation Institute.* Accessed at http://hermes.cde.state .co.us/drupal/islandora/object/co%3A26127 on February 10, 2021.

U.S. Congress, Office of Technology Assessment. (1992). *Testing in American schools: Asking the right questions.* Washington, DC: Author.

Ward, B. A. (1987). *Instructional grouping in the classroom.* Accessed at https://educationnorth west.org/sites/default/files/resources/instructional-grouping-508.pdf on February 10, 2021.

Weisberger, M. (2021). Prehistoric shark was much larger than a great white shark. *Newsela.* Accessed at https://newsela.com/read/prehistoric-giant-shark/id/2001014588/?search_id =9c37bcbf-dc2a-4793-9e5b-7fa1811bdb91 on January 23, 2021.

Weyer, M. (2019, April 16). *Third-grade reading legislation.* Accessed at http://www.ncsl.org /research/education/third-grade-reading-legislation.aspx on February 10, 2021.

Wigdor, A. K., & Garner, W. R. (Eds.). (1982). *Ability testing: Uses, consequences, and controversies.* Washington, DC: National Academy Press.

Wilkinson, T. (2014). *ACT college readiness benchmark attainment by annual family income level 2014.* Accessed at https://act.org/content/dam/act/unsecured/documents/Info-Brief-2014-22 .pdf on February 10, 2021.

Woodworth, J. (2020, November 25). Due to COVID pandemic, NCES to delay National Assessment of Educational Progress (NAEP) assessment. *National Center for Education Statistics.* Accessed at https://nces.ed.gov/whatsnew/commissioner/remarks2020/11_25 _2020.asp on February 10, 2021.

Xia, N., & Kirby, S. N. (2009). *Retaining students in grade: A literature review of the effects of retention on students' academic and nonacademic outcomes.* Accessed at RAND https://rand .org/pubs/technical_reports/TR678.html on February 11, 2021.

Yoakum, C. S., & Yerkes, R. M. (1920). *Army mental tests.* New York: Henry Holt and Company.

Zwick, R. (2013, May). *Disentangling the role of high school grades, SAT scores, and SES in predicting college achievement* [Research report]. Princeton, NJ: Educational Testing Service.

Index

U

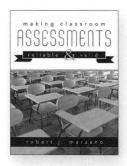

Making Classroom Assessments Reliable and Valid
Robert J. Marzano
Classroom assessments (CAs) have key advantages over large-scale interim, end-of-course, and state assessments. This resource details why CAs should become the primary method for formally measuring student learning and outlines how to revamp your CAs to ensure validity and reliability.
BKF789

The New Art and Science of Classroom Assessment
Robert J. Marzano, Jennifer S. Norford, and Mike Ruyle
Shift to a new paradigm of classroom assessment that is more meaningful and accurate. Step by step, the authors outline a clear path for transitioning to a holistic mode of assessment that truly reflects course curriculum and student progress.
BKF788

Formative Assessment & Standards-Based Grading
Robert J. Marzano
Learn everything you need to know to implement an integrated system of assessment and grading. The author explains how to design, interpret, and systematically use three different types of formative assessments and how to track student progress and assign meaningful grades.
BKL003

The New Art and Science of Teaching Writing & The New Art and Science of Teaching Reading
The New Art and Science of Teaching framework has helped educators around the globe transform instruction. Written by subject-matter experts, these content-specific books detail how to make the most of Dr. Robert J. Marzano's groundbreaking model in the areas of reading and writing.
BKF796 BKF811

The New Art and Science of Teaching Mathematics
Nathan D. Lang-Raad and Robert J. Marzano
Discover how to make the most of the groundbreaking New Art and Science of Teaching model in mathematics classrooms. Readers will discover myriad strategies and tools for articulating learning goals, conducting lessons, tracking students' progress, and more.
BKF810

MARZANO Resources

Visit MarzanoResources.com or call 888.849.0851 to order.